In recent years, the evil-god challenge has become a highly debated topic in the philosophy of religion. *Defeating the Evil-God Challenge* by Jack Symes stands as a pioneering, comprehensive exploration of this contentious subject, providing both depth and intrigue. It not only marks a pivotal milestone in the field but also serves as a must-read for theists, atheists, and anyone navigating the expansive intellectual landscape in between.

> Yujin Nagasawa, Kingfisher College Chair of the Philosophy of Religion and Ethics and Professor of Philosophy, University of Oklahoma, USA

Symes' book – the first book on the evil-god challenge to date – provides a clear and concise overview of key arguments and thinkers. It's a great place to start.

> Stephen Law, Director of the Certificate in Higher Education and Director of Studies in Philosophy at the University of Oxford, Department of Continuing Education, UK

This is the most thorough treatment of the widely-discussed evil-god challenge to date. Symes clearly identifies the strongest version of the challenge and then patiently constructs a robust response, showing how the three main approaches to theology strongly favour attributing goodness rather than evil to god. Required reading for anyone interested in the topic.

> T. Ryan Byerly, Senior Lecturer in Philosophy, University of Sheffield, UK

Engagingly written and accessible, *Defeating the Evil-God Challenge* provides a novel and compelling response to an important argument against the existence of the God of classical monotheism. This book is a must-read for any scholar interested in the fundamental questions of God's existence and nature.

> Asha Lancaster-Thomas, Teacher of Philosophy, Atlanta Classical Academy, USA

Suppose that there is a God, is it more (or at least as) likely that He's bad as it is that He's good? Arguments that the answer to this question is 'Yes' constitute the evil-god challenge as it has been pressed over the last decade. In this, the first book-length engagement with the challenge, Symes makes a sustained, careful, and multi-pronged case that the answer is in fact 'No', a case which will be of cogency and interest to theists, agnostics and atheists alike.

> Tim Mawson, Edgar Jones Fellow and Tutor in Philosophy, University of Oxford, Faculty of Theology and Religion, UK

Defeating the Evil-God Challenge

Also available from Bloomsbury:

Philosophers on Consciousness, edited by Jack Symes
Philosophers on God, edited by Jack Symes
Art, Desire, and God, edited by Kevin G. Grove,
Christopher C. Rios and Taylor J. Nutter
Classical Theism and Buddhism, by Tyler Dalton McNabb and Erik Baldwin
Explaining Evil, edited by W. Paul Franks

Defeating the Evil-God Challenge

In Defence of God's Goodness

Jack Symes

BLOOMSBURY ACADEMIC
LONDON • NEW YORK • OXFORD • NEW DELHI • SYDNEY

BLOOMSBURY ACADEMIC
Bloomsbury Publishing Plc, 50 Bedford Square, London, WC1B 3DP, UK
Bloomsbury Publishing Inc, 1359 Broadway, 12th Floor, New York, NY 10018, USA
Bloomsbury Publishing Ireland, 29 Earlsfort Terrace, Dublin 2, D02 AY28, Ireland

BLOOMSBURY, BLOOMSBURY ACADEMIC and the Diana logo
are trademarks of Bloomsbury Publishing Plc

First published in Great Britain 2024
This paperback edition published in 2026

Copyright © Jack Symes, 2024

Jack Symes has asserted his right under the Copyright,
Designs and Patents Act, 1988, to be identified as Author of this work.

For legal purposes the Acknowledgements on pp. xv–xvi constitute an
extension of this copyright page.

Cover image: The Fall of the Rebel Angels, Pieter Brueghel the Elder
(1526/1530–1569), Royal Museums of Fine Arts of Belgium

All rights reserved. No part of this publication may be: i) reproduced or transmitted in any form, electronic or mechanical, including photocopying, recording or by means of any information storage or retrieval system without prior permission in writing from the publishers; or ii) used or reproduced in any way for the training, development or operation of artificial intelligence (AI) technologies, including generative AI technologies. The rights holders expressly reserve this publication from the text and data mining exception as per Article 4(3) of the Digital Single Market Directive (EU) 2019/790.

Bloomsbury Publishing Inc does not have any control over, or responsibility for, any third-party websites referred to or in this book. All internet addresses given in this book were correct at the time of going to press. The author and publisher regret any inconvenience caused if addresses have changed or sites have ceased to exist, but can accept no responsibility for any such changes.

A catalogue record for this book is available from the British Library.

ISBN: HB: 978-1-3504-1928-5
PB: 978-1-3504-1932-2
ePDF: 978-1-3504-1929-2
eBook: 978-1-3504-1930-8

Typeset by Integra Software Services Pvt. Ltd.

For product safety related questions contact productsafety@bloomsbury.com.

To find out more about our authors and books visit www.bloomsbury.com
and sign up for our newsletters.

To Andrew and Oliver

Contents

List of Figures	x
List of Tables	xi
Preface	xii
Acknowledgements	xv
Introduction	1
Chapter One Constructing the Challenge	5
Chapter Two The Greatest Conceivable Being	37
Chapter Three The Bloody Watchmaker	71
Chapter Four God Revealed	117
Conclusion	157
Notes	160
Bibliography	191
Index	201

Figures

1. The Combined Evil-god Challenge © Jack Symes — 17
2. The Woman's Hand – A Section of Claude Monet's *Woman with a Parasol*. Public Domain via Wikimedia Commons — 98
3. Claude Monet, *Woman with a Parasol*. Public Domain via Wikimedia Commons — 99
4. Thomas (left) and James (right) – A Section of Leonardo da Vinci's *The Last Supper (restored)*. Public Domain via Wikimedia Commons — 100
5. Leonardo da Vinci, *The Last Supper (restored)*. Public Domain via Wikimedia Commons — 100
6. Beautiful Embroidery – A Section of Quentin Massys's *An Old Woman (The Ugly Duchess)*. Public Domain via Wikimedia Commons — 102
7. Quentin Massys, *An Old Woman (The Ugly Duchess)*. Public Domain via Wikimedia Commons — 103
8. Torture in Hell – A Section of Fra Angelico's *The Last Judgement*. Public Domain via Wikimedia Commons — 103
9. Fra Angelico, *The Last Judgement*. Public Domain via Wikimedia Commons — 104

Tables

1	A (Possible) Response to the Evil-god Challenge – Against Accepting Evil God's *A Priori* Absurdity. © Jack Symes	28
2	The (Hypothetical) Pragmatic Effects of Good-god Theism and Evil-god Theism. © Jack Symes	30
3	An Analysis of Grounding God's Moral Character through Perfect-being Theology. © Jack Symes	69
4	An Analysis of Grounding God's Moral Character through Creation Theology. © Jack Symes	115
5	An Analysis of Grounding God's Moral Character through Revelation Theology. © Jack Symes	156
6	An Analysis of Grounding God's Moral Character through Philosophical Theology (Conclusion). © Jack Symes	159

Preface

This book is about the evil-god challenge, the question of why we should believe in a good god rather than an evil god. I have spent the best part of eight years thinking about this question. In fact, I remember the moment when it first took hold. Dressed in matching wax jackets and bomber hats, my mentor Daniel J. Hill and I were crunching through Liverpool's frosty gardens as we rushed to catch the last trains home. We had been discussing objections to god's goodness, and Daniel's train was running slightly earlier than mine. 'I'm afraid we'll have to leave it there,' he said, breathlessly, as he rushed off into the snow, 'but I recommend that you seek out Stephen Law's paper on the evil-god challenge. I think you'd rather enjoy it!'

I spent the next few years researching the evil-god challenge under Daniel's supervision. Our conversations were sustained and enriched by the continued popularity of this fascinating topic. Published in *Religious Studies*, the international journal for the philosophy of religion, Law's paper on the evil-god challenge is one of the most downloaded and cited papers of the past decade, with a cumulative multimedia audience – across podcasts, videos and essays – in the millions. It may surprise readers, therefore, that this is the first academic book to be published on the topic.

The evil-god challenge asks why belief in a good god (i.e. the god of traditional monotheism) is significantly more reasonable than belief in a (hypothetical) evil god. Those who defend the challenge – ominously known as 'the evil-god challengers' – imitate traditional arguments for good god in favour of evil god in order to establish a symmetry between the two hypotheses.[1] Once they have demonstrated this symmetry, challengers claim that theists are unjustified in believing in one god over the other. Therefore, in order to justify their belief in good god, orthodox monotheists must respond to the evil-god challenge: the question of *why* belief in good god is more reasonable than belief in evil god. That's the heart of the debate: challengers aim to establish and maintain the symmetry, and their opponents try to refute it.

The central thesis of this book is that it is more reasonable to attribute goodness to god than it is to attribute evil to god, and, therefore, we have reason to favour belief in good god over evil god. To this end, I examine the structure of the evil-god challenge before exploring the main branches of philosophical theology: perfect-being theology, creation theology and revelation theology. In each area, I argue for a range of asymmetries – drawing from metaphysics, ethics, aesthetics and epistemology – that collectively undermine the alleged parallels between good god and evil god. At the end of the book, I conclude that the evil-god challenge can not only be defeated, but that the response is simple and compelling.

While writing this book, I have had the pleasure of discussing the challenge with philosophers from across the world. Most rewarding of all were the conversations I enjoyed with the evil-god challengers, both before and after my conversion. You see, when I set out to write this book, I did so with the intention of defending the evil-god challenge as an argument against theism. However, as I pushed ahead with my defence of the challenge, I found myself confronting more problems than I had expected. I started to take note of the more minor issues, and, before long, they were beginning to pile up. In the end, I was writing in the shadow of an elephant: a large, obvious, awkward problem that my fellow challengers didn't want to talk about. This realization marked a profound shift in my thinking, as well as, admittedly, a significant obstacle to this work. Alas, by the time I had spotted the elephant, half of this book had already been written; in a nearby possible world, it had a very different ending. Still, I went back to the start, and I believe this book is better for it. Atticus Finch was right, if you want to get to know somebody, it's best to 'climb inside of his skin and walk around in it'.[2]

In recent years, several leading evil-god challengers have also reformed their views. Stephen Law, for example – who served as the external examiner to an earlier draft of this work as part of my doctoral defence – has begun to use the challenge more narrowly. These days, Law is more focused on discrediting traditional responses to the problem of evil than attacking the rest of the arguments for god. Another prominent challenger, Asha Lancaster-Thomas, has progressed in the same direction. For Lancaster-Thomas, the evil-god challenge should be regarded as a tool for understanding why theists believe in god's goodness, rather than an argument against the rationality of theism. Still, Law and Lancaster-Thomas both remain defenders of the challenge, which is no longer my position; nevertheless, both have supported my change of heart. I have omitted many of their kind words about the argument presented in this book, as the majority were induced by Liverpudlian beer (Stephen) and Japanese wine (Asha).

It is worth clarifying some key points before we begin. First, because much of my preceding work has been dedicated to the promotion of public philosophy, it may disappoint some readers to learn that this is not a book for the general public. Any decent philosophical work ought to be clear and accessible – goals which I hope to have achieved here – but we must accept, and I concede this through gritted teeth, that there is a time and a place for making jokes at Adam Sandler's expense. To those in search of an engaging and accessible guide to the philosophy of religion, I recommend my previous book, *Philosophers on God: Talking about Existence*.[3] With that said, I hope this book – despite its density – serves as a helpful guide to anybody interested in the analytic study of philosophy. Whether you are new to philosophical theology, the evil-god challenge or philosophy of religion more generally, I hope you find something valuable within its pages.

Second, I have done my best to capture the thought that precedes my own, but this book is not intended as a history of the evil-god challenge, nor as a catalogue of the merits and shortfalls of the arguments from philosophy's past. Additionally, given the popularity of the challenge, I expect that several papers will have been published on this topic between my writing of this sentence and your reading of it. I trust that the reader will forgive me for such exclusions.

Third, this book is not really about arguments for god's existence. Instead, my focus is philosophical theology. While philosophical theology tries to understand the nature of god by defining god through its main schools of thought – perfect-being theology, creation theology and revelation theology – it does not seek to establish god's existence. Most discussions of the evil-god challenge focus on whether the arguments for good god's *existence* are as strong as those for evil god's *existence*; in contrast, my task is to examine whether the evil-god challenge can be applied to the arguments for god's *attributes*. With that said, I will allow myself short comments on the topic of god's existence when my argument reveals interesting implications.

My fourth and final qualification is that my task is not to show that theism is a reasonable position to hold. The sole conclusion of this book is that the evil-god challenge does not constitute a successful argument against theism. Further still, my argument is not part of some wider project in which I hope to convince my readers of a particular worldview. To avoid any speculation, I wish to confess the following: I am an agnostic who is agnostic about being agnostic … in fact, I'm almost sure of it.

Acknowledgements

I would like to thank all of those who have contributed to the completion of this work. First, I would like to thank Daniel J. Hill for all of his guidance and encouragement. Any virtues of my work are indebted to Daniel's ingenuity, good humour and unrivalled attention to detail; he is the mentor than-which-no-greater-can-be-conceived. Fortunately, as I have discovered first-hand, it is possible for there to be multiple metaphysically maximal beings, which leads me to thank another mentor, Barry Dainton. Conversations with Barry, as well as being intrinsically worthwhile, have inspired many of the ideas presented throughout this book, for which I am tremendously grateful.

I would like to thank the following people for their helpful comments, suggestions and conversations on all or part of the text: Thom Atkinson, Christopher Bartley, Kristian Brindley, Anthony Cashio, Rose de Castellane, William Lane Craig, Harry Drummond, Richard Gaskin, Dale Glover, Philip Goff, Laura Gow, Jonathon Hawkins, Andrew Horton, Lucy James, Asha Lancaster-Thomas, Casey Logue, Oliver Marley, Gregory Miller, Yujin Nagasawa, Manish Popat-Szabries, Lauren Stephens, Richard Swinburne, Paul Taylor and Eric Thomas. I am particularly thankful to Michael Hauskeller and Stephen Law for their thorough examination of an earlier draft of this book during my doctoral defence; their insightful feedback was invaluable to the refinement and enhancement of this work. I would also like to thank the anonymous reviewers at Bloomsbury for their supportive feedback throughout the book's various stages.

I wish to express my gratitude to my students at King Edward VI High School for Girls, the University of Liverpool, the University of Chester and Durham University – as well as all of those who have attended *The Panpsycast*'s monthly discussions – for contributing to the ideas within this work.

This book was produced during my time at the University of Liverpool, whose Department of Philosophy inspired and sustained my work for over a decade. The opportunity to complete my research at Liverpool was a tremendous honour for which I am forever indebted. I also wish to thank the various institutions who graciously funded my research. In addition to the School of the Arts at the University of Liverpool, thank you to Culham St Gabriel's Trust, Durham

University, the Global Philosophy of Religion Project, Hockerill Educational Foundation and Westhill Endowment. Without your support, this project would not have been possible; thank you for this tremendous honour. I am also grateful to the audiences and participants for their feedback at the institutions and conferences where I presented earlier drafts of this book, with special thanks to the Joint Session of the Aristotelian Society and Mind Association (University of Kent, 2020 and St Andrews University, 2022), the University of Liverpool Graduate Conference (2020 and 2021), the University of Nottingham (2020), the AHRC North West Consortium (Keele University, 2020) and the Global Philosophy of Religion Project (Waseda University, 2023).

I am indebted to my agent, Donald Winchester, and to Colleen Coalter, Suzie Nash, Benedict O'Hagan, Ayyan Ejilane and the editorial board at Bloomsbury for their unwavering belief and encouragement. A heartfelt thank you to Michelle, Gary, Alvin, Lisa, Stevie, Joshua, Freddie, Ziggy, Maddison, Adam, Autumn, Samuel, Mia, Rupert and Mollie for their love and support. A very special thank you to Asha Lancaster-Thomas for our many lively and illuminating discussions on the evil-god challenge, to Casey Logue for her guidance throughout the project, to Manish Popat-Szabries for composing the book's epigraphs and to Rose de Castellane for her limitless enthusiasm and insight.

Finally, my deepest acknowledgement is reserved to the dedicatees of this book, whose years of friendship have brought me so much joy.

Introduction

The evil-god challenge: why is belief in a maximally good god significantly more reasonable than belief in a maximally evil god?

The evil-god challenge was popularized in 2010 by Stephen Law's paper of the same name.[1] Published in *Religious Studies*, Law's article is the journal's most downloaded and third most cited paper of the past twelve years.[2] Fundamentally, the challenge depends on what Law has called 'the symmetry thesis', which states that the good-god hypothesis (the belief that good god exists) is roughly as reasonable as the evil-god hypothesis (the belief that evil god exists).[3] Therefore, in order for the orthodox theist's belief in good god to be considered reasonable, one must offer a sufficiently powerful reason for rejecting the symmetry thesis in favour of good god. This book develops a case against the symmetry thesis on behalf of the traditional theist.

My response to the evil-god challenge relies on a distinction that I draw between two types of arguments: those that claim to *ground* god's moral character and those that claim god is (or is not) *compatible* with some argument for (or against) god's existence. To establish a grounding symmetry, one must have roughly symmetrical reasons for attributing goodness or evil to god. In other words, arguments for grounding claim that we have reasons for identifying god as good or evil. In contrast, compatibility symmetry maintains that there are roughly symmetrical reasons for believing that good god and evil god exist. In this work, I focus on arguments that aim to ground (i.e. establish) god's moral character. My analysis shows that when we compare grounding arguments, rather than arguments for compatibility, we find that the arguments for grounding good god are significantly stronger than those for grounding evil god.

In the proceeding chapters, I develop an argument to say that it is more reasonable to attribute goodness to god than it is to attribute evil to god. Drawing from the three major schools of philosophical theology – perfect-being theology, creation theology and revelation theology – I argue that the underlying principles of orthodox theologies (which attribute goodness to god) are significantly more plausible than those required of what I call 'unorthodox theologies' (which attribute evil to god). I intend to show that there are stronger reasons for thinking that god is good rather than evil, and, consequently, that the evil-god challenge can be defeated.

In Chapter One, I outline the nature of the evil-god challenge. I examine several ways of constructing the challenge, highlight different versions of the symmetry thesis, discuss the various methods of establishing the symmetry thesis and identify the different approaches to solving the evil-god challenge. At the end of the chapter, I explain the difference between arguments that establish god's moral character (grounding) and arguments that claim god exists and can be reconciled with otherwise contradictory evidence (compatibility). I argue that in order for the evil-god hypothesis to be considered as reasonable as the good-god hypothesis, the challenger must offer similarly reasonable arguments for attributing evil to god; I examine their ability to do so in the chapters that follow.

In Chapter Two, I discuss the possibility of grounding god's moral character in perfect-being (or maximal-being) theology. I develop three arguments for attributing goodness to god. The first argument claims that goodness (and not evil) is a great-making property; therefore, as god is the greatest conceivable being who possesses all great-making properties, god must be good and not evil. The second argument claims that 'Being Itself' is good and not evil, and, therefore, as god is by definition Being Itself, god must be good and not evil. The third argument maintains that moral statements are true, and that motivation to perform acts is internal to morally true statements (that is to say, true statements such as 'we ought to help people in need' contain, within themselves, a motivation to act), and, thus, god would be motivated to do good but not evil. I attempt to parallel these arguments in favour of evil god – claiming that evil is a great-making property, that Being Itself is evil and that moral motivation is internal to immoral truths (that is to say, 'we ought to hurt innocent people' is true and contains, within itself, a motivation to act in accordance with the statement) – but find these unorthodox principles to be less reasonable than their orthodox counterparts. Therefore, I conclude that it is more reasonable to ground good god in perfect-being theology than it is to ground evil god in perfect-being theology.

In Chapter Three, I consider arguments for grounding god's moral character in creation theology – in other words, I examine arguments for attributing goodness and evil to god through observed goods and evils in the natural world. I develop a case for why the world's extrinsic and intrinsic goods constitute reasons for attributing goodness to god, before attempting to parallel this argument in favour of evil god by appealing to extrinsic and intrinsic evils. Whilst I claim that a parallel argument from extrinsic evils may be effective, I argue that parallel arguments from intrinsic evils – which are outweighed by intrinsic goods – are not as powerful. I then develop an argument that shows additional considerations, such as the aesthetic argument and Reformed epistemology, provide strong reasons for attributing goodness (and not evil) to god. Towards the end of this chapter, I concede that it is difficult to overcome one argument for evil god, which states that the totality of the world's natural evils (extrinsic and intrinsic) counterbalances (or outweighs) the totality of the world's natural goods (extrinsic and intrinsic). Although I accept that this argument may counterbalance appeals to good and evil in the natural world, I claim that it does not address the arguments for attributing goodness to god through Reformed epistemology. Therefore, I conclude that it is more reasonable to ground good god in creation theology than it is to ground evil god in creation theology.

In Chapter Four, I examine the arguments for establishing god's moral character through revelation theology – specifically, I discuss the possibility of attributing goodness and evil to god through scripture, religious experience and miracles. To this end, I appeal to god's (seemingly) malevolent actions in the Christian Scriptures and the (apparent) contradictions between the competing scriptures of different religions; I argue that it is more reasonable to attribute goodness to god once these 'evils' are considered in the light of scriptures' explicit claims about god's goodness. In my discussion of religious experience, I reject the claim that it is roughly as reasonable to ground evil god in 'negative experiences' than it is to ground good god in 'positive experiences'. I argue that those who report negative experiences – unlike positive experiences – rarely (if ever) identify god as the apparent object of such experiences. Finally, I discuss the possibility of attributing evil to god through miracles. Whilst I accept that reports of negative miracles are widespread, I reject that they can be used to form a successful parallel argument for evil god; in short, I claim that god's negative miracles in scripture should be contextualized by scriptures' explicit claims about god's benevolent motivations and that non-scriptural negative miracles (unlike positive miracles) are not said to be performed directly by god, but by lesser supernatural agents. Therefore, I conclude that it is more reasonable to attribute goodness (than evil) to god through revelation theology.

The conclusion of this book is that we have strong reasons for favouring the good-god hypothesis over the evil-god hypothesis, and, therefore, my argument constitutes a solution to the evil-god challenge. Why is belief in a maximally good god significantly more reasonable than belief in a maximally evil god? Because we have significantly stronger reasons for attributing goodness than evil to god.

Chapter One

Constructing the Challenge

Way off the map where dragons be,
And all the lines are blurred,
There evil god may rear his head:
Is faith in him absurd?[1]

1.1 Introduction

Aimed at traditional monotheists, the central claim of the evil-god challenge is that belief in a maximally good god ('good god') is no more reasonable than belief in a maximally evil god ('evil god').[2] If true, as Law has argued, then orthodox monotheists are unjustified in believing in good god over evil god. In other words, if there exists a symmetry between the two competing monotheisms, then belief in good god over evil god should be considered (at best) unreasonable. Therefore, in order to justify their belief, good-god monotheists must respond to the following challenge: why is belief in good god significantly more reasonable than belief in evil god?[3]

Although many aspects of the evil-god challenge (including its label) are unique to Law, the argument's general approach – arguing for evil god to contest belief in good god – is not a novel one.[4] Law recognizes this himself, claiming that the first discussion of the evil-god challenge (on creation theology) appears in 1968 with Edward Madden and Peter Hare's book *Evil and the Concept of God*.[5,6,7] In point of fact, an earlier version of the challenge was presented by Madden at the Brown Philosophy Colloquium in 1962 and published two years later in the journal *Philosophy and Phenomenological Research*.[8] More controversially, there was also some discussion of the evil-god challenge prior to the twentieth century. For example, in 1641, René Descartes discussed his worry that the world was devised by a 'malicious demon of the utmost power and cunning,'[9] in 1779, David Hume proposed that the first cause of the universe was a being of 'perfect malice'[10] and in 1802, William Paley offered a lengthy reply to the suggestion that god 'created the human species' because 'he wished their misery'.[11] With the exception of references to Descartes from Max Andrews and Wallace Murphree,[12, 13] and Angus Ritchie's citation of Hume,[14] these early versions of the challenge have been overlooked in the literature, assumedly because they fail to offer developed arguments and defences for evil god. Nonetheless, it is clear that the new wave of interest and specialization was generated by Madden's work in the 1960s. Following Madden, the challenge was later developed by David and Marjorie Haight (1970),[15] Steven Cahn (1977),[16] Peter Millican (1989),[17] Edward Stein (1990),[18] Christopher New (1993),[19] Thomas S. Vernon (1994),[20] Murphree (1997),[21] Wes Morriston (2004)[22] and Law (2005,[23] 2010,[24] 2011a,[25] 2019[26], 2024[27]), and has since been defended by John Zande (2015),[28] Raphael Lataster (2018),[29] Asha Lancaster-Thomas (2018a,[30] 2018b,[31] 2018c,[32] 2019,[33] 2020a,[34] 2020b[35], 2020c[36]) and John Collins (2019).[37] The listed challenges vary significantly in their structure, application and efficacy; therefore, as Lancaster-Thomas has pointed out, the evil-god challenge should be considered a family of problems rather than a single argument.[38]

It is the aim of this chapter to examine the different versions of the challenge and their constitutive arguments. I begin by outlining four ways of presenting the challenge (Section 1.2), two methods of establishing a symmetry between the two hypotheses (Section 1.3) and two methods of constructing parallel arguments in favour of the evil-god hypothesis (Section 1.4). I proceed to draw a distinction between three categories of arguments for good god (Section 1.5) and four classifications of possible solutions to the challenge (Section 1.6). In each of these sections, I identify the version of the challenge and the types of solutions that I will discuss in the proceeding chapters of the book. At the end of the chapter, I draw a distinction between arguments for grounding (establishing god's moral character) and arguments for compatibility (claiming that god is compatible with the available evidence). I continue to explain the significance of this distinction in the context of my wider argument (Section 1.7). I conclude in Section 1.8.

1.2 Presenting the challenge

Lancaster-Thomas has argued that evil-god challenges follow one of three general approaches.[39] The first aim of this section is to develop Lancaster-Thomas's three definitions. My second aim is to contest the popular view that the evil-god hypothesis is absurd. If, as I propose, belief in evil god's absurdity is roughly as reasonable as belief in evil god's non-absurdity, then challengers are unjustified in presenting the popular version of the challenge (the 'absurdity challenge', which depends on evil god's absurdity) over its counterpart (the 'exclusivity challenge', which does not depend on evil god's absurdity). Third, I argue that the evil-god challenger can (and should) present both versions of the challenge (the absurdity challenge and the exclusivity challenge) simultaneously – this, I claim, overcomes the debate concerning evil god's (non-)absurdity. Finally, I suggest that all versions of the challenge can be met by refuting the symmetry thesis (which I outline in Section 1.3).

I begin by identifying some of the challenge's central features. All evil-god challenges contest good-god theism by arguing for the existence of an evil god. Following Law, I label the two competing hypotheses 'the good-god hypothesis' and 'the evil-god hypothesis'.[40] As per classical beliefs within the Abrahamic religions – Judaism, Christianity and Islam – I understand good god to be necessary, personal (possessing consciousness and free will), omnipotent, omniscient and maximally good.[41] These general attributes are widely accepted by traditional good-god theists, although there may be conceptual differences amongst scholars. Where these differences are minor, I expect that the arguments presented also apply, *mutatis mutandis*, to the reader's preferred definition of good god.[42, 43] From here on, a being that possesses the five listed qualities will be referred to as 'good god'. Similarly, I define the concept 'evil god' as necessary, personal, maximally powerful, maximally knowledgeable and maximally evil. The only difference between good god and evil god is their moral character. I refer to a being that possesses the first four qualities, but whose moral character is yet to be determined, as 'god'.[44]

I turn now to the three formulations of the challenge that are present in the existing literature. Lancaster-Thomas labels the first approach the 'weak evil-god challenge'.[45] This challenge claims that the good-god hypothesis is no more reasonable than the evil-god hypothesis, and, therefore, there is no justification for favouring one hypothesis over the other. The structure of weak evil-god challenges can be presented as follows:

1a. The good-god hypothesis is no more reasonable than the evil-god hypothesis. (Premise)
2a. It is unreasonable to favour the good-god hypothesis over the evil-god hypothesis. (Conclusion)

Lancaster-Thomas states that she is '[un]aware of any scholars who have seriously advocated the weak evil-god challenge'[46] – note her use of the term 'seriously'. However, in a separate article prepared in the same year, Lancaster-Thomas claims that advocates of the weak evil-god challenge include Haight & Haight and New.[47] We should be cautious when attributing different versions of the challenge to its earlier proponents, as their arguments are often compatible with multiple interpretations. Throughout this section, I refrain from referencing ambiguous cases; irrespective of whether Haight & Haight and New defend the weak evil-god challenge, it suffices to say that the weak evil-god challenge is unpopular.[48]

To understand why the challenge is unpopular, we need only to consult what the argument attempts (or does not attempt) to establish. The challenge is 'weak' because it does not claim that the good-god hypothesis is absurd (unlike the second approach) or that it ought not to be considered true (unlike the third approach).[49] Instead, the weak evil-god challenge allows for the possibility that both hypotheses are reasonable, but that the orthodox theist faces a problem: they are unjustified in favouring the good-god hypothesis over the evil-god hypothesis. In short, weak evil-god challenges present the problem – favouring one hypothesis over the other is unreasonable – whereas 'strong evil-god challenges' conclude that belief in good god is absurd or that it ought not to be considered true.

Strong evil-god challenges pose a significant threat to good-god theism by introducing what proponents consider to be a small number of uncontroversial premises. As I argue throughout this section, I believe that some of these premises *are*, in fact, controversial. However, this does not prohibit us from developing an equally potent form of the challenge. As I shall argue, a stronger version of the challenge is available to us – one whose premises are no more controversial than those of the weak evil-god challenge – and this new version of the challenge should, therefore, be preferred. Before we discuss this new version of the challenge, let us consider the second and third approaches.

The second and third approaches (strong evil-god challenges) move from the presentation of the problem to the conclusion that belief in good god is absurd or highly unreasonable. The second method, which Lancaster-Thomas labels the 'strong evil-god challenge from incoherence' (I call this the 'absurdity challenge'), begins with the claim that the evil-god hypothesis is absurd. It proceeds to argue that the good-god hypothesis is just as reasonable as the evil-god hypothesis, and, therefore, that the good-god hypothesis is also absurd. Notably, this is the preferred method of Madden,[50] Cahn,[51] Millican,[52] Morriston[53] and Law,[54] which makes it the most popular version of the evil-god challenge to date. The absurdity challenge can be constructed as follows:

1b. The evil-god hypothesis is absurd. (Premise)
2b. The good-god hypothesis is no more reasonable than the evil-god hypothesis. (Premise)
3b. The good-god hypothesis is absurd. (Conclusion)

Unlike the absurdity challenge, the third formulation does not claim that the evil-god hypothesis is absurd. It goes on to state that if the good-god hypothesis ought to be considered true, and if belief in good god is no more reasonable than belief in evil god, then the evil-god hypothesis ought to be considered true. However, as two mutually exclusive monotheisms cannot both be true, it is not the case that the good-god hypothesis ought to be considered true. This is what Lancaster-Thomas calls the 'strong evil-god challenge from inconsistency'; 'if the good-god hypothesis is true, then the evil-god hypothesis is also true, which constitutes an impossible state of affairs, and, therefore, both must be false'.[55] I present the argument as follows:

1c. It is no less reasonable to consider the evil-god hypothesis true than it is to consider the good-god hypothesis true. (Premise)
2c. The good-god hypothesis ought to be considered true. (Assumed for *reductio*)
3c. The evil-god hypothesis ought to be considered true. (1c–2c)
4c. Both the good-god hypothesis and the evil-god hypothesis ought to be considered true. (2c–3c)
5c. For any mutually exclusive hypotheses, it is not the case that one ought to consider both of those hypotheses true. (Premise)
6c. The good-god hypothesis and the evil-god hypothesis are mutually exclusive. (Premise)
7c. It is not the case that one ought to consider both the good-god hypothesis and the evil-god hypothesis true. (5c–6c)
8c. It is not the case that the good-god hypothesis ought to be considered true. (Conclusion)

Although the exclusivity challenge has been discussed in the literature – see Lancaster-Thomas[56] and Millican[57] – no version of this argument has been endorsed over the absurdity challenge. There appear to be two reasons for this. The first, although speculative, concerns the wider framework in which the evil-god challenge exists. It seems that defenders of the challenge, typically non-theists, are reluctant to concede (even hypothetically) that the good-god hypothesis enjoys a high degree of plausibility. Built into this concern is the lurking possibility that the exclusivity challenge may be used as an argument for dualistic polytheism – a version of which has recently been put forward by Kirk Lougheed.[58] The plausibility of polytheism and non-theism goes beyond the scope of the traditional evil-god challenge and our current project, and, therefore, it suffices to say that the evil-god challenge *simpliciter* should be presented against orthodox monotheism unconstrained by our wider spiritual commitments.[59]

The second motivation for overlooking the exclusivity challenge concerns absurdity: the popular view being that the evil-god hypothesis is absurd, as held by the absurdity challenger. Let us consider this reason in detail. Broadly put, there are three reasons as to why the evil-god hypothesis might be considered absurd. First, one might hold the view that the evil-god hypothesis is *a priori* incoherent. Cases of internal absurdity occur when a proposition contains a logical contradiction (such as in the statement, 'married-bachelors exist') or is metaphysically incoherent (such as in the statement, 'numbers are smelly'). It is also worth noting that many objectors to the evil-god challenge – including Peter Forrest,[60] Andrews,[61] Charles Daniels,[62] Edward Feser,[63, 64] Keith Ward[65] and Christopher Weaver[66] – have claimed that evil god is internally incoherent. Second, one might consider the evil-god hypothesis absurd in the light of external considerations: that is, the evil-god hypothesis is absurd because evil god's attributes contradict facts about the world. Some evil-god challengers (most prominently Law[67]) and many orthodox monotheists (such as Swinburne and Paley[68]) have suggested that it is absurd to believe in evil god because the world contains a significant amount of good. Third, one might argue that the evil-god hypothesis is intuitively absurd.[69] To take one example, whilst the proposition 'there is no such thing as an external world' contains no contradictions, it may be reasonable to believe the statement is absurd until it is shown otherwise. Thus, by the same token, the evil-god hypothesis might be considered pre-theoretically absurd.

I argue that when constructing the challenge, the purported absurdity of the evil-god hypothesis is problematic on all three accounts. First, the evil-god challenger cannot accept that evil god is internally incoherent alongside the view that good god is internally coherent; if they do so – as I argue in Section 1.6 – then this may constitute a significant asymmetry in favour of good god. On the other hand, the challenger may accept evil god's *a priori* absurdity but wish to maintain a symmetry between the two hypotheses by claiming that both hypotheses are *a priori* absurd. Advocates of this approach include Lancaster-Thomas, who writes, 'A final tactic the strong evil-god hypothesizer can employ is to argue that the good-god hypothesis is also impossible, therefore leaving the symmetry thesis intact.'[70] However, if an argument demonstrating the internal incoherence of good god were successful, then this would make the evil-god challenge obsolete: if the good-god hypothesis is *a priori* absurd, then good god does not exist.

Second, Law's assertion that 'almost everyone considers the suggestion that the universe is the creation of an evil god absurd' because 'the universe contains far too much good for it to be the creation of such a malevolent deity' is highly contentious.[71] The sentiment of this claim – which is defended by Law in most presentations of his argument – has also been echoed by Lancaster-Thomas, who states that the 'problem of good is perhaps the biggest problem one could pose' against the evil-god hypothesis.[72] Before responding to Law, let us be clear on how this argument for evil god's *a posteriori* absurdity is structured. I present Law's argument as follows:

1d. If the world contains a significant amount of good, then the evil-god hypothesis is absurd. (Premise)
2d. The world contains a significant amount of good. (Premise)
3d. The evil-god hypothesis is absurd. (Conclusion)

This argument plays a central role in Law's wider challenge, in which he claims that belief in evil god is obviously absurd given the amount of good in the world and that – by the same reasoning – the good-god hypothesis should also be considered absurd given the amount of worldly evils.[73] There are two possible ways of motivating premise 2d: either there is a rough symmetry between the world's goods and evils (that the world contains both a significant amount of good as well as a significant amount of evil) or the world contains significantly more good than it does evil.[74] Let us consider both claims, beginning with the second. The challenger should avoid making the second claim, for if the world does contain significantly more good than evil, then – as William Paley and Richard Swinburne have argued – good god could be grounded in the world's goods (there is enough good), but evil god could not be grounded in the world's evils (there is not enough evil).[75] Instead, for the purpose of constructing the evil-god challenge, I suggest the challenger states the following: the claim that the world contains significantly more good than evil is not significantly more reasonable than the claim that the world contains significantly more evil than good. If this hypothesis is true, then Law's assertion that the evil-god hypothesis is *a posteriori* absurd is no more reasonable than belief in its *a posteriori* non-absurdity; this is my claim here. However, if the hypothesis is false – and the orthodox theist's belief that the world contains significantly more good than evil is highly plausible, while the evil-god challenger's assertion that the world contains significantly more evil than good is highly implausible – then the orthodox theist may have a solution to the evil-god challenge. It's worth noting that Law himself rejects this reply to the challenge, stating that 'appeals to subjective estimations can carry little weight'.[76]

Let us consider the first, and more modest claim – that there is a rough but significant symmetry between the world's goods and evils – as a motivation for premise 2d. Here again, I believe that Law's wider argument can be reversed in favour of the evil-god hypothesis's non-absurdity. As Law suggests himself, orthodox theism maintains that it is reasonable to ground good god in creation given the amount of observed goods in the natural world.[77] Subsequently, the good-god defender may offer theodicies (and defences) to maintain the reasonableness of their view in response to the problem of evil. Let us consider two examples. First, the traditional theist may appeal to the extrinsic free-will defence, one version of which states that for agents to be considered morally praiseworthy for their actions (a great good), good god must allow agents to choose between morally virtuous and morally vicious outcomes. As a world of praiseworthy beings is better than a world of do-gooding automata, it is reasonable to hold that good god may have justified reasons for permitting the existence of some moral evils. Second, one may offer a character-building defence, according to which agents need to experience pain and suffering (evils), so that they can overcome their hardships and develop their moral and spiritual characters (a great good). Therefore, the defence states, good god may have justified reasons for permitting the existence of some natural evils. As evidenced by the prevalence of orthodox monotheism, the popular resulting view is that good-god theism should not be considered absurd. Herein lies the problem with Law's argument for evil god's absurdity: the same approach can also be applied to the evil-god hypothesis, as Law explains in detail.[78] After grounding evil god in worldly evils, the challenger can respond to the problem of good with reverse-theodicies and reverse-defences.[79] To illustrate this move, let us reverse our two previous examples. First, the evil-god defender may construct a pessimistic version of the extrinsic free-will defence. The argument claims that for agents to be considered morally blameworthy for their actions (a great evil), evil god must allow agents to choose between virtuous and vicious outcomes. Therefore, as a world of morally blameworthy beings is worse than a world of evil-doing automata, it is reasonable to hold that evil god may have reasons for permitting the existence of some goods. Second, consider what Law has labelled the 'character-destroying' defence, which states that agents need to experience pleasure and happiness (goods), so they can experience the loss of these goods, which contributes towards their moral and spiritual destruction. Therefore, evil god may have reasons for permitting the existence of some natural goods.[80] The conclusion: if the good-god hypothesis should not be considered to be an obvious *a posteriori* absurdity (as held by the majority of monotheists), then why should the evil-god hypothesis be considered absurd on symmetrical grounds? The onus is on the evil-god challenger to show why their argument for evil god's *a posteriori* absurdity is more reasonable than evil god's *a posteriori* non-absurdity. I summarize the argument as follows:

1e. If it is reasonable to believe the good-god hypothesis despite the problem of evil, then it is reasonable to believe the evil-god hypothesis despite the problem of good. (Premise)
2e. It is reasonable to believe the good-god hypothesis despite the problem of evil. (Premise)
3e. It is reasonable to believe the evil-god hypothesis despite the problem of good. (Conclusion)

The argument presented is not intended as an irrefutable proof of evil god's non-absurdity. Rather, it serves to demonstrate that belief in the evil-god hypothesis's *a posteriori* non-absurdity is not obviously and significantly less reasonable than belief in its *a posteriori* absurdity. After constructing an argument in the same spirit as my own, Perry Hendricks concludes, 'It follows that – since the problem of good fails – premise (2) [that belief in evil god is unreasonable (1b)] is groundless.'[81]

The absurdity challenger may contest this line of argument, claiming that the question is not whether the evil-god hypothesis is *actually* absurd, but whether the orthodox theist considers it to be absurd. If the good-god defender claims that 'the world's goods rule out the possibility of evil god' then – if the world contains a similar amount of good and evil – they should apply this same reasoning to their own religious belief and conclude that the world's evils rule out the possibility of good god. Notably, Law argues that good-god defenders do, in fact, take the evil-god hypothesis to be *a posteriori* absurd. Law writes, 'Theists typically dismiss the evil-god hypothesis out of hand because of the problem of good.'[82] However, several traditional theists – including William Lane Craig,[83] Hendricks[84] and Ben Page & Max Baker-Hytch[85] – have argued, in response to Law, that theists do not rule out the evil-god hypothesis because of the world's goods. If this is true, there are a significant number of theists that Law's argument does not apply to, as well as many who may choose to abandon the problem of good (there is too much good in the world for evil god to exist) as a reason to reject the evil-god hypothesis – note that they may also claim that the world's goods significantly exceed the world's evils. For these reasons, the absurdity challenger's claim that evil god *is* (or is *typically held to be*) absurd, is contentious.

Before proceeding, it is worth emphasizing that these considerations also apply to Law's most recent formulations of the challenge. In 2024, Law offers the following clarification: 'My argument is this: if you can reasonably reject the evil-god hypothesis because of the problem of good, and I think you can, then you can reasonably reject the good-god hypothesis because of the problem of evil.'[86] As I have argued, however, we have no more reason to *reject* than *accept* the absurdity of the evil-god hypothesis on the basis of observed goods. Law must explain *why* we should rule out an evil god on the basis of observed goods. Otherwise, to defeat Law's version of the challenge, the theist needs only to claim that one cannot demonstrate the absurdity of the evil-god challenge through the problem of good. From here, the theist may argue that they have *other* reasons for favouring the good-god hypothesis over the evil-god hypothesis. It is these other reasons that constitute the focus of the proceeding chapters.

Third, let us evaluate the claim that the evil-god hypothesis is intuitively absurd. We should note that positions that seem absurd in the first instance should be revised in the light of supporting evidence – evidence that (as we shall see) the evil-god hypothesizer claims to provide. We should also recognize that many worldviews do not consider malevolent gods and deities to be absurd. Within polytheistic faiths, consider the *Ju/'hoansis's //gangwa matse*,[87] the Egyptians' conception of Apophis[88] and the Marcionites' interpretation of the Hebrew god.[89] Many non-theistic perspectives also attribute evil to what they consider to be the greatest metaphysical entity, whether it be the naturalistic existential pessimist who claims that 'the world is generally [bad] and that we should [not] be happy and grateful to live in it',[90] or the Buddhist philosophers who speak of the world as bracketed in pain and sorrow.[91] For many adherents of non-theistic pessimistic worldviews, it is the good-god hypothesis and not the evil-god hypothesis that strikes them as absurd. To take one example, consider the following passage from Schopenhauer's autobiographical writing:

> In my 17th year, lacking all scholarly education, I became deeply moved by the misery of life as Buddha in his youth, when he caught sight of disease, old age, pain and death. The truth that the world so very clearly revealed to me soon overcame the Jewish dogmas that I too had engrained, and I concluded that this world could not be the work of an infinitely good being, but might very well

be that of a devil who brought creatures into existence so he could revel in the spectacle of their agony.[92]

Finally, to take a monotheistic example, consider the Indonesian Hindus' belief in Sang Hyang Widhi: a supreme deity that is both good and evil. Mark Hobart recalls the following anecdote from his fieldwork with the Balinese Hindus:

> Late one evening after a long discussion with a group of villagers ... I remarked that ... in Christianity there was a paradox that, if God were good, omnipotent and omniscient, how could evil exist? To my surprise I was met with hoots of laughter ... One of them explained the matter to me, to mutters of agreement from the others. Of course God – in Bali Sang Hyang Widhi, the highest, all-embracing Divinity – was bad ... How else could there be bad in the world?[93]

I acknowledge that this is an example of a monotheistic deity with a mixed moral character, but my point is a more general one: if the monotheistic good-god hypothesis, the polytheistic evil-god hypothesis, the non-theistic pessimistic hypothesis and the monotheistic morally-mixed-god hypothesis are not considered intuitively absurd, then why should we think differently of the evil-god hypothesis? It is impossible to determine how widespread this intuition is from the armchair. I expect that the intuition will differ significantly from person to person and from culture to culture.

In all three cases, my claim is not that the evil-god hypothesis is reasonable but that the jury is out as to whether or not the evil-god hypothesis should be considered absurd. Although we should remain open to the possibility that the evil-god hypothesis is absurd (as argued by the aforementioned philosophers), in the light of the above, I propose that the evil-god challenger should not commit themselves to a specific form of the strong evil-god challenge. Instead, they should present the absurdity challenge and the exclusivity challenge simultaneously.

To understand how and why the evil-god challenger should present both versions of the argument, consider the following proposal. Rather than defending or rejecting the absurdity of the evil-god hypothesis, suppose that we presented the challenge in the form of a dilemma. On this approach, the challenger would begin by asking the following question: 'Is the evil-god hypothesis absurd?' If the good-god theist affirms evil god's absurdity, then they face the absurdity challenge. On the other hand, if the good-god theist denies evil god's absurdity, then they must respond to the exclusivity challenge. Hypothetically, an 'evil-god dilemma' would alleviate the challenger's burden of arguing for evil god's (non-)absurdity, whilst allowing the good-god defender to select between the two arguments. I present the evil-god dilemma as follows:

1f. Either the evil-god hypothesis is absurd or the evil-god hypothesis is not absurd. (Premise)
2f. If the evil-god hypothesis is absurd, then the good-god hypothesis is absurd. (1–3b)
3f. If the evil-god hypothesis is not absurd, then it is not the case that the good-god hypothesis ought to be considered true. (1–8c)
4f. The good-god hypothesis is absurd or ought not to be considered true. (Conclusion)

Although this approach appears to offer a solution to the contentious question of evil god's absurdity, we should refrain from presenting the challenge as a dilemma for the following reason. As I discuss in Section 1.5, arguments supporting the evil-god hypothesis can be constructed in one of two ways. First, an argument for evil god may be built upon the epistemic and metaphysical foundations of orthodox good-god monotheism. Or, second – and most importantly – an argument for evil god may deviate from the foundations of good-god theism when a principle the challenger seeks to replace is not significantly more reasonable than its replacement. It is this second type of argument that creates a problem for the evil-god dilemma. Simply put, when the good-god defender claims that the evil-god hypothesis is absurd or not absurd, the challenger may contest their answer. By rejecting the good-god theist's answer to the evil-god dilemma's initial question, the challenger forces the good-god defender to address the adjacent challenge – see Figure 1.

Consequently, it does not matter whether the good-god theist believes they face the absurdity challenge or the exclusivity challenge: in reality, they must address both, and so the evil-god challenger should be prepared to present both. Significantly, this approach strengthens the challenge, as it does not rely on the truth of premise 1b (that the evil-god hypothesis is absurd) which several opponents of the challenge – most notably Hendricks[94] – have rejected in their own responses to Law. Given that the truth of premise 1b is no more reasonable than its falsity, those who rely solely on the absurdity challenge (such as Madden, Cahn, Millican, Morriston and Law) leave themselves vulnerable to the rejection of premise 1b. By offering what I call the 'combined challenge' rather than the absurdity challenge, opponents such as Hendricks must respond to premise 2b/1c – that is, the symmetry thesis. Note that this move is only legitimate if the

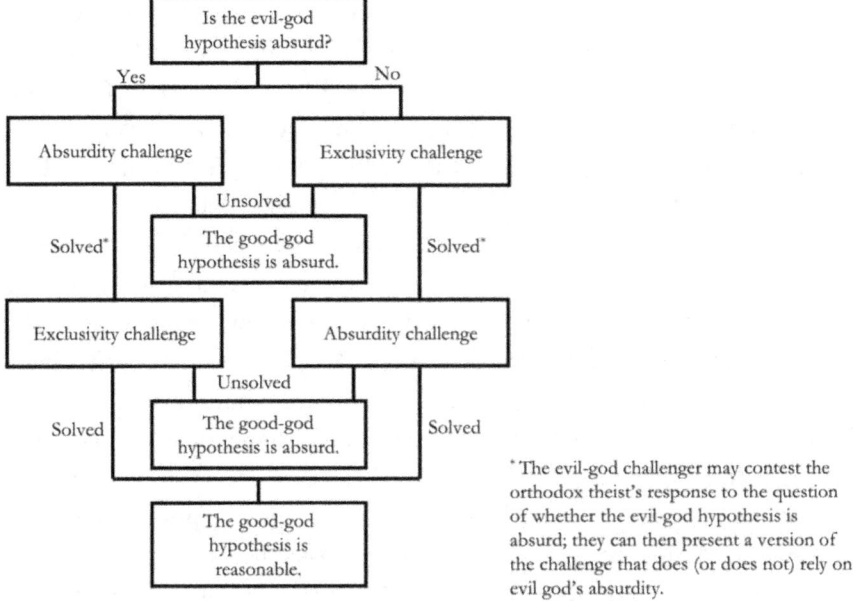

Figure 1 The Combined Evil-god Challenge.⁹⁵© Jack Symes

evil-god hypothesis's absurdity is not significantly more reasonable than its non-absurdity, which for the aforementioned reasons I take to be true.

To answer both forms of the challenge, the orthodox theist should address the evil-god challenge directly and reject both arguments' central claim: that the good-god hypothesis is no more reasonable than the evil-god hypothesis.

1.3 Symmetry

All evil-god challenges rest on the claim that the good-god hypothesis is no more reasonable than the evil-god hypothesis. As Law points out, this premise can be interpreted in one of two ways: according to the 'exact parallel thesis' or the 'symmetry thesis'.⁹⁶ In this section, I outline both theses before advocating the symmetry thesis.

According to the exact parallel thesis, for every argument for (such as cosmological and teleological arguments) or against (such as arguments from evil and hiddenness) the existence of good god, there is an exact parallel argument for or against the existence of evil god. Before Law reframed the discussion, this seems to have been the predominant view amongst evil-god challengers, including Hume,[97] Madden and Hare,[98] Haight & Haight,[99] Cahn[100] and Stein.[101] Law attributes the exact parallel thesis to Madden, Hare, Cahn and Stein, but only in reference to the problem of evil, theodicies and defences ('the problem of evil literature').[102] While it is true that the challenges cited by Law held that the problem of evil literature was perfectly isomorphic with respect to the problem of good, many thinkers preceding Law applied the exact parallel thesis to a range of arguments for and against god's existence, including the cosmological argument,[103] the argument from religious experience,[104] the ontological argument[105] and ethical arguments.[106] Cahn appears to be the single exception to this rule, restricting his focus to the problem of evil literature.[107] We should keep in mind that, pre-Law, many of the earlier challengers did not state whether they supported the exact parallel thesis and, instead, may have favoured the symmetry thesis. Therefore, let us accept that prior to Law it is likely that the only thesis offered by challengers was the exact parallel thesis, whilst remembering that the views of Law's forerunners may be compatible with the symmetry thesis.

Since the publication of Law's seminal paper, proponents of the challenge have shifted their focus away from the exact parallel thesis towards Law's symmetry thesis. Unlike the exact parallel thesis, the symmetry thesis rejects the view that for every argument for or against good god's existence there is an exactly parallel argument for or against evil god's existence. In its place, the symmetry thesis maintains that once we evaluate all of the available evidence and considerations pertinent to both hypotheses, the reasonableness of each hypothesis will be 'roughly' as similar.[108]

In Law's view, if an asymmetry in favour of good god is presented, there are – broadly put – two reasons why this may not constitute a solution to the challenge.[109] First, an asymmetry may not have a significant amount of explanatory power or constitute an effective argument in itself, and, in such cases, it is insufficient as a reason for favouring the good-god hypothesis over the evil-god hypothesis. For example, one may argue – like Ward[110] – that while good god is an appropriate object of prayer, the same is not true of evil god; however, minor asymmetries such as being the appropriate object of prayer appear to have little effect on the probability of either hypothesis, as they do not increase the alethic plausibility of either hypothesis. Second, an asymmetry favouring the good-god hypothesis may be neutralized or outweighed by a separate asymmetry favouring the evil-god hypothesis. For example, good god – but not evil god – can be grounded in the Christian Scriptures, which claim that god is good. However, evil god – but not good god – may be grounded in the significant amount of evil in the natural world.[111] In these examples, despite there being two asymmetries, neither is 'significant' as each one is counterbalanced (or arguably outweighed) by the other. In order to reject the symmetry thesis, those responding to the challenge must, therefore, provide (i) a powerful and effective argument that uniquely favours the good-god hypothesis, which (ii) cannot be neutralized or outweighed by a separate asymmetry uniquely favouring the evil-god hypothesis. If an argument meets these criteria, then it should be considered a 'significant reason' for favouring the good-god hypothesis over the evil-god hypothesis.

Throughout the forthcoming chapters, I respond to a version of the challenge that incorporates Law's symmetry thesis over his predecessor's exact parallel thesis. In rejecting the exact parallel thesis, Law offers two examples of asymmetries: the first purported asymmetry relates to Augustine of Hippo's theodicy from original sin, and the second relates to the claim that free will is an intrinsic good. I make a case for several additional asymmetries in the proceeding chapters.

Finally, there are two ways of understanding the symmetry thesis: as part of a *narrow* evil-god challenge and a *broad* evil-god challenge. Narrow evil-god challenges compare particular arguments (X) for good god with parallel arguments (of X) for evil god. In such cases, the challenger does not wish to examine whether there is more evidence *on the whole* for good god or evil god. There are at least four examples of narrow evil-god challenges in the literature: Descartes (who concentrates on epistemology), Hume (who focuses on design), Paley (who also focuses on design) and Haight & Haight (who concern themselves with the ontological argument). In contrast, *broad* evil-god challenges claim that the symmetry thesis holds across *all* of the various aspects of classical monotheism. Although broad challenges can motivate the symmetry thesis, which requires a symmetry across 'all of the available evidence', narrow evil-god challenges are significantly less powerful. A narrow evil-god challenge can only highlight what a particular argument is missing – namely, a consideration that favours good god over evil god – however, narrow challenges can be overcome if the theist accepts that the relevant argument can be supplemented by further arguments or evidence that cannot be paralleled by the challenger. I also take it that a sufficient discussion of the broad challenge will catalogue notable symmetries that can be used as part of narrow evil-god challenges, and, therefore, for these reasons, I focus on the broad evil-god challenge throughout this book.

1.4 Structure

All evil-god challenges to date, whether they incorporate the exact parallel thesis or the symmetry thesis, build their case by constructing arguments that parallel – or roughly parallel – those for or against good god ('symmetrical arguments'). The only difference between the two theses is that challengers favouring the symmetry thesis are not required to mirror every argument for good god with an exact parallel argument for evil god, whereas the exact parallel defender must defend a perfect isomorphism. In all cases, the evil-god defender should aim to base their arguments on the epistemic and metaphysical assumptions of good-god theism. In this section, I explain why, and the circumstances in which the challenger is permitted to deviate from the principles of orthodox theism.

When the evil-god challenger constructs parallel arguments supporting evil god's existence, they are not required to present arguments for the underlying metaphysical or epistemic assumptions of their view (I discuss the exception to this rule below) or believe that the arguments they offer are inherently persuasive. Instead, they present the challenge as an internal problem for good-god theism, constructing arguments solely for the purposes of establishing a symmetry between the two hypotheses. Drawing from Yujin Nagasawa, Lancaster-Thomas sees this as one of the evil-god challenge's greatest strengths.[112] Rather than disputing the underlying claims of orthodox monotheism, the evil-god challenger attempts to develop parallel arguments that are 'as metaphysically and epistemically sympathetic as possible',[113] in order to avoid the 'contentious, deep philosophical complexities' to be found in the vast literature on the traditional arguments for and against the existence of good god.[114] (Note that this virtue is limited; as we shall see, the evil-god challenger will have to challenge some of the underlying assumptions of good-god theism.) To take one example, consider the Kalām cosmological argument as presented by Craig:

1g. Whatever begins to exist has a cause. (Premise)
2g. The universe began to exist. (Premise)
3g. The universe has a cause. (Conclusion)[115]

Rather than disputing the underlying assumptions of the Kalām cosmological argument, the evil-god challenger argues that the conclusion favours the good-god hypothesis no more than it favours the evil-god hypothesis. The evil-god defender is not expected to defend the underlying philosophical structure of the Kalām cosmological argument, as the parallel is intended as a challenge, and not as a serious proof for evil god's existence. In such cases, the challenge is as follows: why is argument X for good god significantly more reasonable than the same argument (X) for evil god?

There are circumstances in which the evil-god defender may deviate from the epistemic and metaphysical foundations of good-god theism. Such a move is permitted only when the epistemic or metaphysical principles that the evil-god challenger seeks to replace are not significantly more reasonable than their replacements.[116] Where the epistemic or metaphysical foundations of an orthodox argument are altered, the challenge adopts the following structure: why are principle X and the argument built upon X significantly more reasonable than an alternative principle (Y) and the argument built upon Y?[117] To take an example, let us consider one of Collins's developments to the challenge.[118] Following Gottfried Leibniz, the good-god theist may claim that our universe constitutes 'the best of all possible worlds'.[119] Building upon this principle, one may proceed to develop an argument for god's goodness:

1h. If we exist in the best of all possible worlds, then god is good. (Premise)
2h. We exist in the best of all possible worlds. (Premise)
3h. God is good. (Conclusion)

To construct a parallel argument and maintain the symmetry thesis, the evil-god defender must replace the argument's metaphysical claim (2h) with a similarly reasonable principle. Here, the challenger may introduce the claim that we exist in the worst of all possible worlds. The parallel argument could be presented as follows:

1i. If we exist in the worst of all possible worlds, then god is evil. (Premise)
2i. We exist in the worst of all possible worlds. (Premise)
3i. God is evil. (Conclusion)[120]

The challenge here is to explain why the belief that 'we exist in the worst of all possible worlds' is significantly more reasonable than Leibniz's original claim. In some cases, a deviation from good-god theism's framework may be subtler. To take an example, whilst the good-god hypothesizer may appeal to Scripture's revelation of god's love, the evil-god defender might appeal to contradictions between the world's competing scriptures. The evil-god challenger should avoid altering the underlying principles of good-god theism wherever possible, as doing so increases the possibility of notable asymmetries.[121]

In contrast to symmetrical arguments, I label arguments that cannot be paralleled by the opposing hypothesis as 'independent arguments'. When constructing independent arguments for good god or evil god, as in the case of parallel arguments, the challenger may employ premises or underlying principles that are widely accepted by orthodox theists, as well as premises that are roughly as reasonable as those used by good-god theists. Independent arguments for evil god may also introduce new premises, if and only if the premises are highly plausible.

1.5 Arguments

In the previous section, I identified one of the main virtues of the evil-god challenge: that the challenge attempts to avoid complex debates relating to the underlying assumptions of good-god theism wherever possible. The second primary virtue of the challenge – again, drawing from Lancaster-Thomas[122] – is that the evil-god challenge can be applied to all arguments for and against the existence of good god. In this section, I distinguish between three types of arguments and show how each of them can be incorporated into the challenge.

First, some arguments do not aim to establish god's moral character. Arguments of this sort do not rely on god's goodness as an underlying principle or a hidden premise, and god's goodness is not implied by the argument's conclusion. To recycle our previous example, although the Kalām cosmological argument infers a timeless, spaceless, necessary being with the power to create something out of nothing, it says nothing about god's moral character. Arguments that meet this criterion are typically presented as part of a cumulative case for the existence of good god; however, they can also be used to form a collective case for the existence of evil god. For arguments of this type, the evil-god challenger does not need to construct parallel arguments or alter the target argument's premises. (There is one minor exception to this rule: the challenger may need to replace the term 'God' with 'evil god'.)

Second, some arguments do not claim that god is good, but assume an underlying principle or hidden premise that favours the good-god hypothesis from which – in conjunction with the argument's conclusion – one can infer that god is good. To take an example, consider Anselm of Canterbury's ontological argument from *Proslogion II*, as presented by Millican:

1j. The Fool understands the phrase: 'something-than-which-nothing-greater-can-be-thought'. (Premise)
2j. Hence something-than-which-nothing-greater-can-be-thought exists at least in the Fool's mind. (1j)

3j. It is greater to exist in reality than to exist in the mind alone. (Premise)

4j. So if that-than-which-nothing-greater-can-be-thought existed only in the Fool's mind, then it would be possible to think of something greater (i.e. something existing in reality also). (2j–3j)

5j. But this would be a contradiction, since it is obviously impossible to think of something greater than that-than-which-nothing-greater-can-be-thought. (4j)

6j. Therefore, something-than-which-nothing-greater-can-be-thought must exist both in the Fool's mind and in reality also. (Conclusion)[123]

Although the argument appears to be silent on god's moral character, god's goodness – according to Anselm and advocates of perfect-being theology – can be inferred from the concept 'something-than-which-nothing-greater-can-be-thought'. As Anselm writes, 'He must therefore be living, wise, powerful and all-powerful, true, just, happy, eternal and whatever similarly it is absolutely better to be than not to be.'[124] As Anselm implies, the argument contains a hidden principle or premise, which maintains that the greatest conceivable being holds all great-making properties to the highest possible degree and that goodness is a great-making property. If we were to accept these assumptions in conjunction with the argument's conclusion, then the argument says that good god (and not evil god) exists. For arguments of this type, the evil-god defender should construct parallel arguments that are roughly as reasonable as the orthodox arguments, and they should do so by preserving or deviating from the epistemic and metaphysical foundations of good-god theism. In attempting to construct a parallel of Anselm's ontological argument, the evil-god challenger must do the latter: propose that evil is a great-making property or that it is worse to exist than it is not to exist.[125]

Finally, there are arguments that make an explicit case for god's goodness. Arguments of this sort will either claim to establish god's goodness (consider forms of the moral argument) or god's goodness in addition to a number of other divine attributes (consider Thomas Aquinas's fourth way). Depending on the target argument, parallel arguments may need to deviate from the underlying principles of good-god theism (as we saw with the Leibnizian argument for god's goodness), whilst other parallels can be constructed within the existing framework of good-god theism. To take an example, consider Craig's moral argument:

1k. If good god does not exist, then objective moral values and duties do not exist. (Premise)

2k. Objective moral values and duties do exist. (Premise)
3k. Therefore, good god exists. (Conclusion)[126]

In order to construct a parallel, the evil-god defender needs only to replace 'good god' with 'evil god':

1l. If evil god does not exist, then objective moral values and duties do not exist. (Premise)
2l. Objective moral values and duties do exist. (Premise)
3l. Therefore, evil god exists. (Conclusion)

As moral values can be measured against the objective yardstick of either maximal goodness or maximal evil – says the challenger – it appears that the symmetrical argument functions just as effectively as the target argument.[127] If the good-god hypothesizer wishes to respond to the challenge, in this case, they must explain why the orthodox moral argument (1–3k) is significantly more reasonable than the parallel moral argument (1–3l).

1.6 Responses

According to Lancaster-Thomas, critics of the challenge have offered four types of responses: asymmetry objections, impossibility objections, well-being objections and fideistic objections.[128] In this section, I develop a brief account of each objection. I begin with the most popular objection and end with the least popular objection.

Asymmetry objections reject the symmetry thesis by arguing that the two hypotheses are not roughly symmetrical. The proposed asymmetry or asymmetries, says the critic, demonstrates that the good-god hypothesis is significantly more reasonable than the evil-god hypothesis. Advocates of this approach include Paley (1802),[129] John King-Farlow (1978),[130] Michael Bergmann and Jeffrey Brower (2007),[131] Craig (2011,[132] 2024[133]), Forrest (2011),[134] Glenn Peoples (2011),[135] Ritchie (2012),[136] Nagasawa (2017),[137] Hendricks (2018,[138] 2023[139]), B. Kyle Keltz (2019),[140] Lougheed (2020),[141] Page & Baker-Hytch (2020),[142] Calum Miller (2021)[143] and Carlo Alvaro (2022),[144] making asymmetry objections by far the most popular method of responding to the challenge. There are two types of argument that can be presented as part of an asymmetry objection: asymmetrical arguments and independent arguments. Asymmetrical arguments claim that an orthodox argument for the good-god hypothesis is significantly more effective than its parallel argument for the evil-god hypothesis. Asymmetrical arguments can also be cumulative, claiming that several independently insignificant asymmetries may constitute a significant asymmetry when they are considered collectively. Second, an independent argument may be presented in favour of an asymmetry. Such arguments will provide compelling evidence for the good-god hypothesis, but they cannot be paralleled in favour of (or outweighed by further considerations favouring) the evil-god hypothesis. The advantage of asymmetry objections is that they address the challenge head-on: if the objector can provide a significant asymmetry in support of the good-god hypothesis, then the evil-god challenge can be met. The argument that I develop in the forthcoming chapters is a type of asymmetry objection; I discuss this further in Section 1.7.

Impossibility objections attempt to undermine the symmetry thesis by rejecting the possibility of the evil-god hypothesis. As suggested by Lancaster-Thomas, impossibility objections are closely related to asymmetry objections; however, while asymmetry objections accept that the evil-god hypothesis is at least a coherent concept, impossibility objections claim that the evil-god hypothesis is *a priori*, *a posteriori* or intuitively absurd, and, therefore, 'it is senseless to postulate [the evil-god hypothesis] … in the first place'.[145] Arguments of this sort place evil god in the non-obtaining world of married–bachelors, smelly–numbers and water as CO_2. The objector declares: just as no symmetry thesis can be established between smelly-numbers and non-smelly-numbers, no symmetry thesis can be established between good god and evil god. The resulting view, says the critic, is that the evil-god challenge is a non-starter. This is the second most popular response to the challenge, whose proponents include Daniels (1997),[146] Feser (2010[147], 2011[148]), Andrews (2012),[149] Ward (2015)[150] and Weaver (2015).[151]

Unlike asymmetry objections, there is an ongoing debate as to whether a compelling impossibility objection would constitute a solution to the evil-god challenge. To understand why, let us consider Law's response to Feser's argument for evil god's *a priori* incoherence. In short, Feser argues that the concept of evil god is an *a priori* absurdity, as he puts it himself:

Nothing that is omnipotent could possibly be less than perfectly good, and indeed that nothing that is divine could possibly be less than perfectly good. … The God of classical theism isn't the same kind of thing as Law's "evil god" at all. … It is blindingly obvious that Law's "evil-god challenge" is completely irrelevant.[152]

Responding to Feser's attempt to undermine the challenge, Law argues that the evil-god challenge can still function despite evil god's *a priori* absurdity. In his response to Feser – as well as in his original paper[153] – Law states that:

> Even if there were a conceptual problem with the idea of an evil god … that does not prevent the evil-god challenge from being run. … Assume an evil god is conceptually impossible. Nevertheless, there might also be powerful empirical evidence against an evil god. In fact there is – far too much good in the world. And if that empirical evidence is sufficient to rule an evil god out beyond reasonable doubt … why then isn't the evil we see sufficient to rule a good god out beyond reasonable doubt[?][154]

Note that Morriston, an earlier proponent of the evil-god challenge, makes use of this same approach:

> In the first place, many theists would claim that demonism [(evil-god theism)] is logically incoherent. … Even if demonism is incoherent in just the way that some theists believe, I think it is still useful to ask whether there is any other way to show that demonism is false. Specifically, I want to ask whether there is some range of facts about our world, relative to which demonism is sufficiently unlikely to warrant the judgment that the Demon [(evil god)] does not exist. … Are there straightforward empirical grounds for thinking that demonism is false? Is something about the character of the world that makes demonism unlikely enough to warrant the judgment that there is no such demon?[155]

To illustrate this tension, let us assume that Feser's assertion is correct: the good-god hypothesis is *a priori* possible, but the evil-god hypothesis is *a priori* impossible. Furthermore, let us give Morriston and Law's argument the benefit of the doubt and accept that evidence can count for or against a hypothesis despite it being *a priori* absurd.[156] Morriston and Law's claim that the evil-god challenge can still function despite evil god's *a priori* absurdity relies on the following assertion: that in addition to evil god's hypothetical *a priori* absurdity, evil god should also be considered absurd, *a posteriori*, because there is 'far too much good in the world'. Morriston and Law proceed to isolate the second part of this argument and reverse it to form an *a posteriori* argument against good god: although the good-god hypothesis is *a priori* reasonable, they say, it is *a posteriori* absurd because there is far too much evil in the world. Ultimately, this argument relies on two claims: first, that the amount of good in the world is sufficient for ruling out the evil-god hypothesis, and second, that the world contains a similar amount of good and evil (or a greater amount of evil than good). Thus, Morriston and Law's argument has the following structure:

1m. The evil-god hypothesis should be considered absurd because the world contains a significant amount of good. (Premise)
2m. The world contains a similar amount of good and evil – or the world contains a greater amount of evil than good. (Premise)
3m. If the evil-god hypothesis should be considered absurd because the world contains a significant amount of good – or the world contains a greater amount of evil than good – then the good-god hypothesis should be considered absurd because the world contains a significant amount of evil. (Premise)
4m. The good-god hypothesis should be considered absurd. (Conclusion)

For our current purposes – that is, to illustrate the power of impossibility objections – it is worth outlining two responses to the argument presented (1–4m). First, let us consider premise 1m. As we saw in Section 1.2, this is not a premise that the orthodox theist must (or is even necessarily likely to) accept. As the good-god hypothesis is *a posteriori* reasonable and the arguments within the problem of evil literature (for and against good god) are roughly symmetrical to the arguments within the problem of good literature (for and against evil god), so says Morriston and Law's hypothetical critic, then the evil-god hypothesis is also *a posteriori* reasonable. In other words, given the symmetry between theodicies (and defences) for good god and reverse-theodicies (and defences) for evil god, the orthodox theist might concede that the amount of good in the world is not sufficient for ruling out the existence of evil god (see 1–3e), therefore, rejecting premise 1m. Second, the orthodox theist may reject premise 2m – that the world contains a similar amount of good and evil (or a greater amount of evil than good). Instead, one may claim that the world contains significantly more good than evil. As we shall see in Chapter Three, 'life', says Swinburne, 'is a tremendous good in itself', and in life, 'the good outweighs the bad'.[157] This point is shared by Paley: 'Happiness is the rule; misery, the exception',[158] and from this observation, 'we are authorized to ascribe to the Deity the character of benevolence'.[159] If my suggestion is true – that the question of evil god's *a posteriori* absurdity is contentious – then the challenger should not bite the *a priori* absurdity bullet for the following reason: if the good-god hypothesis and the evil-god hypothesis are *a posteriori* reasonable, but the evil-god hypothesis is *a priori* absurd and the good-god hypothesis is *a priori* reasonable, then belief in evil god is absurd and belief in good god is reasonable. (Similarly, the evil-god challenger cannot accept an *a posteriori* asymmetry of this type either: if both hypotheses are *a priori* reasonable, but the evil-god hypothesis is *a posteriori* absurd and the good-god hypothesis is *a posteriori* reasonable, then belief in evil god is absurd and belief in good god is reasonable.)

To illustrate the point further, consider the following example, in which Lancaster-Thomas defends Morriston and Law's view by rejecting the significance of evil god's *a priori* (non-)absurdity:

> Susan is attempting to prove to her friend, Steve, that some markings through a woodland area are the tracks of a unicorn by pointing out particular characteristics of the markings. ... In an attempt to enlighten Susan ... Steve proposes that they originated from "a werewolf that has never existed in human form". Susan objects to Steve's argument to say that anyone who knows anything about lycanthropy knows that werewolves must necessarily have had human form at some point, yet it does not seem to be absolutely integral for Steve's *reductio* argument that "a werewolf that has never existed in human form" is possible. Even if this being is impossible, Steve can still hypothesise its existence to demonstrate the ridiculousness of Susan's unicorn claim.[160]

This approach is reinforced in the wider literature, such as in the work of Joshua Mugg.[161] Drawing from the work of developmental psychologist Allan Leslie,[162] Mugg endorses a cognitive 'decoupling mechanism', which holds that we are able to 'represent an object as what it is while simultaneously representing it as having incompatible properties'.[163] Rather than representing the world, our 'pretend' concepts – such as unicorns and banana–phones[164] – are not a representation of the world, 'but [a] representation of [a] representation'.[165] The upshot, says the evil-god challenger, is that we can utilize concepts such as 'evil god' or 'a werewolf that has never existed in human form' regardless of their *a priori* incoherence, as they are not intended to be direct reflections of the world.

Ultimately, all of these arguments – as used by Morrison, Law and Lancaster-Thomas – rely on the *a posteriori* absurdity of the evil-god hypothesis. (Recall that I remain agnostic on the question of evil god's *a posteriori* absurdity; see 1–3e.) With this in mind, let us consider a different example, in which the balance of

Table 1 A (Possible) Response to the Evil-god Challenge – Against Accepting Evil God's *A Priori* Absurdity. (Here, a tick (✓) represents non-absurdity and a cross (✗) represents absurdity.) © Jack Symes

	A priori	*A posteriori*	**Pre-theoretically**
Good god	✓	✓	✓
Evil god	✗	✓	✓

a posteriori evidence is unknown. Competing at your weekly pub quiz, suppose the quizmaster proposes the following question: 'What is the prime minister's marital status?' Stumped, you ask your team for help. Your husband says, 'The prime minister is married.' Whilst your best friend proclaims, 'The prime minister is a married–bachelor!' Your husband *could* be wrong, but all else being equal, his answer (which is internally coherent) should clearly be preferred over your friend's (which is internally incoherent).

In any case, this debate is largely academic. In the chapters that proceed, I defend the view that the evil-god hypothesis is neither *a priori* nor *a posteriori* absurd.[166] Furthermore, I do not commit myself to a view on whether the good-god hypothesis or the evil-god hypothesis should be ruled out by the problem of evil or the problem of good. As I argue in Section 1.7, my response is a cumulative asymmetry objection: I claim that we have better reasons for attributing goodness than evil to god.

Third, fideistic objections maintain that belief in good god does not need to be justified on rational grounds – for example, one may claim that religious belief can be grounded in faith rather than alethic considerations. Within the evil-god literature, this approach has been defended only by King-Farlow (1978)[167] and Forrest (1998),[168] making it second to the most unpopular response to the challenge (well-being objections). As argued by Lancaster-Thomas, those who favour fideistic objections accept the symmetry thesis, but place their faith in good god nonetheless.[169] As the symmetry thesis underlies the evil-god challenge – and the evil-god challenge states that orthodox theistic arguments cannot establish the truth of the good-god hypothesis over the evil-god hypothesis – the fideistic objector sacrifices their ability to employ philosophical arguments for good god's existence. The resulting worldview is beyond the scope of the evil-god challenge *simpliciter*; if the orthodox theist maintains that their view is not based on alethic considerations, then the evil-god challenge does not apply. This critique also applies to other forms of fideistic objections, such as the argument that some reasons for believing in good god cannot, or are yet to be, be expressed in language; ineffable arguments for good god cannot be incorporated into the evil-god challenge, and the same applies to ineffable arguments for evil god.

Finally, well-being objections start from the premise that belief in good god promotes well-being and moral actions, whilst belief in evil god is detrimental to well-being and leads to immoral actions.[170] Arguments of this type do not dispute the symmetry thesis on alethic grounds, but argue that we have pragmatic reasons for favouring the good-god hypothesis over the evil-god hypothesis. Let us consider two types of well-being objections: *weak* well-

Table 2 The (Hypothetical) Pragmatic Effects of Good-god Theism and Evil-god Theism. (Here, a tick (✓) represents a positive outcome and a cross (✗) a negative outcome.) © Jack Symes

	Well-being	Moral outcomes
Believe in good god	✓	✓
Believe in evil god	✗	✗

being objections and *strong* well-being objections. Weak well-being objections claim that it is reasonable to believe in good god over evil god for its pragmatic benefits. Consider, for example, a finite wager on the pragmatic benefits of good-god theism versus evil-god theism, as illustrated in Table 2.

The rational decision would be, says the critic – once they have made their case for the positive effects of good-god theism and the negative effects of evil-god theism – to wager in favour of good god: to believe that a maximally loving parent watches over us, that they want us to perform moral actions and that union with this parent awaits us after death. Although the wager may appear reasonable, weak well-being objections cannot offer a solution to the challenge. To break the symmetry thesis, the objector must provide reasons that increase the likelihood of the good-god hypothesis and decrease the likelihood of the evil-god hypothesis. Whilst weak well-being objections might show that belief in good god would increase our quality of life, they do not show that our quality of life increases the truth value of the good-god hypothesis.

Unlike weak well-being objections, strong well-being objections aim to establish a link between the pragmatic benefits of orthodox theism and the increased likelihood of the good-god hypothesis. According to Anastasia Scrutton, within the framework of pragmatic encroachment – 'the idea that practical considerations about what to believe can also constitute epistemic reasons'[171] – the practical benefits of orthodox theism give us strong epistemic grounds for favouring the good-god hypothesis over the evil-god hypothesis. With the exception of Scrutton, there are few (if any) contemporary proponents of the well-being objection. There appear to be four reasons for the view's unpopularity. First, weak well-being objections cannot constitute solutions to the evil-god challenge: orthodox theists are welcome to adopt their belief for its practical benefits, and this has no impact on the symmetry thesis. Second, strong well-being objections rely on unpopular and contentious epistemologies, such as pragmatic encroachment. Given that the evil-god challenge is constructed (largely) within the framework of orthodox good-god theism, the objector should aim to provide orthodox arguments in favour of the good-god hypothesis – arguments that would be welcomed by a higher proportion of orthodox theists – before reaching for unorthodox epistemologies.[172] Third, it is not self-evidently true that belief in evil god leads to a decrease in well-being and moral outcomes. For example, Lee found that the *Ju/'hoansi*, who believed in a morally defective god, were a happy and ethical people. Lee writes, 'They live in a moral universe of high caregiving standards, in which the ideal seems to be that every person is directly obligated to meet the needs of every other person all the time.'[173] Finally, as Lancaster-Thomas has argued in her reply to Scrutton, well-being objections overlook the intention behind the evil-god challenge.[174] Rather than offering a serious alternative to orthodox theism, the evil-god challenger only argues for the existence of evil god to demonstrate that the good-god hypothesis is unreasonable. The evil-god hypothesizer does not claim that people should become evil-god theists, and, therefore, arguments that compare genuine belief in the two gods are obsolete: even if we accept all of Scrutton's premises, the evil-god challenge remains unaffected.

1.7 Grounding and compatibility

Throughout the forthcoming chapters, I develop a cumulative asymmetry objection in response to the evil-god challenge. The asymmetries that I propose ultimately rely on a distinction that I draw between arguments for grounding and compatibility. In this section, I outline the differences between grounding and compatibility before explaining how the distinction relates to my wider thesis.

There are some arguments that aim to establish god's nature: these are grounding arguments. Arguments for grounding maintain that *if* god exists, *then* god would possess certain attributes. Traditionally, these arguments are the focus of philosophical theology. Philosophical theology attempts to understand god's nature, but it does not seek to demonstrate or defend god's existence; furthermore, it does not *assume* god's characteristics either. Consider the following example. Suppose the good-god defender claims that the world contains significantly more good than evil and, from this observation, maintains that creation offers a positive reason for attributing benevolence (rather than malevolence) to god. In this case, the argument aims to ground god's moral character in nature; however, to emphasize the point once more, it says nothing about god's existence. Arguments for grounding god's attributes are found in the three main schools of philosophical theology: perfect-being theology, creation theology and revelation theology. I explore each of these theological traditions in the proceeding chapters.[175] In summary, a consideration is said to ground the good-god hypothesis (or its counterpart) if the evidence or argument is sufficient for attributing goodness (or evil) to god.

In contrast to grounding arguments, an argument ought to be considered an argument for compatibility if it aims to show that a pre-established or hypothetical conception of god is compatible with some evidence for or against god's existence. There are two different types of compatibility argument. First, compatibility arguments may aim to establish that some conception of god is, or is not, *compatible* with some argument for god's existence. For example, in the context of the evil-god challenge, the challenger may argue that evil god is compatible with – and can also be supported by – the traditional arguments for god's existence (such as the ontological, cosmological or teleological arguments). Similarly, one could develop a compatibility argument *against* either hypothesis being reconcilable with some evidence (e.g. by way of the problem of evil, good or hiddenness). Unlike arguments for grounding, compatibility arguments do not attempt to develop a concept of god but focus on demonstrating the existence (or non-existence) of a god with a pre-established or assumed set of attributes. In other words, arguments for compatibility remain silent on *why* we ought to think that god is benevolent or malevolent.

Second, other arguments on compatibility aim to show that god is compatible with some consideration that would otherwise count against god's existence. In the literature, for example, such arguments usually take the form of theodicies and defences in response to arguments from evil and hiddenness. Unlike the first type of compatibility argument, this second type of compatibility argument does not offer *positive* reasons for why some conception of god exists – after all, one might assume god's existence and proceed to claim that some otherwise contradictory evidence is compatible with one's assumed hypothesis. To take an example, suppose we have a large number of reports involving positive religious experiences, in which Jesus and his angels are believed to cause happy and pleasurable experiences. The challenger may argue that evil god is *compatible* with such evidence because evil god has reasons for allowing such goods to exist; after all, evil god wants to deceive us of his true intentions. Within this example, we find no reasons that increase the *initial* probability of the evil-god hypothesis – as it relies on the assumption that there are reasons for evil god's existence – and, therefore, it may be distinguished from the first kind of compatibility argument. Significantly, however, all compatibility arguments have the following in common: no compatibility argument attempts to *ground* god's character. In other words, compatibility arguments do not propose reasons for thinking that god is good or evil.

The distinction between grounding and compatibility is not original to this work. Rather, it is effectively a reformulation of the ancient distinction between philosophical theology and arguments concerning god's existence. In the chapters that follow, I focus on arguments for grounding rather than arguments for compatibility. To borrow from Thomas Morris:

> In these pages, I attempt to focus on some purely conceptual issues. My centre of attention is how we think about, or conceive of, God. … Questions concerning the rationality of religious belief, the nature of faith and the cogency of arguments for the existence of God … those topics are not at the centre of my attention here, but the issues which are treated in the present book will be found to hook up with those other topics in numerous and interesting ways.[176]

In the light of this distinction, I maintain that an imagined hypothesis, all else being equal, is less reasonable than a grounded hypothesis. To illustrate why, let us consider an example. Suppose I claimed that one of my colleagues was, unjustly, plotting my demise. Consider the following argument for compatibility, in which I argue for my colleague's existence, but not their moral character: 'Look over there! See, that's my evil colleague leaving the soup kitchen; I told you he existed!' The argument offers no evidence for why my colleague is evil, and, therefore, you shouldn't take my hypothesis too seriously. Now consider a second kind of compatibility argument, in which I defend my evil-colleague hypothesis against contrary evidence: 'Of course he's volunteering at the soup kitchen; he's trying to deceive me of his true intentions!' That shouldn't convince you either; after all, you want to know *why* I believe my colleague is evil in the first place. Now, suppose I offered a grounding argument in which I claimed to establish my colleague's moral character: 'Why is he evil? Look! He's running toward me with an axe! He's swinging it at m–' The likelihood of my hypothesis has increased significantly.

A review of the literature reveals that every proponent of the evil-god challenge to date *imagines*, *proposes*, *assumes*, *supposes* or *introduces* the logical possibility of a malevolent god, rather than arguing for god's malevolence. Of course, it is worth noting that the grounding of a hypothesis is not sufficient for it to be deemed reasonable; as Law argues, it may turn out that the evil-god hypothesis is incompatible with the world's goods and that the good-god hypothesis is incompatible with the world's evils, making both hypotheses unreasonable. It is worth noting, however, that in order to defend such a view, one must respond to the argument I proposed earlier in this chapter (1–3e). With these qualifications in mind, I maintain that my central claim is not a radical one; I propose that, all else being equal, a grounded hypothesis is significantly more reasonable than a non-grounded hypothesis.

Throughout the forthcoming chapters, I present many arguments that favour the attribution of goodness (over evil) to god. Although I accept that the arguments for grounding good god and evil god in the totality of the world's goods and evils appear roughly as reasonable (Chapter Three, Section 3.8), the arguments from perfect-being theology (Chapter Two), Reformed epistemology (Chapter Three, Section 3.9) and revelation theology (Chapter Four) tip the weight of evidence in favour of orthodox theism. I intend to show that this cumulative asymmetry objection undermines the symmetry thesis and constitutes a successful solution to the evil-god challenge.

1.8 Conclusion

In this chapter, I have given an overview of the nature of the evil-god challenge. First, I outlined four variations of the challenge and defended a non-partisan approach to the question of evil god's absurdity. We have seen that the evil-god challenge can be presented without committing oneself to evil god's absurdity or non-absurdity, and that the objector should develop asymmetries as they attempt to solve the challenge. Second, I discussed the distinction between the exact parallel thesis and the symmetry thesis and outlined the criterion for undermining the symmetry between the two hypotheses. As we saw, in order for an objection to be considered significant, responses to the challenge must provide (i) a powerful and effective argument that uniquely favours the good-god hypothesis, which (ii) cannot be neutralized by a separate asymmetry uniquely favouring the evil-god hypothesis. Third, I discussed two ways in which the challenger can develop arguments supporting the evil-god hypothesis and three types of target argument that the challenger should aim to parallel. Notably, we saw that the challenger can deviate from the underlying principles of traditional theism when necessary, but in doing so, they may increase the number of possible asymmetry objections. Fourth, I considered four broad objections to the evil-god challenge and argued that asymmetry objections should be pursued over impossibility, fideistic and well-being solutions. We also saw that the challenger should not be willing to concede the impossibility of the evil-god hypothesis, as this may constitute a solution to the evil-god challenge. Finally, I drew a distinction between establishing god's moral character (grounding) and showing that a pre-established understanding of god is compatible with the available arguments and evidence (compatibility). I argued that – all else being equal – a grounded hypothesis is more reasonable than a non-grounded hypothesis.

In Chapter Two, I discuss the possibility of grounding god's moral character through perfect-being theology. I outline a number of asymmetries between the two hypotheses and claim that the arguments for grounding good god are stronger than the arguments for grounding evil god.

Chapter Two

The Greatest Conceivable Being

When stranded in the Sea of Doubt,
  In deep ontology,
Perfection as god's evil good
  Could be the hidden key.

2.1 Introduction

We saw in Chapter One that several critics of the evil-god challenge have proposed impossibility objections – that is, critiques which reject the possibility of evil god. According to such objections, it is senseless to postulate an evil god in the first place, and, therefore, no symmetry can be established between the evil-god hypothesis and the good-god hypothesis. There are several versions of this objection in the literature, which – broadly stated – fall into two categories: those which focus on great-making properties and maximal greatness ('great-making objections') and those which focus on moral motivation ('motivation objections'). This chapter focuses on the most promising formulations of both objections. In my discussion of great-making objections, I draw from the work of Anselm and Aquinas. In considering motivation objections, I examine arguments from Swinburne and Weaver.

In this chapter, I offer a series of reasons for thinking that it is more reasonable to attribute goodness (and not evil) to god. At the same time, I defend the evil-god hypothesis against impossibility objections. I do so by offering coherent parallel arguments in favour of evil god. Ultimately, however, I conclude that theism's orthodox principles are more plausible than their parallels.

This chapter has the following structure. I begin, in Section 2.2, by distinguishing between two different god theses: the omni-god thesis and the maximal-god thesis. Although the challenger can parallel both theses, I argue that favouring the maximal-god thesis over the omni-god thesis puts the orthodox theist at an unnecessary disadvantage, and, therefore, I favour the omni-god thesis. In Section 2.3, I proceed to discuss an Anselmian argument for god's goodness – namely, that goodness is a great-making property and that god (as the greatest metaphysically possible being) possesses all great-making properties to the highest possible degree. In this same section, I discuss the significance of perfect-being theology in connection to the ontological argument. In Section 2.4, I reject several parallel versions of perfect-being theology which define god as 'the worst conceivable being'. In their place, I argue that – in order to offer a coherent argument for grounding evil god – the challenger should claim that 'evil is a great-making property'. In Section 2.5, however, I reject this parallel by defending the view that it is more reasonable to believe that goodness (and not evil) is a great-making property. In Section 2.6, I construct a Thomistic argument for god's goodness, which relies on a privation theory of evil. I go on to develop a parallel version of Aquinas's argument, in Section 2.7, which depends on the claim that good is the privation of evil. In Section 2.8, I evaluate the two privation theories, arguing in favour of the privation theory of evil (for good god) and against the privation theory of good (for evil god). In Sections 2.9 and 2.10, I turn my attention to moral motivation arguments for good god. According to the view I discuss – if motivation is intrinsic to moral truth and if god knows all truths – god can be motivated only to do good. In Section 2.11, I offer a number of responses on behalf of the challenger, before rejecting them in favour of orthodox theism. I conclude in Section 2.12.

2.2 Omni-god and maximal-god

Followers of good-god theism have traditionally adopted the omni-god thesis. According to this view, good god is maximally great and necessarily omniscient, omnipotent and omnibenevolent.[1,2] To date, the majority of evil-god challengers have concentrated on undermining an omni good god by constructing arguments in favour of an omni evil god. More recently, however, Lancaster-Thomas has proposed that evil-god challengers can parallel a separate good-god thesis: the maximal-god thesis.[3] The most developed version of the maximal-god thesis is presented by Nagasawa, who states that good god 'is the being that has the maximal consistent set of knowledge, power and benevolence'.[4,5] The main benefit of this approach is its modesty. Rather than being committed to an 'unnecessarily specific' claim – that is, good god *must* be omniscient, omnipotent and omnibenevolent – the maximal-god thesis does not specify the level of good god's attributes.[6] By defining good god in this way, Nagasawa maintains that the orthodox theist can avoid a significant number of arguments traditionally presented against good-god theism. These arguments fall into three categories: those which claim (i) that good god's individual attributes are internally incoherent, (ii) that good god's different attributes are mutually inconsistent and (iii) that good god's attributes are inconsistent with facts about the world.[7] While omni-god theists must address these arguments on a case-by-case basis, maximal-god theists believe they can avoid these problems entirely. If successful, the three types of arguments listed show that the omni-god thesis is false; however, because the maximal-god thesis is open to limiting good god's attributes, it cannot be falsified.[8]

If the omni good-god thesis (a more ambitious version of the maximal good-god thesis) can be paralleled in favour of evil god, then so too can the maximal good-god thesis. This is because the omni-god thesis is the strongest version of the maximal-god thesis, as well as being the most challenging to parallel. If an omni good god can be defended against the three types of argument listed, then the maximal good-god theist may believe in an omni-god. As Nagasawa puts it, 'The maximal God thesis suggests that, while God is certainly very knowledgeable, very powerful and very benevolent, He *might* or *might not* be omniscient, omnipotent and omnibenevolent.'[9] Therefore, if the strongest version of the maximal-god thesis can be paralleled for omni evil god, then so too can a weaker version (i.e. a maximally evil god).

I maintain that orthodox theists and challengers should focus on the omni-god thesis rather than the maximal-god thesis. There are four reasons for this. First, the evil-god literature (to date) has focused almost entirely on the omni-god thesis. I believe that, given the following considerations, converting the existing literature would be an unnecessary feat. Second, we should keep in mind that belief in good god is a genuine belief held by sincere believers. Therefore, we should ask how many theists would favour the maximal-god thesis over the omni-god thesis. I expect that the answer would be few, especially given that the maximal-god thesis involves being open to the possibility that good god's attributes are severely limited.[10, 11] Third, the maximal-god thesis risks making the evil-god challenger's task too easy. Once the evil-god hypothesis is grounded, the challenger may circumvent a significant number of objections. Take, for example, the asymmetry objection from worldly goodness – which states that the evil-god hypothesis is unreasonable because the world contains significantly more good than evil. Given the flexibility of the maximal evil-god hypothesis, conceding a limitation on evil god's malevolence is insignificant, as the maximal evil-god thesis avoids specifying the level of evil god's attributes in the first place. Attempting to avoid arguments against good-god theism (perhaps unnecessarily),[12] the good-god theist allows the evil-god defender to dodge problems of their own, and the flexibility of both maximal-god hypotheses will result in fewer asymmetries than the omni-god hypotheses. As our current project is to identify and assess notable asymmetries between the good-god hypothesis and the evil-god hypothesis, we should therefore focus on the omni-god thesis over the maximal-god thesis. Fourth, following Lancaster-Thomas, it seems that adopting the maximal-god thesis puts the good-god defender at a further disadvantage.[13] According to the 'threshold argument', if there exists a threshold under which god could no longer be described as 'good', then orthodox maximal-god theists cannot guarantee that good god's benevolence will fall above the 'good' threshold. In other words, because the maximal-god thesis *does not* commit god to a level of goodness – as all of god's attributes are entirely flexible – it may turn out that god's character is not sufficiently 'good'. The reverse is true of the maximal evil-god hypothesis: one cannot guarantee that evil god's malice rises above the 'evil' threshold. The resulting view is that both hypotheses may collapse into one another. As Lancaster-Thomas puts it, 'Since benevolence (and, correspondingly, malevolence) is a scaling property, it must be admitted that when the benevolence levels fall below a certain level, the maximal good-god thesis collapses into the maximal evil-god thesis; the two are indistinguishable.'[14] Note that this is a problem for the good-god defender, but not a problem for the evil-god challenger. The evil-god challenger defends the view that the good-god hypothesis is not significantly more reasonable than the evil-god hypothesis; on the other hand, the good-god defender has to show that the good-god hypothesis is significantly more reasonable than the evil-god hypothesis. The force of Lancaster-Thomas's argument is as follows: the goal of the orthodox theist cannot be achieved if the two hypotheses are indistinguishable. It is worth noting that the threshold argument is limited in three important senses. First, the argument assumes that there is a threshold for good and evil. Second, the argument goes through *only if* god does not meet the threshold for 'good'. Third, in reality, very few orthodox good-god monotheists would accept that god is anything but perfectly good – although god may sacrifice a degree of power or knowledge for some greater good, god would never sacrifice his goodness. (The Abrahamic god is not 'good' or 'very good', but *perfectly* good.) Here, I do not claim that Lancaster-Thomas's argument is successful; I present it simply as a problem that the good-god theist may wish to avoid. The omni-god thesis is not subject to these four limitations, and, therefore – in order to steelman the good-god theist (as we shall the evil-god challenger) in search of a solution to the challenge – we ought to focus on the omni-god thesis.

2.3 Anselm's armchair

Perfect-being theologians deduce god's attributes from the perfect-being thesis, which states that god 'is the greatest metaphysically possible being'.[15] On this view, the greatest metaphysically possible being must, by definition, possess all great-making properties to the optimal degree. According to Nagasawa, there are at least four types of great-making properties: those that are great for oneself (the property of being strong is great for weightlifters because it benefits weightlifters), those that benefit the world and others (it is great for a therapist to be empathetic for the sake of their patients), those that are great in the context of one's character or capacity (flavour adds to the greatness of wine but not to the greatness of numbers) and those that are intrinsically great (properties that are great in themselves, regardless of whether they are great in the other three senses).[16] Orthodox theists maintain that god is *intrinsically* great. Stated formally, a property is an intrinsic great-making property if and only if, all else being equal, an object possessing that property is made greater solely in virtue of possessing that property.[17,18] In other words, god's qualities are to be pursued for their own sake: they are great independently of wider circumstances. One popular method of determining which properties constitute great-making properties is to consult our intuitions through thought experiments.[19,20,21,22] Nelson Pike offers a useful example:

> Consider the following game: There are two doors. Behind each door is an object. On the front of each door is written the name of a quality. On the second door is written the contradictory of the name written on the first. ... The object behind each of the doors bears the quality indicated on the front. ... You are to choose a door. The point of the game is to pick the door concealing the object that ought to be preserved. You are to use only the information given on the front of the door.[23]

Suppose I was to write 'powerful' on the first door and 'not powerful' on the second. Knowing nothing else about the objects behind the doors, the intuitive value judgement is to preserve the object behind the 'powerful' door. As Daniel J. Hill writes, 'I think most people think powerlessness a worse thing than power, which is one reason why people are always trying to expand their power by modern technology or exercise or the acquisition of money or getting promoted at work.'[24] The same is said to be true of the remaining attributes. To take some examples, Pike believes we ought to pick the 'knowledgeable' door over the 'not knowledgeable' door;[25] Morris the 'conscious' door over the 'not conscious' door;[26] and Augustine the 'free' door over the 'not free' door.[27] Finally – according to perfect-being theologians[28] – we would pick the 'good' door over the 'not good' door. In the literature, few justifications are offered in favour of this intuition. However, one of the more detailed explanations can be found in the work of J. L. Schellenberg:

> A person who's open and sharing, willing to give of herself in relationship, has a quality we admire, as well as desire for ourselves; we rightly think *it's good in itself for a person to be this way*, and not just that we can get or give something by being loving. Consider for a moment this sharing, relational love in its various human manifestations: the love of friends, the love of siblings, the love of spouses. It is not only because of what it produces in the way of happiness or personal and societal growth that we value it.[29]

As Schellenberg proposes, we value that which is good and loving for the sake of itself. Plugging this intuition into perfect-being theology, we may say that as the greatest metaphysically possible being will possess the greatest possible array of intrinsic great-making properties to the highest possible degree – and that, as goodness is an intrinsic great-making property – we can successfully ground god's goodness.

According to Nagasawa, perfect-being theology is 'arguably the most widely accepted form of traditional monotheism'[30] – see Anselm,[31] Descartes,[32] Craig,[33] Hill[34] and Alvin Plantinga.[35] If true, then perfect-being theology strikes at the heart of the evil-god challenge: god is, by definition, a perfect being and a perfect being must be good. When we talk of 'evil god', says the orthodox theist, we're not talking about the concept of 'god', but some lesser deity. God is a perfect being and we can deduce god's attributes from the perfect-being thesis; however, we cannot arrive at the concept of evil god through the perfect-being thesis. The idea of a perfect being who is evil is a non-starter, says the objector, because good is a perfection and evil is an imperfection.

Although perfect-being theology can be traced back to Greco-Roman philosophy,[36] Anselm is undoubtedly the best-known of the perfect-being theologians. Anselm's original contribution to the field was importing perfect-being theology into a deductive proof for good god's existence in what has come to be known as 'the ontological argument'. Numerous variations have appeared since, including those from Descartes,[37] Leibniz[38] and Moses Mendelssohn.[39] More recently, a number of prominent philosophers – such as Craig,[40] Kurt Gödel,[41] Charles Hartshorne,[42] Norman Malcolm,[43] Nagasawa[44] and Plantinga[45] – have defended the view that ontological arguments count as strong evidence for the existence of good god.

Recall Millican's presentation of Anselm's first ontological argument, which he takes from the second chapter of *Proslogion* (see 1–6j).[46] For Anselm, the perfect being – who is good and not evil, as 'it is better to be just rather than unjust, and happy rather than unhappy'[47] – is not only a coherent concept, but one that exists in reality. According to the orthodox view, as a perfect being cannot be evil, the ontological argument cannot show that evil god exists. Several evil-god defenders have contested this view, maintaining that Anselm's ontological argument can be paralleled in favour of evil god. Examples include Robert J. Richman,[48] Haight & Haight,[49] Millican,[50] New,[51] Murphree,[52] Timothy Chambers,[53] Law,[54] Zande[55] and Lancaster-Thomas.[56] Note that each of these philosophers believes that the traditional ontological argument is just as effective as its parallel. As Millican writes, 'A parallel adaptation is equally successful with Descartes' Ontological Argument in *Meditations 5*, and also the various modern versions by Hartshorne, Malcolm and Plantinga.'[57] Law summarizes the purported parallel as follows:

> I can conceive of an evil god – a being than whom no worse can be conceived. But it is worse for such being to exist in reality than in the imagination. Therefore, the being of which I conceive must exist in reality.[58]

Law's parallel ontological argument is not as powerful as its orthodox counterpart. In short, this is because it overlooks the distinction I drew in Section 1.7: the difference between arguments for grounding and compatibility. Orthodox perfect-being theology and the traditional ontological argument attempt to ground god's goodness and demonstrate good god's existence; in contrast, Law's parallel argument argues only that evil god can be reconciled with the ontological argument (an argument for evil god's compatibility with the argument). As we have seen, perfect-being theology begins by filling in the concept of god by picking out the great-making properties which make a being perfect, whereas Law – like many evil-god challengers – begins by *assuming* evil god's moral character. As Law writes:

> *Suppose* the universe has a creator. *Suppose* also that this being is omnipotent and omniscient. But *suppose* he is not maximally good. Rather, *imagine* that he is maximally evil.[59]

Orthodox theists do not suppose or imagine that god is omnipotent, omniscient and maximally good; rather, they offer reasons and arguments for why god would possess these attributes. If the parallel ontological argument is to carry similar weight, the challenger must ground evil god in a perfect-being theology of their own – a task to which we now turn our attention.

2.4 The worst conceivable being

As we saw in Chapter One, the evil-god challenge does not attack orthodox theologies or arguments for good god *directly*. Instead, it proceeds *indirectly* by developing parallel cases for evil god that are roughly as reasonable as their corresponding arguments for good god. In the previous section, we saw how arguments from perfect-being theology claim that good god (and not evil god) can be deduced from the idea of a greatest conceivable being; therefore, in order to maintain a grounding symmetry, the challenger must develop a similarly reasonable perfect-being theology that favours the attribution of evil (and not goodness) to god. I begin this section with one such account, which maintains that god's malevolence can be deduced from a *worst-being* thesis. I go on to reject this approach and, instead, suggest that the challenger stays true to the framework of perfect-being theology, but that they propose an alternative underlying principle: that evil, and not goodness, is a great-making property.

Recall that in Anselmian terms, god is 'something than which nothing greater can be thought'.[60] Following Mohammad Saleh Zarepour, we should interpret this foundational belief as a 'single-divine-attribute' doctrine, which claims that there is a fundamental divine property (in this case 'being the greatest conceivable being') from which we can deduce all of the other divine attributes.[61] Several evil-god challengers – including Haight & Haight,[62] Millican,[63] New,[64] Murphree,[65] Law,[66] Zande[67] and Lancaster-Thomas[68] – have proposed that, in order to parallel Anselm, we should define evil god as 'the worst being that can be conceived'. There are two ways of understanding this claim and, on both accounts, there are reasons for avoiding this definition of evil god.

First, according to one reading, 'the worst' refers to the opposite of 'the greatest' in a broadly metaphysical sense. In other words, 'the worst being that can be conceived' will possess a maximal set of bad-making properties, rather than a maximal set of great-making properties. According to the orthodox framework, one bad-making property would be omnimalevolence. However, because omnipotence, omniscience and existence are great-making properties, the 'worst being' would also be maximally weak, maximally ignorant and non-existent – that is to say, evil god would be *necessarily* non-existent or impossible.[69] As the evil-god hypothesis states that evil god is omniscient, omnibenevolent and (hypothetically) exists, it appears that evil god cannot be grounded in a broadly metaphysical 'worst-being theology'.[70] Second, the challenger may argue that 'the worst being' does not refer to a broad set of metaphysical properties but, specifically, to moral properties. On this view, the most immoral being would be one who manifests their evil disposition in reality to the greatest conceivable extent. Therefore, as well as being omnimalevolent, 'the worst being' must also be omniscient (to know how to maximize evil), omnipotent (to have the power to maximize evil) and exist in reality (to bring evil into reality). Note that this 'worst being' cannot be grounded in a broadly metaphysical worst-being theology or a perfect-being theology. As we have seen, the worst-being thesis (which interprets 'the worst' in a broadly metaphysical sense) does not result in evil god's existence, and the perfect-being thesis (which interprets 'perfect' in a broadly metaphysical sense) leads to an omnibenevolent god rather than an omnimalevolent one. Instead, this view – that god holds all great-making properties, with the exception of moral character (which is a bad-making property) – is better described as a worst-being-mis-match thesis (the 'mis-match thesis'). The mis-match thesis claims that god possesses a combination of great-making and bad-making properties. However, the problem with the mis-match thesis is that it does not offer a justification as to *why* god's moral character is the outlier. Therefore, we should favour the perfect-being thesis on the grounds of simplicity. Law notes this point himself, writing:

> For example, we might suggest that a good god can be defined in a simple way, e.g. as possessing every positive attribute. As goodness is a positive attribute, it follows that this god is good. The concept of an evil god, by contrast, is more complex, for he possesses both positive attributes (omniscience and omnipotence) and negative attributes (evil). Principles of parsimony require, then, that we favour the good-god over the evil-god hypothesis. I acknowledge that there may indeed be asymmetries between the good – and evil-god hypotheses in terms of simplicity and economy.[71]

Following Law and Zarepour, let us acknowledge that the mis-match thesis is not a 'single-divine-attribute' doctrine – which maintains that god is X (where X is the greatest being, the worst being or the Necessary Existent[72]) – from which all of god's other attributes can be deduced. Instead, the mis-match thesis should be understood as a 'dualistic-divine-attribute' doctrine, according to which god is X *and* evil. As the parallel argument (god is X and evil) does not maintain the same logical structure as the target argument (god is X), we should favour the orthodox framework to the unorthodox framework on the grounds of parsimony.[73] Therefore, I conclude, we have more reason to favour the perfect-being thesis (for good god) than the mis-match thesis (for evil god).[74]

We should note that Law claims that as regards the argument from good god's simplicity, this asymmetry may be insignificant in the light of further considerations. For example, arguments for good god may be inherently unreasonable, and other arguments may be more effective in supporting evil god than good god.[75] I have two responses. First, in the spirit of the evil-god challenge, I develop my argument by granting the orthodox theist the benefit of the doubt, that their metaphysics and epistemology provide reasons for thinking that belief in god is reasonable. Again, as we saw in Section 1.4, the evil-god challenge attempts to undermine orthodox theism indirectly (by offering a parallel case for evil god) rather than directly (by analysing arguments for good god). This allows the challenger to avoid complex and contentious debates regarding good-god theism's underlying epistemic and metaphysical principles. Second, throughout this book, I argue that in the context of grounding there are numerous arguments for good god that cannot be sufficiently paralleled in favour of evil god; however, there are no arguments for evil god that cannot be sufficiently paralleled by the traditional theist.

Before proceeding, let us consider a further, connected problem with the mis-match thesis. As suggested by Law, one might also hold the view that god's *evil* moral character is inconsistent with the *goods* that are god's intelligence and power.[76] In other words, the argument states that evil god's other attributes (knowledge and power) are not just *great*-making properties but *good*-making properties; therefore, even if the mis-match thesis were as simple as the perfect-being thesis, the mis-match thesis would not ground evil god but a morally-mixed god. Miller alludes to this point in the following extract:

> [I] seem to lean in favour of knowledge and power being intrinsically good. For it is plausible that the scientific thirst for knowledge is good in and of itself, and that ignorance is bad. It is also plausible that aiming at truth is intrinsically and not just instrumentally good. Indeed, this seems to be one of the key reasons why deceit is wrong, even when relatively innocuous. ... If so, then maltheism [(evil-god theism)] combines positive and negative properties, while theism combines only good properties, and so is more uniform and hence simpler.[77]

If either objection is true – whether it be that the perfect-being thesis is simpler than the mis-match thesis, or that the mis-match thesis fails to ground evil god – then we should conclude that the perfect-being thesis is more reasonable than the mis-match thesis. Moreover, it is worth noting a further problem with the mis-match thesis in reference to the ontological argument. If evil god does not hold all great-making properties to the highest possible degree, then we can conceive of a being with a greater nature (1j) – namely, good god. As the being with a-nature-than-which-no-greater-nature-can-be-thought must be instantiated in reality (6j), the Anselmian ontological argument for good god (a perfect being) will be significantly more reasonable than an Anselmian ontological argument for evil god (an imperfect being). Therefore, it appears that we have several strong reasons for favouring orthodox perfect-being theology over its parallel.

With these considerations in mind, I propose that the evil-god challenger does not attempt to ground evil god in the worst-being thesis or the mis-match thesis. Before proposing a solution on behalf of the challenger, I wish to reject one more attempt at developing a logically coherent parallel for evil god. Lancaster-Thomas has claimed that the evil-god challenger should begin their parallel argument by reversing one of perfect-being theology's non-moral underlying principles. Rather than accepting that it is greater to exist than not to exist, says Lancaster-Thomas, the challenger should propose that it is greater *not* to exist than it is to exist.[78] This argument relies on what Lancaster-Thomas calls 'the principle of the inferiority of existence', which states that 'any nature that is instantiated is lesser than any nature that is not instantiated (or any nature that is conceived only in the mind)'.[79] This anti-natalist approach, says Lancaster-Thomas, is roughly as reasonable as its natalist counterpart. However, as an attempt to parallel orthodox perfect-being theology, an anti-natalist framework cannot ground evil god. Suppose we accept Lancaster-Thomas's suggestion (that it is better to not exist than it is to exist) and suppose we attempt to develop a conception of evil god from a single-divine-attribute doctrine. If we begin from a broadly metaphysical worst-being theology (which maintains that god possesses a maximal set of bad-making properties), evil god will exist (as it is worse to exist), but he will not be omnipotent or omniscient (as it is better to be powerful and intelligent). In contrast, if we begin from the claim that god is the 'greatest being', god will be omnipotent, omniscient and omnibenevolent, but he will not exist (following the principle of the inferiority of existence). Finally, the anti-natalist view has no significant impact on the efficacy of the mis-match thesis, which – as we have seen – is inherently more complex and fails to ground evil god over a morally-mixed god. Therefore, an anti-natalist view of existence's intrinsic value cannot be used to form a similarly reasonable parallel argument for evil god.[80]

In my view, the challenger should accept that 'god is the greatest being that can be conceived'. However, rather than accepting that *benevolence* is a great-making property, I suggest that the challenger argues that *malevolence* is a great-making property. Although, as I argue in Section 2.5, this principle is not as reasonable as the orthodox view (that goodness is a great-making property), it allows the challenger to form a logically coherent conception of evil god, and, therefore, avoids the charge that an evil god is logically impossible. I end this section by discussing some reasons for why one might believe that evil is a great-making property.

Proponents of good-god perfect-being theology justify the attribution of benevolence to god by appealing to intuitions or revelation. In this chapter, I have restricted our discussion to intuitions. (Grounding god's goodness in revelation is the focus of Chapter Four.) Our earlier example from Schellenberg stated that benevolence is a great-making property, and that 'we rightly think it's good in itself for a person to be this way, and not just that we can get or give something by being loving'.[81] Attempting to parallel this view, Lancaster-Thomas has argued that 'some people might have the Machiavellian intuition that malevolence is greater than benevolence'.[82] There are two reasons to be sceptical of this proposal. First, in the quotation – 'some people might'[83] – we are not told whether or not people hold this 'Machiavellian' intuition. In reality, it is unlikely that many people hold the intuition that evil is an *intrinsic* great-making property – I discuss this further below – however, I accept that many people believe that evil is an *extrinsic* great-making property. Second, a 'Machiavellian' intuition does not involve the claim that malevolence is intrinsically greater than benevolence. For Niccolò Machiavelli, evil is an extrinsic great-making property – rather than an intrinsic great-making property – which benefits the possessor, the world or others.[84] As we see in one of *The Prince*'s most notorious lines, 'one must be a fox *in order to recognize traps*, and a lion *to frighten off wolves*'.[85] In order to develop a similarly reasonable parallel argument, the challenger must establish that evil is not just extrinsically great but intrinsically great.

With these considerations in mind, I maintain that rather than claiming 'some people' hold the intuition that evil is intrinsically great, the challenger should argue that they don't see why benevolence but not malevolence should be seen as an intrinsic great-making property. Real greatness, says the challenger, consists in rejecting and transcending one's conscience, laws and commandments: to do evil despite the pressure to do good. One might build such a view upon a (pessimistic) interpretation of Friedrich Nietzsche's philosophy, which involves – for the greatest among us – 'the self-overcoming of the moralist, into their opposite'.[86] On this view, a being is greater if they transcend moral values rather than conform to them. This is, says the challenger, the same phenomenon we observe in our world leaders such as Napoleon Bonaparte and Vladimir Putin; their overall characters are considered great in the light of (not despite of) their moral character.[87] The challenge, then, can be presented as follows: why is the intuition that *benevolence* is a great-making property significantly more reasonable than the intuition that *malevolence* is a great-making property? Just as the evil-god challenge (and belief in evil god) may be presented in the absence of genuine evil-god theism, so too can the claim that evil is a great-making property. The onus, then, is on the good-god hypothesizer to provide an asymmetry to justify their belief. If the traditional theist cannot justify why their underlying premise (goodness is intrinsically great) is more reasonable than the challenger's (evil is intrinsically great), then it is no more reasonable to attribute goodness to god through perfect-being theology than it is to attribute evil to god through perfect-being theology.

Before we analyse this response, it is worth noting why the challenger should not claim that neither goodness nor evil is an intrinsic great-making property. Let us consider two consequences of asserting such a view. First, if the challenger concedes that it is unreasonable to propose that evil is a great-making property – and argues instead that goodness cannot be a great-making property – then they concede the ground of perfect-being theology to the good-god hypothesizer. In other words, as soon as the challenger accepts that evil cannot be a great-making property, they present the contest as one between god's goodness and non-goodness, rather than a contest between god's benevolence and malevolence. Second, if the challenger wishes to argue that goodness is not a great-making property, then they move away from the evil-god challenge *simpliciter*. The evil-god challenge argues against orthodox theism by developing parallel arguments for evil god; once the challenger argues against theism directly (in this case, by attacking the claim that goodness is a great-making property), they sacrifice the challenge's central virtues – as discussed in Sections 1.4 and 1.5. If it can be shown that goodness is not a great-making property, then an orthodox perfect-being theology that aims to ground good god would be obsolete, and, therefore, there would be no need to develop an unorthodox perfect-being theology in the first place. To put it simply, if goodness is not a great-making property, then there is no point in developing an evil-god challenge within the remit of perfect-being theology.

In summary, if it is roughly as reasonable to believe malevolence is a great-making property (than it is to believe that benevolence is a great-making property), then perfect-being theology can ground evil god's central attributes: omniscience, omnipotence and omnimalevolence. This approach would overcome the Anselmian impossibility objection, which states that the greatest conceivable being cannot be evil. Moreover, it lays the groundwork for a parallel ontological argument – an argument which, at face value, will be indistinguishable from the traditional version (1–6j). I maintain that positing evil as a great-making property is the best approach for the evil-god challenger; however, as I argue in the following section, this view faces a number of problems.

2.5 Imaginary evidence

In this section, I identify three responses to the hypothetical claim that evil is a great-making property. The first response is weak, the second is stronger and the third constitutes a clear asymmetry favouring the attribution of good (over evil) to god.

First, let us consider the *argument from inherent asymmetries*. According to this objection, the reengineering of perfect-being theology and the relationship between god's attributes are themselves significant asymmetries. As the challenger has removed some of the central underlying principles of good-god theism, the evil-god hypothesis is no longer a parody of the good-god hypothesis. In other words, removing core tenets of good-god theism (in itself) constitutes a significant difference between the two hypotheses.

This approach appears to run together the fact that there are 'big differences' between the two hypotheses and the view that these differences constitute 'significant asymmetries'. When the challenger asks for 'significant asymmetries', they mean something particular: a *reason* for favouring the good-god hypothesis over the evil-god hypothesis. Merely identifying differences between the two hypotheses is insufficient: one must also state why an orthodox argument is significantly more reasonable than its parallel. Moreover, the challenger can accept that the evil-god hypothesis is not a parody of the good-god hypothesis, and, therefore, circumvent the accusation that it is 'no longer' a parody. A parody argument is a type of *reductio ad absurdum*, which must, necessarily, retain the framework – underlying principles, premises and logical structure – of its opponent's argument or worldview and, from there, deduce an absurd conclusion.[88] However, as I outlined in Section 1.4, this is different to the structure of the evil-god challenge. Although open to the use of parody arguments, the evil-god challenge typically appeals to parallel arguments. Parallel arguments claim that similarly reasonable arguments can be presented in favour of an alternative hypothesis, and these arguments are not beholden to the principles, premises and structure of their opponent's. In other words, parallel arguments are not parody arguments. In order to respond to the challenge, then, the good-god believer must offer reasons for why their principles and premises are significantly more reasonable than the challenger's.

Second, let us consider the argument from *transcending moral principles*. As we saw, one argument for the view that evil is a great-making property claimed that a being is greater if they reject and transcend moral principles than conform to them. At face value, this approach does not seem to be more reasonable than its counterpart – that it is greater to conform to moral principles than reject them. However, the claim that it is greater to be moral than immoral has the (added) benefit of being intuitively appealing. This is a powerful intuition, one that plays a significant role in our day-to-day lives: we do not want to purge morality from ourselves or other people, we want to be good. Once more, as Schellenberg put it, 'A person who's open and sharing, willing to give of herself in relationship, has a quality we admire, as well as desire for ourselves.'[89] There is a second problem. As we saw, the challenger may claim that some characters – such as Putin – are considered great in the light of (not despite of) their moral character. Here, there are three responses available to the orthodox theist. First, they may claim that Putin's evil does not contribute to his *intrinsic* greatness, but that his moral character contributes only to his Machiavellian greatness – that is to say, his evil is an extrinsic great-making property which benefits himself or others. (For what it's worth, I think it is unlikely that people praise Putin because he is intrinsically evil; it seems more likely that they praise him for his ability to function as a strong leader.) Second, it seems that we also have *a posteriori* reasons for thinking that goodness (and not evil) is a great-making property. People are typically more likely to aim to acquire more knowledge, power and goodness for their intrinsic value than their counterparts – ignorance, weakness and evil – for their intrinsic value. Such *a posteriori* observations, which I discuss in more detail in the forthcoming sections, also provide grounds for rejecting one of Lancaster-Thomas's central claims, that 'the good-god hypothesizer's kaleidoscopic belief system is based *only* on metaphysical intuition.'[90] I maintain that such *a posteriori* observations – as well as properly basic beliefs (see Section 3.9) and revelation accounts which attribute goodness and not evil to god (see Chapter Four) – provide sufficient reason to reject Lancaster-Thomas's conclusion that belief in good god (over evil god) is grounded solely in intuitions. Let us consider a third problem with this view. If the challenger insists that Putin is intrinsically praiseworthy, one should question whether they are praising his moral character or his intelligence and power. (In reality, it seems more likely that people praise Putin as being intrinsically powerful than being intrinsically evil.) When Putin's attributes – power, intelligence and moral character – are combined, it may turn out that his overall greatness is higher than that of *moral characters*, such as Mahatma Gandhi. (His lack of benevolence may allow him to be more powerful in the world than his virtuous counterparts.) However, when we compare the moral characters of Gandhi and Putin in isolation from their other attributes, it seems that Gandhi possesses the intrinsically greater moral character.[91]

Finally, let us consider the most promising objection to the claim that evil is a great-making property: the *evil-world response*. According to this response there are no convincing reasons for believing that evil is an intrinsic great-making property in the world we inhabit. Although many people hold the intuition that goodness is an intrinsic great-making property, the same is not true of evil. This response highlights an important asymmetry between the two hypotheses, one that is akin to Bergmann and Brower's response to an earlier version of Law's evil-god challenge. 'If Law wants to mount a real attack on traditional theism', write Bergmann and Brower, 'he will need at the very least to engage some of the *actual* support that has been identified here on earth.'[92] Evil-god perfect-being theology, says the critic, is built upon imaginary evidence. Although we can imagine a world in which evil is a great-making property, that's not the world we inhabit. In contrast, the god of traditional perfect-being theology can be grounded in tangible evidence. To illustrate the point, suppose an anti-theist claimed that 'being a pumpkin' was a great-making property. A similar response – 'Nobody believes that pumpkin-ness is a great-making property!' – seems appropriate.[93] The asymmetry is, therefore, as follows: we can deduce the good-god hypothesis from perfect-being theology by appealing to real-life (non-hypothetical) intuitions, but we cannot deduce the evil-god hypothesis from perfect-being theology from real-life (non-hypothetical) intuitions.

One popular response to this objection – recently championed by Lancaster-Thomas[94] – is that an evil god would have obvious reasons for instilling the false intuition that goodness is a great-making property. As Lancaster-Thomas puts it, 'if evil god did exist, it seems likely that it would desire us to believe that it was benevolent in order to deceive humans, therefore perhaps evil god would want us to intuit that benevolence makes a being greater.'[95] Like many arguments in the evil-god literature, this rebuttal overlooks grounding in favour of compatibility. As we have seen, the goal of perfect-being theology is to ground god's attributes – recall that a consideration grounds good god (or its counterpart) if the evidence is sufficient for attributing goodness (or evil) to god. If the challenger avoids grounding evil god – *assuming* god's malevolence (and appealing to the compatibility between evil god and evidence for good god) *before* they ground evil god's moral character – then the grounded hypothesis (all else being equal) should be preferred over the non-grounded hypothesis (see Section 1.7).

Murphree and Lancaster-Thomas have also argued that our intuition that 'benevolence is a great-making property could be explained away by wishful thinking and confirmation bias'.[96] In fact, Murphree goes as far to say that 'the arguments have historically led to the belief in the presence of a heavenly God, rather than a hellish anti-God ... because of the predispositions of the people considering them: historically people have been metaphysical optimists'.[97] There are two problems with this approach. First, rather than paralleling good-god theism, this response constitutes a direct attack against the underlying premises of orthodox theism: in essence, claiming that orthodox perfect-being theology amounts to nothing more than optimism. As we have seen, this is against the spirit and beyond the scope of the evil-god challenge, which aims to argue against theism indirectly without raising complex and contentious debates. Second, suppose the challenger insists on arguing against theism directly – that is, rather than developing a parallel case for the view that evil is a great-making property, suppose that the challenger cuts to the chase and claims that goodness is not a great-making property. In this case, they open themselves up to the following problem: if, once all of the available evidence is considered, the good-god believer is successful in showing that goodness is a great-making property (and not merely wishful thinking), then the challenger must accept that the asymmetry falls strongly in favour of the good-god hypothesis. In other words, by conceding that a parallel argument for evil god is highly implausible, the challenger opens themself up to a potentially significant asymmetry.

Before proceeding, I wish to outline (and respond to) another objection on behalf of the challenger. The evil-god defender may bite the bullet and accept that their hypothetical intuition (that evil is an intrinsic great-making property) is precisely that: hypothetical. Recall that the asymmetry is as follows: people hold the intuitive belief that being good is intrinsically great (and this can be used to ground good god in perfect-being theology), but there is no intuitive belief that being evil is intrinsically great (and, therefore, evil god cannot be grounded in perfect-being theology). The challenger – in the spirit of New's imaginary Encyclopaedia article for evil god[98] – may be tempted to state the following: although people do not intuit the belief that evil is a great-making property in *this* world, I can *conceive* of a possible world in which people hold the intuition that evil is a great-making property. As god – at least for perfect-being theists – exists in every possible world, there is a world in which its inhabitants believe that god (who holds all purported great-making properties) is evil. Belief about god's moral character, then, is contingent upon the world that we occupy.

Unfortunately for the challenger, this evidence is not only hypothetical, but it contrasts with the underlying principles of orthodox theism. For the good-god defender, intrinsic great-making properties are necessary truths – that is to say, there are no worlds in which power, knowledge and goodness are not great-making properties. In other words, if one thinks that great-making properties are contingent then one cannot do the cross-world comparison necessary to state that god is the greatest possible being. The challenger can respond to this belief only by claiming that evil (and not goodness) is a necessary great-making property. (However, as we have seen, this parallel principle is not as reasonable as the orthodox principle.) Alternatively, if the challenger wishes to reject the idea that intrinsic great-making properties are necessary truths – but are, instead, contingent truths – then they abandon the evil-god challenge in favour of a direct attack against orthodox theism. (However, as we have seen – in the context of the evil-god challenge – this would place the weight of evidence in favour of good god.) Therefore, it seems that perfect-being theology favours the attribution of goodness (and not evil) to god.[99]

2.6 Maximally good

Several proponents of orthodox theism – including Bergmann and Brower,[100] Ward,[101] Keltz[102] and Feser[103] – have developed Thomistic responses to the evil-god challenge. In this section, I focus on Feser's version of the argument. According to Feser, the classical theists (such as Aristotle, Augustine and Aquinas) maintained that evil is parasitic on the good – that is to say, the classical theists defended a version of the privation theory of evil. On this view, goodness consists in an entity achieving its final cause: realizing its ideal form in accordance with its essence.[104] To take an example, a squirrel who can swim, leap between trees, stockpile nuts, reproduce and raise their young is a 'good' squirrel, and the opposite is a 'bad' squirrel. Here we see the concepts of *moral goodness* and *goodness as correct function* coincide, as for Aquinas, 'the essence of goodness consists in this'.[105]

For Aquinas, all beings desire perfection, but Being Itself, if it lacks goodness, cannot be desirable. Therefore, Being Itself must be good, as we do, in fact, desire it. As Aquinas puts it, 'Hence it is clear that goodness and being are the same really. But goodness presents the aspect of desirableness, which being does not present.'[106] If we accept this view – that goodness and Being are two sides of the same coin – then we may describe that which is incomplete, that which does not fulfil its function, as 'lacking good'. Rather than having Being, evil is a *lack* of Being: a privation of good. Aquinas summarizes this view in the following passage:

> [I]t cannot be that evil signifies being, or any form or nature. Therefore it must be that by the name of evil is signified the absence of good. And this is what is meant by saying that *evil is neither a being nor a good*. For since being, as such, is good, the absence of one implies the absence of the other.[107]

As god constitutes Being Itself, god must also be good and not evil. Therefore, says Feser, the evil-god challenge 'is completely irrelevant to classical theism'. If 'God is Being Itself, the claim "If God exists, then He is good" is metaphysically necessary, while the claim "If God exists, He might be evil" is necessarily false'.[108]

Just as perfect-being theology may be developed into an argument for good god's existence, Feser's Thomistic conception of god can be developed into an argument to the same effect. In fact, Aquinas already had such an argument in mind. Aquinas's fourth way can be stated as follows:

1n. The fourth way is taken from the gradation to be found in things. Among beings there are some more and some less good, true, noble and the like. (Premise)

2n. But 'more' and 'less' are predicated of different things, according as they resemble in their different ways something which is the maximum, as a thing is said to be hotter according as it more nearly resembles that which is hottest; so that there is something which is truest, something best, something noblest and, consequently, something which is uttermost being; for those things that are greatest in truth are greatest in being, as it is written in *Metaphysics ii*. (Premise)

3n. Now the maximum in any genus is the cause of all in that genus; as fire, which is the maximum heat, is the cause of all hot things. (Premise)

4n. Therefore, there must also be something which is to all beings the cause of their being, goodness and every other perfection; and this we call God.[109] (Conclusion)

The fourth way identifies goodness as a scaling property (i.e. some entity can have more goodness than another, just as some entity can be hotter than another) and that some entity must hold this property to a maximal degree (i.e. there must be a maximally good thing that other entities participate in).[110] If the underlying premises cannot be paralleled in favour of evil god, then the argument may show that the good-god hypothesis (but not the evil-god hypothesis) is highly reasonable. Just as the ontological argument relies on perfect-being theology, the fourth way relies on the privation theory of evil: that goodness consists in Being and evil in a lack of Being. Without this underlying premise, it would be no less reasonable – following the structure of the fourth way – that there be a maximum in the genus of evil: a yardstick of maximal evil against which all other evils are measured.[111]

2.7 The privation theory of good

In order to defend the symmetry thesis against Feser's Thomistic objection, the challenger must reverse the claim that evil is the privation of good.[112] I propose – following Collins and Lancaster-Thomas[113, 114] – that the challenger claims that goodness is nothing more than the privation of evil (call this the 'privation theory of good'). As Aquinas's argument builds from the assertion that Being Itself coincides with goodness, our parallel principle must maintain that Being Itself coincides with evil. In developing such an account, I draw from the work of Schopenhauer.[115] According to one interpretation of Schopenhauer, Being Itself has no value. When we reflect on existence or achieve (what Aristotle would call) our final end or purpose, we are left empty and bored. Schopenhauer describes this view in his essay, 'On the Vanity of Existence':

> Boredom is direct proof that existence is in itself valueless, for boredom is nothing other than the sensation of the emptiness of existence. For if life, in the desire for which our essence consists, possessed in itself a positive value and real content, there would be no such thing as boredom: we take no pleasure in existence except when we are striving after something.[116]

In this passage, Schopenhauer claims that Being Itself is valueless; however, for our purposes, this is insufficient. In order to develop a parallel account – in which existence is not valueless but evil – the challenger must take Schopenhauer a step further. Instead, the challenger must claim that an empty, boring existence is not valueless, but has negative value. On another reading of Schopenhauer, we can see that he takes this step himself. Consider the following quotation:

> I therefore know of no greater absurdity than that absurdity which characterizes almost all metaphysical systems: that of explaining evil as something negative. For evil is precisely that which is positive, that which makes itself palpable; and good, on the other hand, i.e. all happiness and all gratification, is that which is negative, the mere abolition of a desire and extinction of a pain.[117]

On this approach, achieving our final end – purported perfection or Being Itself – is not what contains value. Instead, only in the state of deficiency can we find happiness, which consists in relief from evil and suffering. The only goodness we find in the world 'springs from lack, from deficiency and thus from suffering'.[118]

In short, while Aquinas claims that we desire alignment with our final cause, the pessimistic Schopenhauerian argues that we desire the state of striving. If we take the view that goodness consists in a state of deficiency rather than a state of 'perfection' – and plug this into the Thomist's belief that what we naturally desire coincides with what is good – then perfection consists in evil and not the good. If evil is part and parcel of Being Itself, then we may describe the lack of fulfilment of an entity's final cause as the 'privation of evil'. This underlying metaphysical principle can be imported into a parallel Thomistic argument for evil god's existence, which I present as follows:

1o. The fourth way is taken from the gradation to be found in things. Among beings there are some more and some *less evil*, true, and the like. (Premise)
2o. But 'more' and 'less' are predicated of different things, according as they resemble in their different ways something which is the maximum, as a thing is said to be hotter according as it more nearly resembles that which is hottest; so that there is something which is falsest and *most evil* and, consequently, something which is uttermost being; for those things that are greatest in truth are greatest in being, as it is written in *Metaphysics ii*. (Premise)
3o. Now the maximum in any genus is the cause of all in that genus; as fire, which is the maximum heat, is the cause of all hot things. (Premise)
4o. Therefore, there must also be something which is to all beings the cause of their being, *evil*, and every other perfection; and this we call *evil god*.[119] (Conclusion)

The orthodox fourth way and the parallel version both uphold that 'good' and 'evil' are scaling properties (they come in degrees) and that the relevant properties – *good* for the orthodox view and *evil* for the parallel argument – are what Hill calls 'maxi-optimality properties' (i.e. their maximal degree coincides with their optimal degree).[120] If the privation theory of good is roughly as reasonable as the privation theory of evil, the challenger can accept Aquinas's principle that there must be 'something which is to all beings the cause of their being' and that this being is maxi-optimally evil. (It is worth noting that, in the light of the above, Feser's claim that the evil-god hypothesis is internally incoherent and 'completely irrelevant' overlooks this parallel: we can conceive of a logically coherent conception of evil god, in which good and not evil is a privation, and, therefore, an evil god is not impossible.[121, 122]) Now, the task lies at the feet of the good-god hypothesizer who must provide a significant asymmetry to justify favouring the orthodox privation theory over its parallel. Such a reason will need to answer the following question: why is the *privation theory of evil* significantly more reasonable than *the privation theory of good*? I answer this question in the following section.

2.8 A privation of intuition

One version of the argument outlined in Section 2.7 – which claims that goodness is the privation of evil – has been defended by Collins.[123] Since the publication of Collins's paper, three notable responses have appeared in the literature. In this section, I examine each of these responses and conclude in favour of orthodox theism.

First, Page and Baker-Hytch offer at least two arguments in response to the privation theory of good. The first is a metaphysical one, which is – in essence – a reframing of the motivations for adopting the privation theory of evil. 'Good and bad', say Page and Baker-Hytch, 'signify the success of a thing at fulfilling the function proper to a given kind and the deficiency of a thing at performing the function proper to a given kind, respectively'. They conclude, 'We can see no way for this approach to be mirrored.'[124] Their second argument is a linguistic one, according to which ordinary usage of the terms 'good' and 'bad' conforms to the privation theory of evil rather than the privation theory of good. We typically describe things that are good – good tables, good coffees, good students – as those which fulfil their desired function. This is *the* natural way of expressing things. It would be unnatural to describe a sturdy table as a bad table, a tasty coffee as a bad coffee and a hard-working student as a bad student. Through some awkward linguistic engineering, it may be possible to rephrase these ways of describing an entity's function, but the 'simplest' and 'most natural' expression of goodness and badness in relation to function will always be captured by the privation theory of evil.[125]

The first of Page and Baker-Hytch's arguments does not undermine the parallel, and the second only provides a (very minor) asymmetry favouring the traditional privation theory. First, let us consider the metaphysical argument.

As we saw in the previous section, the mirror of the functional argument, following Schopenhauer, is that 'good' signifies the *failure* of a thing at fulfilling the function proper to a given kind, and that 'bad' signifies the *success* of a thing at performing the function that is proper to a given kind. This is motivated by the 'boredom' and 'evil' of Being Itself, and the 'happiness' and 'gratification' of striving (i.e. deficiency). To reject the privation theory of good in favour of the privation theory of evil, one must say why this approach is less reasonable than its counterpart. Page and Baker-Hytch's second argument provides one reason for adopting the privation theory of good over the privation theory of evil – that is, that the privation theory of good leads to an unnatural way of describing the world. If the privation theory of good were true, then we would have to say things like 'the table is bad because it is sturdy', 'the coffee is bad because it is tasty' and 'the student is bad because they are hard-working'. The challenger should concede that the privation theory of evil sounds more unnatural (if not absurd) in comparison to the privation theory of good. At the same time, the traditional theist should concede that *linguistic appeal* does little to raise the probability of the orthodox privation theory.

Second, in Keltz's paper, we find at least three arguments against the privation theory of good. Those relevant to our inquiry rely on the claim that if the privation theory of good were true, then all agents would be naturally inclined towards their own destruction rather than their completeness. Keltz writes:

> Plants would naturally be dead or sick if unimpeded, while only occasionally being healthy, if at all. Animals would seek their destruction and naturally be dead or sick if unimpeded, while only occasionally being healthy, if at all. Humans would naturally be dead or sick (with occasional health) and would desire to be dead, sick, ignorant and unhappy. However, since it is obvious that the privation view of good is not warranted based on what we see in nature, then a deep asymmetry holds regarding the Thomistic privation view of evil.[126]

In response to Keltz, the challenger should claim that 'what we desire' is evil, but what we desire is not 'our own destruction'. This is because the completed state is not one in which nothing exists – so we should not expect the world's entities to move towards their own destruction – but one that has negative (and not positive) *value*. Keltz believes that this argument misses the point:

> If all things in nature tend toward the perfection of their natures, it does not matter if this is called 'evil' or anything else. The concept would remain while only the labels would change because being would still be desirable (yet called 'evil') and non-being would be undesirable (yet called 'good').[127]

This, however, is close to the nature of the parallel: the teleological framework (all things tend to fulfil their natures) remains the same, but the value and what is desirable (that fulfilment is 'bad' and not 'good', so says the challenger) is what changes. The challenger's question: why is the switching of the labels, and what is good and desirable, more reasonable than the orthodox view? As we have seen, Page and Baker-Hytch offer a linguistic reason; another reason has been offered by Miller, to which we now turn our attention.

Finally, Miller's response focuses on the intuitive absurdities that are (purportedly) inherent to the privation theory of good. On the privation theory of evil, we can see how concepts such as 'betrayal' and 'illness' (evils) are corruptions of concepts such as 'loyalty' and 'health' (goods), but it is much harder to see how 'loyalty' and 'health' (goods) could be corruptions of 'betrayal' and 'illness' (evils). One may accept, as Lancaster-Thomas would concede, that Miller's examples favouring good god are more intuitive than their equivalents for evil god.[128] As Miller puts it, 'a privation theory of evil is more intuitively appealing to most than a privation theory of good'.[129]

Miller's is the best response to the challenger. As we saw in Section 2.5, the orthodox theist maintains that our intuitions provide a reliable method for identifying great-making properties. We also saw that the challenger's hypothetical intuitions are less reasonable than the non-hypothetical intuitions of the good-god defender. This same approach can be used in relation to privation theories. As Miller argues, the privation theory of evil enjoys intuitive appeal, but the same cannot be said of the privation theory of good. This constitutes an asymmetry favouring good god over evil god.

Before proceeding, let us consider three objections to Miller's view on behalf of the challenger. First, one may argue that this is not a decisive asymmetry, but that intuitive appeal only constitutes a minor asymmetry. The traditional theist should accept this objection. However, it is important to understand that, on behalf of the theist, my overall case consists of cumulative asymmetries, in which we have many reasons – some minor, some significant – for favouring the grounding of good god over evil god. In contrast, there seem to be very few (if any) arguments for favouring the grounding of evil god over good god. Once all of the evidence pertinent to the grounding of good god and evil god has been considered, I maintain that it is more reasonable to attribute goodness to god than it is to attribute evil to god.

Second, as stated, Lancaster-Thomas has argued that the reasons for favouring good god over evil god are, ultimately, nothing more than a series of positive intuitions. However, as we saw in the case of great-making properties, it seems that we also have *a posteriori* reasons for favouring the orthodox view (that we desire goodness) over the unorthodox parallel (that we desire evil). This same point is made by Keltz when he claims that 'human beings desire happiness and the perfection of their natures' and 'do not desire their destruction'.[130] This strengthens the asymmetry beyond intuitions.

Third, the challenger may argue that we should expect evil god to instil false intuitions in order to deceive his creations. On this view, evil god wants us to think that Being Itself is good (and not evil) to keep us in the dark about his true nature and intentions. This response is supported by Lancaster-Thomas, who claims that evil god produces false intuitions in order to prevent us from ending our lives prematurely. She writes, 'By instilling a false intuition that existence is good in his creations, evil god is preventing them from taking the easy way out. Evil god deceives individuals by programming a "natural" mechanism that desires to preserve life.'[131] Lancaster-Thomas continues:

> [U]nder Thomistic theism, taking one's own life or the life of another is considered an unforgivable sin, such is the force of the belief that existence is good. Again, the deceit-loving evil god might enjoy indoctrinating individuals with the belief that the fail-safe is off limits to anyone who does not want to be destined to a negative relationship with their creator and the determiner of their afterlife.[132]

Following Lancaster-Thomas's argument, the challenger might claim that the intuition favouring the privation theory of evil provides no more reason for believing in good god over evil god. Note that the structure of this response – 'evil god has reasons for wanting us to believe he is good' – can be applied to any of the arguments for grounding good god. (We have already seen this response from the challenger in reply to the intuition that 'goodness is a great-making property'.) The problem with this argument, however, is that it *assumes* the grounding of evil god, rather than offering reasons for attributing evil to god. In other words, Lancaster-Thomas's response is an argument for evil god's compatibility with the available evidence, rather than an argument for establishing evil god's moral character. In terms of grounding, it is more reasonable to attribute goodness to god from the intuitive and *a posteriori* evidence that Being Itself is good, than it is to attribute evil to god from the hypothetical intuition that Being Itself is evil.

2.9 Simply Swinburne

I turn now to motivation objections. Several motivation objections – see Swinburne,[133] Forrest,[134] Miller,[135] Luke Wilson,[136] Weaver[137] and Page & Baker-Hytch[138] – have already been discussed in the literature. Here, I discuss the argument in its strongest form: in the context of non-Humean motivations. (To be motivated by reasons rather than desires is to have a 'non-Humean' motivation.) My focus, therefore, is on motivation objections that claim god is necessarily omnibenevolent (and not omnimalevolent) because god has reasons for being good and has no reasons for being evil. I begin with an argument from Swinburne (in this section), before strengthening Swinburne's case through amendments proposed by Weaver (in Section 2.10). I then propose (and reject) a series of responses from the evil-god challenger.

From god's omnipotence alone, Swinburne believes that we can deduce god's omniscience, perfect freedom and perfect goodness.[139] In order to be concise, let us assume that god is omnipotent, omniscient and perfectly free; our focus is whether god's moral character can be deduced from these attributes. According to Swinburne, agents must have reasons for acting. In his words, 'A movement brought about by an agent would not be an action unless the agent had some reason for bringing it about.'[140] An agent's reasons for acting will either be influenced by rational or non-rational factors. When non-rational (Humean) factors override an agent's will, they fail to act rationally – that is, we act against our better judgement. For example, one might hold the belief that going for a run rather than smoking a cigarette is the (rational) healthier decision but opt for the cigarette because of an overriding (non-rational) desire. In other situations, evil actions emerge from states of ignorance. For example, when shopping for a new sweatshirt, a consumer's limited knowledge of working conditions in Xinjiang may lead to the indirect funding of slavery. Such factors, says Swinburne, explain why people act against what should be their better judgement. However, as a perfectly free agent, god would not be subject to non-rational desires or weakness of will; furthermore, as an omniscient being, god is aware of all true facts, and, therefore, could never suffer from ignorance. Finally, suppose we believe that moral judgements have truth values; in other words, suppose that moral cognitivism is true. On moral cognitivism, statements about certain actions being morally good or morally bad will be true or false, and an omniscient agent would know which actions were good and which actions were bad. Swinburne concludes, 'His judgements about which actions are morally bad and which actions are morally good will be true judgements. Hence a perfectly free and omniscient being can never do actions that are morally bad, and will always do the best action'.[141, 142]

2.10 The webs we Weaver

Weaver claims that Swinburne's argument for god's goodness is insufficient. In the following extract, Weaver explains why:

> Even granting the assumptions Swinburne requires, one cannot soundly derive God's omnibenevolent character from God's freedom and omniscience, for as Michael Martin ... has pointed out, something like the god of evilism [(evil-god theism)] could act wickedly 'not out of ignorance but in a basic and fundamental way' intending 'to do evil knowing that it is evil because it is evil'.[143]

Weaver's response, which states that god's *knowledge* of what is right or wrong does not necessitate his *choosing* right over wrong, constitutes a reason to reject Swinburne's argument for god's goodness. However, Weaver also offers a revision that can be used to regenerate Swinburne's argument. Like Swinburne, Weaver argues that god cannot be evil because god's benevolence is logically necessary. However, in order to necessitate god's choosing right over wrong, Weaver suggests that we *weave* motivation into the fabric of morality itself. That is to say, Weaver proposes that true statements – such as 'we ought to help people in need' – contain, within themselves, motivations to act.

The argument proposed rests on the truth of moral rationalism and what Weaver describes as a 'modest (reasons) internalism'.[144] Moral rationalism states that moral duties contain reasons to act, and modest internalism maintains that having a good reason to act involves having a desire to fulfil that goal. In essence, this involves a non-Humean–Kantian approach to meta-ethics, in which 'the source of the moral ought's normativity is *internal* to morality itself'.[145] The argument is that god would have good reasons to fulfil moral duties, because the desire to be good is internal to moral duties. I construct Weaver's argument as follows:

1p. An omniscient being always deliberates correctly. (Premise)
2p. An omniscient being knows all truths and has no false beliefs. (Premise)
3p. Motivation is internal to moral truth. (Premise)
4p. Statements prescribing morally good actions are true and statements prescribing morally bad actions are false. (Premise)
5p. God can be motivated only to perform morally good actions. (Conclusion)

Thus, Swinburne's missing premise, says Weaver, is that 'motivation is internal to moral truth' (3p). As motivation is internal only to morally true actions (which are good) and motivation is not internal to morally false actions (which are bad), god can *only* have reasons to perform morally good actions and has no reasons to perform morally bad actions.[146, 147, 148] It follows that if the evil-god challenger cannot offer a similarly reasonable parallel argument from moral rationalism and reasons internalism – the conclusion of which being that god can be motivated only to perform morally evil actions – then we have a powerful asymmetry favouring the good-god hypothesis over the evil-god hypothesis. In the following section, I defend this argument against a series of objections.

2.11 Up is down and down is up

In the literature, Swinburne and Weaver's arguments are described as impossibility objections. However, I maintain that they are, in fact, asymmetry objections. As we saw in Section 1.7, an asymmetry objection states that we have evidence for favouring good god over evil god (that is to say, 'on this account, good god has the advantage'), whereas an impossibility objection maintains that evil god is conceptually incoherent (in other words, they say, 'an evil god is impossible'). However, as we have seen, although evil god has a low epistemic probability, an evil god is logically possible – even on Swinburne's account – and, therefore, the challenger may begin their rebuttal by claiming that evil god is not akin to square–circles or married–bachelors. On behalf of the challenger, I now develop (and respond to) four objections to Weaver's asymmetry argument.

First, the challenger may be tempted to argue that a non-Humean account of moral character is implausible. If the challenger can show that a non-Humean account of moral character is implausible, then – so says the objection – we can reject Weaver's asymmetry. This may be true, and such an approach has been suggested by Wilson.[149] However, in his own response to Weaver, Collins (rightly) points out that a 'direct rebuttal' of moral rationalism would go beyond the scope of his article.[150] I want to go a step further: a direct rebuttal of moral rationalism goes beyond the scope of the evil-god challenge. As we saw in Section 1.4, the evil-god challenge functions by paralleling arguments in favour of evil god in order to *indirectly* undermine arguments for good god. There are three points to consider. First, if the challenger does not offer parallel arguments in favour of evil god, then they concede ground to the good-god defender (that is to say, if their direct attack fails, then we have an asymmetry favouring good god). Second, by attacking theism directly, they sacrifice the main virtues of the evil-god challenge – namely, that it avoids complex and contentious debates (see Section 1.4) and can be applied to all arguments for good god (see Section 1.5). Third, recall that, as stated in Section 1.4, the evil-god challenge is an internal problem for theism. Therefore, as Hendricks has put it, 'The popularity of the argument is irrelevant: all that matters is that the good-god theist accepts it, for that would give them reason to reject the symmetry thesis.'[151, 152] For these reasons, I believe the challenger ought to parallel Weaver's argument.

Second, let us consider a parallel version of Weaver's argument. Collins offers the most recent, and the best defence of, a parallel argument of Weaver's argument from moral motivation.[153] Before we explore Collins's parallel, note that he describes Weaver's argument as 'the strongest against the symmetry thesis', the force of which can only be *partially* deflected'.[154] Now, rather than accepting moral rationalism, Collins offers a parallel underlying principle which he labels '*im*moral rationalism'. According to this principle, 'recognition that an action is contrary to one's moral obligations ... is a practical reason to do that action'.[155] This is a straightforward move, one that trades on the question of which moral statements are to be taken to be intrinsically normative. Let us put this in the context of Weaver's argument. The key premises in Weaver's arguments are 3p and 4p. Collins seems to accept 3p, which claims that 'motivation is internal to moral truth'. However, Collins questions *which statements* constitute moral truths. Thus, I take Collins to reverse 4p; instead of claiming that 'morally good actions are true and statements prescribing morally bad actions are false', Collins asserts that 'morally bad actions are true and statements prescribing morally good actions are false'.

Collins's parallel is a novel one, but like many parallel principles, immoral rationalism does not correspond with our understanding of reality. Not only does it lack intuitive appeal, but it also raises several significant meta-ethical problems. To understand why, let us consider some examples. For moral rationalists, moral statements such as 'we should help people in need' are true; however, according to the *im*moral rationalist, such statements are false. Furthermore, for the moral rationalist, immoral statements such as 'we should harm innocent people' are false, whereas for the immoral rationalist, such statements are true. As we can see, immoral rationalism turns meta-ethics on its head and, if it were true, would give agents reasons to do evil actions and not good actions. In reality, we perform good actions because they are good, and we take their goodness to be sufficient for performing them. In contrast, when somebody explains their motivations to do evil, we do not take their prescriptive immoral statements to be true but encourage them to think through their ideas more carefully; in doing so, we hope that they see truth and reason. This point is echoed by Miller, who writes:

> An easy way to see this is that if we ask someone why they did something and they respond, 'because it was good to do so', we could reasonably leave it at that. But the response 'because it was bad to do so' appears considerably less intelligible. That may be all the theist needs to show that theism is more probable.[156]

In short, Collins's parallel principle does not correspond with our understanding of morality. If it were true, we would find ourselves in a very peculiar and, more worryingly, unpleasant world. Believing that 'immoral statements are true' and 'moral statements are false' is like believing 'up is down' and 'down is up'. In the real world, that's just not how things are.[157]

Third, let us consider another attempt at paralleling Weaver's argument. Swinburne and Weaver both accept that god is perfectly free – it is this perfect freedom which will be the focal point of our parallel. I draw from Swinburne here, who offers a well-developed account of divine freedom. The appeal of Swinburne's view is its simplicity. Rather than postulating complex substances – for example, multiple gods or gods with limited attributes – he introduces one 'very simple' kind of person whose attributes can be deduced from omnipotence alone.[158] An omnipotent, omniscient being whose actions were predetermined would be more complex than a being who was free. Therefore, as we should prefer simple explanations over complex explanations, we should take god to be perfectly free. For Swinburne, an action is a free action 'if and only if the agent's choosing to do that action, that is having the intention to produce the result of that action, has no full explanation – of any kind'.[159] It is here where the challenger may be tempted to claim the following: an omnipotent, omniscient and perfectly free god may choose to do evil – with the knowledge that the action is evil – as an act of radical freedom.

This is similar to Weaver's response to Swinburne; however, the suggestion here is that Weaver might have overlooked the fact that this same objection can be levied against his own argument. Weaver accepts that god is perfectly free but *restricts* this freedom – says the challenger – in claiming that god is unable to choose not to adhere to a motivation that is internal to truth. For the challenger, god recognizes that motivation is internal to truth, but can – motivated by the desire to act out of whim and maintain their radical freedom[160] – choose to do otherwise. Again, on this conception of evil god, evil god is able to decide whether to act rationally, whereas good god *has to* act rationally. In summary, the structure of the argument proposed in response to Swinburne and Weaver is as follows: why should the view that *god always acts rationally for the purposes of good* be considered significantly more reasonable than the view that *god acts freely and ir/rationally for the purposes of goods (including whim)*?

In rejecting this argument, the good-god defender may claim that a god who acts rationally is significantly more plausible than a god who would act irrationally. Here I discuss two versions of the rational-god objection. The first response states that it is greater to be rational than it is to be irrational; therefore, as god holds the greatest combination of great-making properties, the concept of an irrational god is implausible. This objection relies on an appeal to perfect-being theology and rationality as a great-making property – however, it does not explain why god's rationality is more important than god's freedom. Therefore, I believe the good-god defender should offer a separate response. The second objection begins by identifying the reason why god, on this account, would perform evil actions: namely, for the purposes of goods (including whim). Therefore, on this account, what god would be doing would be 'good' rather than evil – the evil being an unfortunate outcome, a side-effect, of a greater good. Moreover, there is an additional problem here: the challenger provides no reason as to why, out of whim alone, god would necessarily choose evil actions over good actions. It is inherent to the concept of whim that one's actions are not motivated by reasons, and, therefore, god's actions would essentially be random (rather than aiming at some good or evil). If god acts out of rationality alone, then good god is preferable to evil god; if god acts out of whim (and whim is good), then good god is preferable to evil god; however, if god acts out of whim (and whim is not good), then god will perform both good and evil actions, and, therefore, neither hypothesis would be preferable.

Finally, one may question whether human moral imperatives necessarily apply to god. If god is not subject to the same moral obligations as humans, then Weaver's argument from moral motivation would be ineffective. An argument of this type has been put forward by Lancaster-Thomas, who motivates her objection to Weaver-style arguments in two ways. First, Lancaster-Thomas argues that 'human preferences could be completely unimportant to god',[161] and, second, that the challenger can 'deny that it is necessarily rational to do good'.[162] If human preferences do not apply to god and it is not necessarily rational to do good, says the objection, then – as Weaver fails to ground either hypothesis – Weaver's argument from moral motivation fails to ground good god over evil god.

As we have seen, arguments of this type constitute direct (and not indirect) attacks against orthodox theism. A true parallel would not contest the efficacy of moral rationalism and reasons internalism but make a case, as Collins does, for how moral rationalism and reasons internalism favour evil god. With that said, even if the challenger rejects moral rationalism and reasons internalism – in favour of sceptical theism or Humean moral motivation, for example – then good god will still hold the advantage. To understand why, consider two possibilities. Suppose moral rationalism and reasons internalism apply to god as well as humans; on this account (following Weaver) we have a strong asymmetry favouring good god. Alternatively, if moral rationalism and reasons internalism are false and do not apply to god, then neither hypothesis holds an advantage over the other. The good-god defender either wins or draws; however, the evil-god defender can only draw or lose. Therefore, when we consider both possibilities in conjunction, we see that the attribution of *goodness* to god holds more of the logical-possibility-space than the attribution of *evil* to god. With that said, we need not concern ourselves with such complex and contentious debates, because to do so – as we saw in Section 1.4 – would take us beyond the scope of the evil-god challenge. For these reasons, I believe Weaver and the traditional theist can successfully reject Lancaster-Thomas's rebuttal.

I maintain that Weaver's original argument for good god is more reasonable than the parallels and objections that have been offered for evil god. Therefore, it appears we have more reason to attribute goodness (and not evil) to god through arguments from non-Humean moral motivation.

2.12 Conclusion

Over the course of this chapter, I developed several great-making and motivation-based arguments for attributing goodness (and not evil) to god. First, I drew a distinction between two versions of orthodox theism: the omni-god thesis and the maximal-god thesis. We saw that in order to steelman and offer the most accurate reflection of orthodox theism, we should favour the omni-god thesis over the maximal-god thesis. Second, I developed an argument for why the greatest metaphysically possible being would be good and not evil. After rejecting parallel arguments on behalf of the challenger, we saw that the success of orthodox perfect-being theology (and the ontological argument) relies on the principle that goodness is a great-making property. I then offered three responses to the challenger's parallel claim – claiming that evil is a great-making property – in which we saw how the challenger's intuition, unlike the theist's intuition, has no basis in reality. Third, I presented Aquinas's argument

Table 3 An Analysis of Grounding God's Moral Character through Perfect-being Theology. (Note that in Table 3 and all forthcoming tables arguments less reasonable than their counterparts will be marked with a cross (X), whereas more or similarly reasonable arguments will be marked with a tick (✓).) © Jack Symes

	Great-making properties (and the ontological argument)	Privation theories (and Aquinas's fourth way)	Theories of non-Humean moral motivation
Attribute goodness to god	✓	✓	✓
Attribute evil to god	X	X	X

for god's goodness – that Being Itself is good and not evil – which relied on the privation theory of evil. On behalf of the challenger, I attempted to parallel the privation theory of evil by offering a privation theory of good. I presented three responses to the challenger's claim, in which I argued that the privation theory of good lacked intuitive force, unlike the privation theory of evil. Fourth, I discussed the possibility of grounding god's moral character in arguments from moral motivation. Assuming a non-Humean account of moral agency, in which motivation is internal to moral truth, I explained why god would have reasons to perform good actions but not evil actions. I offered four responses on behalf of the challenger, before arguing that none of these – including the parallel claim that motivation is internal to immoral truth – are sufficient for establishing a similarly reasonable parallel for evil god. I also suggested that the arguments presented do not constitute impossibility objections (as evil god may still be possible), but that they are better described as a series of asymmetry objections. My analysis is illustrated in Table 3.

In Chapter Three, I discuss the possibility of grounding god's moral character in creation theology. Although I concede that the world's cumulative goods and evils constitute evidence favouring both hypotheses, I outline a number of asymmetries favouring the attribution of goodness to god over the attribution of evil to god.

Chapter Three

The Bloody Watchmaker

Evil, evil everywhere,
  The reasons to believe,
In evil god are just as strong
  As those up good god's sleeve.

3.1 Introduction

As we saw in Chapter One, in order to maintain the symmetry thesis, the evil-god challenger must ground god's malevolence as the orthodox believer establishes god's goodness. In other words, the challenger should parallel arguments that attribute goodness to god – such as those from perfect-being theology, creation theology and revelation theology – by arguing that such frameworks can also be used to attribute evil to god. In Chapter Two, we identified the following asymmetry: although evil god could be grounded in an unorthodox version of perfect-being theology, it is more plausible to ground good god in an orthodox version of perfect-being theology. In this chapter, we turn our attention towards grounding god's moral character through creation theology. To this end, I develop a number of strong parallel arguments for attributing evil to god – such as those from extrinsic evil and the totality of evil (extrinsic and intrinsic) – but, ultimately, conclude that the balance of evidence favours the attribution of goodness (rather than evil) to god.

Creation theology centres around the belief that god is the ultimate cause of the universe. On this view, to borrow from Aquinas, 'we arrive at the knowledge of His being, not through God Himself, but through His effects'.[1] Given that god (the cause) created the world (the effect) – and, as Alister McGrath puts it, there are 'physical or metaphysical fingerprints' of causes in their effects[2] – god's attributes can be inferred from the existence and arrangement of the natural world. For example, god's power can be taken from the world's existence, as that which brought the universe into existence must have the power to create something *ex nihilo*.[3] The same can be said of god's knowledge; as Jonathan Edwards writes, 'infinite wisdom must be exercised in order that gravity and motion will be perfectly harmonious',[4] and we should 'take notice of the great wisdom that is necessary in order thus to dispose every atom'.[5] Our question is whether, through observations of the natural world, it is more reasonable to attribute goodness to god than evil.[6]

In the following sections, I develop arguments to say that each of our hypotheses can be grounded in the world's extrinsic goods and evils, before I advance several asymmetries (from the world's intrinsic values) that favour the grounding of good god over evil god. However, towards the end of this chapter, I concede that the totality of the world's evils (extrinsic and intrinsic) may counterbalance the totality of the world's goods (extrinsic and intrinsic). I go on to offer a final asymmetry that cannot be paralleled by the challenger – namely, that good god (and not evil god) can be grounded in Reformed epistemology. For this reason, I conclude that it is more reasonable to ground good god than evil god in the arguments presented throughout this chapter.

This chapter is structured as follows. I begin, in Section 3.2, by outlining three accounts of moral motivation. I do so in order to understand how we can attribute moral character to god through creation theology and the sort of world an omnibenevolent (or omnimalevolent) god would create. I argue that good god will always be motivated or disposed to perform good actions – and that evil god will always be motivated or disposed to perform evil actions – and will do so at every opportunity. In Section 3.3, I develop an observation-based argument for why orthodox theists – such as Paley and Swinburne – believe that we can infer god's goodness from the goods in nature. In Section 3.4, I respond to Paley and Swinburne on behalf of the challenger – appealing to Richard Dawkins, Hume and Nagasawa – by drawing from pessimistic accounts of nature. At the end of this section, I state that it is no less reasonable to attribute evil to god (based on the amount of extrinsic evil in the world) than it is to attribute goodness to god (based on the amount of extrinsic goodness in the world). At the same time, I suggest that intrinsic goods cannot be counterbalanced by intrinsic evils and proceed to examine these asymmetries in the following sections. In Section 3.5, I discuss the intrinsic value of existence, life and consciousness. In doing so, I reject an argument that has been put forward by Lancaster-Thomas, who claims that David Benatar (a prominent anti-natalist) holds existence to be intrinsically evil; I argue that Benatar does not, in fact, reject the intrinsic value of existence. In contrast, I maintain that it is more reasonable to hold that existence is intrinsically good than intrinsically evil. In Section 3.6, I discuss the intrinsic value of free will. I argue that free will is an intrinsic good, before considering two objections from Stein and three objections from Law. I explain how the orthodox theist can overcome four of these objections; however, I leave discussion of Law's most promising response – that the *totality* of the world's goods does not outweigh the totality of the world's evils – to Section 3.8. In Section 3.7, I discuss a final intrinsic asymmetry: the argument from aesthetic value. According to the argument from aesthetic value, goodness (and not evil) can be attributed to god because good god (and not evil god) would be motivated or disposed to create a beautiful world (namely, *our* world) rather than an ugly world. In Section 3.8, I develop Law's argument from the totality of the world's evils, which states that it is no more reasonable to hold that the world's combined total of goods (extrinsic and intrinsic) exceeds the world's combined total of evils, than it is to hold that the world's combined total of evils (extrinsic and intrinsic) exceeds the world's combined total of goods. At this point, I accept that Law's objection threatens to undermine the asymmetries developed in Sections 3.5–3.7. In the light of Law's objection, in Section 3.9, I develop an independent argument for grounding god's goodness in Reformed epistemology. I note that, predominantly, people form a significant number of properly basic beliefs that favour the attribution of goodness to god, but (asymmetrically) people do not form properly basic beliefs that predominantly involve the attribution of evil to god. I maintain that Reformed epistemology supports the grounding of good god over evil god, which (significantly) cannot be neutralized by Law's argument from grounding evil god in the totality of the world's evils. I conclude in Section 3.10.

3.2 Maximal moral character

In order to assess how one might attribute maximal goodness (or evil) to god through creation, I begin by discussing how (or whether) god would exercise his moral power. I focus on three popular accounts of moral character: action-based, motivation-based and disposition-based.[7] My central claim is as follows: when one describes god's moral character through creation, they are not just describing god's actions but the nature of god's motivations or dispositions. To support this claim, I argue that the action-based account of moral character is insufficient as a standalone theory. However, I propose that an (essentially) action-based account of moral character follows from – and becomes sufficient when combined with – the motivation-based or disposition-based accounts of moral character when they are applied to a maximally good (or evil) god. In order to be concise, I shall refer to examples of good characters (but not evil characters) throughout this section. (Note that the ideas discussed are just as applicable, *mutatis mutandis*, to evil characters. In fact, the proponents of these theories typically discuss them in relation to evil rather than good moral characters.)[8]

The *action-based* account is one of the most popular theories of moral character. According to this view – supported by Peter Brian Barry,[9] John Kekes,[10] Luke Russell[11] and Laurence Thomas[12] – an agent is good if they perform frequent or significant good actions. On this approach, we may describe god as good if all of god's actions were good. However, this view faces an important problem. Simply put, it fails to consider an agent's motivations or dispositions. To illustrate why this is a problem, consider the following examples. According to the action-based account, seemingly good actions might be carried out in pursuit of a greater evil (consider the wheeler-dealer selling a faulty product at a 'bargain' price), they might not be done freely (consider the criminal who is forced to engage in community service) or they could occur accidentally (consider the pharmacist who, muddling up prescriptions, ends up saving their patients' lives).[13] These examples indicate that an action-based account (alone) may be insufficient for describing an agent as good. Significantly, this is also a problem for god and creation; if the action-based account is true, then the theist cannot point to the world's goods and infer that god has the appropriate intentions or desires. In its place, then, we require a theory of character that allows us to attribute genuine benevolence to god through nature.

On a *motivation-based* account, as defended by Todd Calder,[14] an agent is good if they are regularly motivated to carry out good actions. Therefore, if an agent only has the desire to cause other agents significant amounts of pleasure and happiness, and never has the desire to bring about gratuitous pain and suffering, then the agent can be considered maximally good. In the case of finite beings, there is a potential problem with this view – that is, we think that acting on our motivations is also morally significant. Consider, for example, the brain in a vat who is always motivated to perform altruistic, generous acts. Should we consider the vatted brain to be just as good as the person who puts these same motivations into action?[15] Crucially, this problem does not arise for an omnipotent, omniscient god, who would have the power and know-how to act on all of their motivations. A motivation-based account, therefore, results in a god who (from the outside) is indistinguishable from an action-based god. Consequently, the strength of the action-based account (god performing the maximal amount of significant good actions) is maintained, whilst its shortcoming (god not having the necessary motivation) is overcome. It follows that – when we import a motivation-based account into the framework of orthodox creation theology – through our observations of the world, we can attribute genuine benevolence to god.

Finally, let us consider the *disposition-based* account. Dispositionalists – such as Barry,[16] Daniel Haybron[17] and Russell[18] – claim that an agent should be considered good if they have a strong disposition to perform good actions whenever the opportunity presents itself. On this view, one does not need a constant motivation to do good in order to be considered good; a good person, says the dispositionalist, is simply one who is inclined to act in accordance with their good intentions whenever the action is possible. Similar to the motivation-based account, dispositionalists face the problem of ability and opportunity. To take a final example, consider the human-rights advocate who – unjustly imprisoned by an authoritarian regime – holds the disposition but never has the opportunity to challenge apartheid; in contrast, consider the non-imprisoned human-rights advocate who possesses the disposition but is successful in their contribution to the eradication of apartheid. The latter has, potentially, the greater of the two characters. If this is correct, then we have reason to think that the action-based account captures an important (and necessary) feature of moral character. In reference to god, we need not get sidetracked by such debates, as the disposition-based account *entails* an (essentially) action-based view of god's character. If a maximally good god has the disposition to perform good actions at every opportunity, then they will always succeed in performing good actions as they have the power and intelligence to act on their dispositions.[19] Together, the disposition-based account (which overcomes the problem faced by the action-based account) and the action-based account (which overcomes the problem faced by the disposition-based account) can sufficiently capture god's goodness.

Therefore, when we attribute moral character to god through creation, let us say that we are claiming something not merely about god's acts, but about god's motivations or dispositions. Furthermore, we may wish to say – given the action-based implications of the motivation-based and disposition-based views – that it would be logically impossible for a maximally good god to create anything other than a perfectly good world, and logically impossible for a genuinely evil god to create anything other than a perfectly evil world. However, as Swinburne has pointed out, while 'often there may be no best action that God can do, it may sometimes be that there is a best kind of action'.[20] In other words, if there is not a uniquely best of all possible worlds, god will create the best *kind* of world. With these considerations in mind, to attribute goodness to god, one must show that our world is the best (or best kind) of possible world; conversely, to attribute evil to god, one must show that we inhabit is the worst (or worst kind) of possible world.

3.3 'It is a happy world after all'

In this section, I appeal to examples of goodness in the natural world in order to motivate an argument for the attribution of goodness to god. From Socrates to Swinburne,[21, 22] philosophers who have argued that the natural world exhibits features of design that aim to benefit rather than disadvantage its creatures. If the world was designed to benefit us rather than harm us, then – so says the argument from creation theology – it is more reasonable to attribute goodness to god than evil. The most thorough defence of this view is found in the penultimate chapter of Paley's book, *Natural Theology*.[23] I begin this section by outlining the central features of Paley's argument.[24] Paley makes two observations about the natural world which, together, are said to be sufficient for attributing goodness to god. The first observation states that 'in the vast plurality of instances … the design of the contrivance is *beneficial*' to the world's creatures.[25] In other words, when we look to nature, we see that it is geared towards the happiness and flourishing of its creatures, rather than their suffering and destruction. If this were true, says Paley, then we should expect to find creatures in the world who are pleased (and not displeased) with their bodies, functions and worldly resources. (I provide some examples below.) According to Paley's second observation, 'the Deity has *superadded pleasure* to animal sensations, beyond what was necessary for any other purpose'.[26] That is to say, there are some pleasures and goods that go beyond what is necessary for survival. Moreover, the natural world not only contains *extrinsic* goods but *intrinsic* goods, and this latter category includes a range of aesthetic experiences (such as smells, sounds, sights and the like) as well as the capacity for conscious experience itself.[27] 'It is by these [two observations]', says Paley, 'that we are to prove, that the world was made with a benevolent design'.[28, 29]

Let us consider each of Paley's observations in detail. First, Paley argues that the world, as a whole, is designed to benefit humans and non-human animals. Therefore, we can expect to observe creatures who are happy to exist in the world.

According to Paley, this is exactly what we do find, as we see in the following extract:

> It is a happy world after all. The air, the earth, the water, teem with delighted existence. In a spring noon, or a summer evening, on whichever side I turn my eyes, myriads of happy beings crowd upon my view. ... A bee amongst the flowers in spring, is one of the cheerfullest objects that can be looked upon. Its life appears to be all enjoyment: so busy, and so pleased.[30]

For Paley, the behaviour of non-human animals offers a window into their inner lives and their experience of nature. When we look through this window, says Paley, we find creatures who are delighted (and certainly not displeased) to play their part in the natural order of things. This delight stems from the fact that the world's creatures see their *teloi* as good – that each species takes the fulfilment of their species-specific-ends as something of positive value, rather than something of negative value. Hence, these creatures are happy to exist, because the total contents of their lives – including the resources that are required for their survival – benefit them far more than harm them. In the following quotation, Paley gives a more detailed example of non-human animals displaying their inner gratitude:

> Walking by the sea side, in a calm evening, upon a sandy shore, and with an ebbing tide, I have frequently remarked the appearance of a dark cloud, or, rather, very thick mist, hanging over the edge of the water. When this cloud came to be examined, it proved to be nothing else than so much space, filled with young *shrimps,* in the act of bounding into the air from the shallow margin of the water, or from the wet sand. If any motion of a mute animal could express delight, it was this: if they had meant to make signs of their happiness, they could not have done it more intelligibly. Suppose then, what I have no doubt of, each individual of this number to be in a state of positive enjoyment, what a sum, collectively, of gratification and pleasure have we here before our view?[31]

According to Paley, if the creatures did not enjoy the world and their activities, then they would not behave in this way. The natural order could have been designed to ensure that our species-specific-ends resulted in the suffering, destruction and misery of our fellow creatures; but thank good god, according to Paley, this is not the world we find ourselves in.

The case of our own species is more problematic, in which celebrations of life and the natural order, so says the critic, are exceptions rather than the rule. (For many of us, jumping and dancing are reserved for birthday celebrations, baby showers and bachelor parties – if at all.) Therefore, the argument goes, if the natural world was designed to make us happy, then why are so few of us skipping through life in a perpetual state of glee? Why, if Paley is right, do we not spend our days celebrating with the shrimp and buzzing with the bees? According to Paley, this is because human beings take the natural world for granted. Humans *should* be pleased – our bodies and functions are appropriate objects of gratitude – but we lack the appropriate response. As Paley puts it:

> Nightly rest and daily bread, the ordinary use of our limbs, and senses, and understandings, are gifts which admit of no comparison with any other. Yet, because almost every man we meet with possesses these, we leave them out of our enumeration. They raise no sentiment: they move no gratitude.[32]

Rather than attack this argument directly, in keeping with the evil-god challenge, let us give Paley the benefit of the doubt and say (for now) that the natural order of things – including the human condition – involves well-functioning bodies and worthwhile ends. Moreover, let us also say – as Paley suggested in the previous extract – that the world contains natural resources which benefit the world's creatures. If these observations are correct, then it points us towards a world that was programmed to support the flourishing of its creatures, and, therefore, we have reason to ground god's goodness in nature. This is a far stretch from the world we would expect from an evil god, says Paley, who would design a world to cause us misery (which is limited) over mirth (which is plentiful).

This brings us to Paley's second observation, that the world's conscious creatures are endowed with surplus pleasures (goods that are not required for a creature's survival). As Paley explains, it would be sufficient for the world's creatures to be guided towards their survival by nature's *necessary* pleasures and pains: 'whether the creation proceeded from a benevolent or a malevolent being, these capacities must have been given, if the animal existed at all'.[33] However, in addition to necessary pleasures and pains, god has also blessed us with *superadded* pleasures – pleasures or goods that, for no other end, are valuable in and of themselves (let us call them '*gratuitous* goods'). Paley offers the following observation in support of this claim, which he takes to be sufficient for making his case:

> A single instance will make all this clear. Assuming the necessity of food for the support of animal life, it is requisite, that the animal be provided with organs, fitted for the procuring, receiving, and digesting of its food. It may be also necessary, that the animal be impelled by its sensations to exert its organs. But the pain of hunger would do all this. Why add pleasure to the act of eating; sweetness and relish to food?[34]

We could, thinks Paley, survive without the flavour of fruits, the serenity of sunbathing and the quench of satisfying our thirst. For, in each case, the negative experience – the pain, the shiver and the thirst – would be sufficient for pushing a creature towards their survival. However, this is not the world that god designed. Our world, finely tuned with all of its gratuitous goods, points towards a designer who wants his creations to enjoy their existence. Again, this is very different from the world we should expect from an evil god, as Paley recognizes himself:

> If he had wished our misery, he might have made sure of his purpose, by forming our senses to be so many sores and pains to us, as they are now instruments of gratification and enjoyment. … He might have made, for example, every thing we tasted bitter; every thing we saw loathsome; every thing we touched a sting; every smell a stench; and every sound a discord.[35]

As the extract suggests, Paley rejects the suggestion that pains and evils are gratuitous, for, if they were, then life would be stripped of its enjoyment. However, as we have seen, Paley believes that creatures are (or at least should be) happy to experience the world, and he takes this to be sufficient for ruling out the likelihood of a preponderance of gratuitous evils.

In the light of Paley's observations, the good-god defender may conclude that, according to the natural order of things, 'happiness is the rule' and 'misery, the exception'.[36] Therefore, say Paley and his followers, 'we are authorized to ascribe to the Deity the character of benevolence' rather than malevolence.[37, 38] We are now in a position to formulate Paley's argument, which I present this in its simplest form in order to accommodate further appeals to goods that are to be found in the natural world:

1q. If the natural world contains a significant amount of good, then it is reasonable to attribute goodness to god through creation. (Premise)
2q. The natural world contains a significant amount of good. (Premise)
3q. It is reasonable to attribute goodness to god through creation. (Conclusion)

Paley's view (at least in spirit) remains popular amongst traditional theists. To take one such example, Swinburne – in the penultimate section of his book, *Providence and the Problem of Evil* – claims that the world's goods significantly outweigh the world's evils.[39] In fact, Swinburne goes as far as to say that this is one of the main reasons why people choose not to end their lives through suicide: 'One reason why they so desire [to go on living] is that they think that … the good outweighs the bad … even if they think that at present the bad outweighs the good, they live in hope of better times.'⁴⁰ Furthermore, Swinburne argues that life, in itself, is *intrinsically* valuable:

> [M]any others do not commit suicide because they want (i.e., desire) to go on living, even when life is unexciting or painful. ... They must therefore think that merely going on having experiences is a good which outweighs so much bad. Life is a tremendous good in itself.⁴¹

For Swinburne, life is not only good because of the things *within* life (happiness and pleasure), but because life is valuable in itself. In order to motivate this view, recall Pike's game from Section 2.3, in which we were forced to choose between two objects – to save one and destroy the other. Knowing nothing else about the two objects, with one labelled 'living' and the other 'not living', the intuitive value judgement is to preserve the 'living' thing over the 'not living' thing. (This is a point we shall return to in Section 3.5.) This bolsters Paley's argument significantly. Included in the category of gratuitous goods is life itself (as life is not necessary to the existence of entities), in addition to (as I shall argue) the intrinsic value of existence, consciousness, free will and the world's beauty. I maintain that each of these intrinsic values constitutes a notable asymmetry that favours the attribution of goodness (and not the attribution of evil) to god.

In summary, for Paley and Swinburne, the world is designed to benefit us rather than harm us, and it is a world that we should be grateful for. If we plug these observations into creation theology, and an appropriate theory of moral character (motivation-based or disposition-based), then it may be said that goodness can be reasonably attributed to god (1–3q).

3.4 The cosmic sin

Several evil-god challengers have developed parallel arguments from creation theology, including Cahn,⁴² Millican,⁴³ Stein,⁴⁴ New,⁴⁵ Morriston,⁴⁶ Law,⁴⁷ Zande⁴⁸ and Lancaster-Thomas.⁴⁹ In this section, I follow in their footsteps by developing an argument for grounding evil god's moral character in the world's evils. In order to construct a successful parallel argument, the challenger ought to reverse the observations from the previous section. That is to say, the challenger should provide a similarly reasonable case in support of the following propositions:

1r. The world was designed to make us suffer. (Conclusion)
2r. The world contains gratuitous evil. (Conclusion)

Before we proceed, it is worth keeping in mind that the philosophers and scientists I draw from throughout this section do not believe in an evil god – in fact, some of them believe in a good god. However, as we saw in Section 1.6, this difference is immaterial, for the evil-god hypothesizer does not conclude that we should become evil-god theists, but non-theists. Similarly, it is worth noting that the scholars discussed vary in what they believe to be the implications of their observations and arguments. The most common position, however, is that the good-god believer ought to abandon the project of grounding god's moral character in creation. To take one example, consider the following extract from Hume:

> No decisive proofs can ever be produced against this authority; nor is it possible for you to compute, estimate and compare all the pains and all the pleasures in the lives of all men and of all animals: And thus by your resting the whole system of religion on a point, which, from its very nature, must for ever be uncertain, you tacitly confess, that that system is equally uncertain.[50]

It is on this (purported) uncertainty that the challenger builds their case for grounding evil god in nature.

Let us turn to the challenger's first claim (1r), that 'the world was designed to make us suffer'. According to evolutionary biology, says Dawkins, the world is a miserable place for those who find themselves in the state of nature. Dawkins writes:

> The total amount of suffering per year in the natural world is beyond all decent contemplation. During the minute that it takes me to compose this sentence, thousands of animals are being eaten alive, many others are running for their lives, whimpering with fear, others are slowly being devoured from within by rasping parasites, thousands of all kinds are dying of starvation, thirst and disease.[51]

From this observation, which is no more anecdotal than Paley's, the challenger may claim that the world was designed to make its creatures suffer. In fact, Dawkins himself argues that if one were to believe in the efficacy of creation theology, then the world's evils provide reason to attribute evil (rather than goodness) to god.[52] As Dawkins puts it in *The God Delusion*, 'It is childishly easy to overcome the problem of evil. Simply postulate a nasty god.'[53] Dawkins's observation is a good starting point; however, in order to parallel Paley's argument, the challenger must also provide *specific* examples of suffering in the natural world. Let us consider two, both of which are borrowed from Felipe

Leon's short list of teleological evils.[54, 55] In our first example, the jungle cat's call deceives its victims in order for the cat to attack, kill and devour its prey:

> Imagine being a pied tamarin monkey living in the Brazilian rainforest and suddenly a baby's voice cries out in distress; the urge to go out and help would be overwhelming. But in reality it's a lure set by a margay, a jungle dwelling wild cat with remarkable mimicry skills.[56]

As the example suggests, the natural order – a system which involves the killing of innocent creatures in order for other creatures to survive – strikes us as malevolent rather than benevolent. Moreover, beyond deceiving and ending the lives of other creatures, we also see predators cause their victims prolonged periods of suffering, as illustrated in our second example:

> The North American short-tailed shrew, Blarina brevicauda, secretes venom from salivary glands in its lower jaw to paralyze prey. But the point of the paralysis is not to kill the prey, but to keep it alive for an extended period of time to allow for prolonged feeding. A tiny shrew can infect a mouse, for example, and then graze on it for days and days until it eventually succumbs to its physical injuries.[57]

If the natural order had been configured by a benevolent benefactor, then it is reasonable to expect a world without internal torture mechanisms. Instead, a world in which creatures are forced to keep one another alive in their suffering in order to bleed them dry of their nutrients, is the sort of world we would expect from an evil god. Let us keep this point in mind as we consider the role of humans in the natural order of things.

Human-'kind', says the challenger, is responsible – in the minute it takes me to compose this sentence – for the slaughter and torture of thousands of non-human animals in factory farms and research facilities.[58] As Schopenhauer writes, 'It can truly be said: Men are the devils of the earth and the animals are the tormented souls.'[59, 60] Moreover, we humans, like our fellow creatures, also find ourselves in a world that is designed to harm us. As Hume puts it:

> And why should man, added he, pretend to be an exemption from the lot of all other animals? The whole earth, believe me, Philo, is cursed and polluted. A perpetual war is kindled amongst all living creatures. Necessity, hunger, want, stimulate the strong and courageous: Fear, anxiety, terror, agitate the weak and infirm. The first entrance into life gives anguish to the new-born infant and to its wretched parent: Weakness, impotence, distress, attend each stage of that life: And it is at last finished in agony and horror.[61]

As we see, Hume argues that the human condition is not as delightful as Paley and Swinburne would have us believe – that is to say, it is not that we take our human condition for granted, but that we have little to be grateful for. From these observations, the challenger may claim that the natural world is not geared towards the happiness and flourishing of its creatures, but their suffering and destruction.

Before I present a case for gratuitous evils (2r), it is worth considering an additional argument – taken from Hume and developed by Nagasawa – for the evil *of* nature, rather than the evils that are to be found within nature. Hume offers the following observation: 'every animal is surrounded with enemies, which incessantly seek his misery and destruction'.[62] In other words, in the state of nature, it is a war of every natural creature against the other, where no security is possible and life is full of horror. As I have suggested, in the extract quoted, I believe that Hume is on the verge of appealing to a third category of evil that is gaining traction in contemporary philosophy of religion: *systemic evil*. According to Nagasawa, himself a proponent of good-god theism, the existence of systemic evil rules out the possibility that the natural world is, on the whole, a good place of which we should be happy and pleased to be a part.[63] Typically, proponents of orthodox theism and atheism give examples of *specific* goods and evils (the jump of a shrimp and the venom of a shrew) and different *types* of good and evil (dancing and torture), but they fail to identify this third category, which lies beyond the standard dichotomy between natural and moral evil. For Nagasawa, systemic evil refers to the whole *process* of evolution by natural selection, the 'violent, cruel and unfair system' on which our 'entire biological system' is based.[64] In other words, when we're considering systemic evil, we're not just referring to instances of evil, but the structure that underpins the existence of all sentient creatures: the mechanism of evolution itself. Nagasawa summarizes the problem as follows:

> Suppose I filled a cage with lots of different animals – lions, lizards, leopards and the like – and a small amount of food and water. If I were to lock the cage and watch these animals fight for their survival, you would think I was playing an extremely horrible game! Yet, this is the state of the natural world. ... [How can we] stand on the bones of countless intelligent creatures – animals who died painfully and miserably – and proclaim that we should be happy and pleased to live in such a cruel and violent world? The costs that these animals paid for our survival seems unjustifiably high.[65]

For Nagasawa, when we peel away the surface-level goods and evils, we find a system which guarantees pain and suffering for an enormous number of creatures. That is to say, contrary to the optimistic observations of Paley and Swinburne, the underlying nature of the material world is evil through and through: the roots of evil run much deeper than the roots of goodness. The question is: what sort of a god would create a world that is *fundamentally* evil? The challenger concludes that this is the work of an evil god – a god who does not want us to be happy but wants us to suffer (1r).

The challenger's second claim (2r) – which, again, is intended to parallel observations made by the orthodox theist – is that the world contains gratuitous evil. Here, I believe that the challenger can reverse Paley's observation concerning what is (according to Paley, pain) and what is not (according to Paley, pleasure) necessary for our survival. However, at the end of this section, I suggest that there are some intrinsic goods – such as those put forward by Swinburne – that cannot be paralleled by the challenger. These form the basis of our discussion in Sections 3.5–3.7.

Let us begin with survival-based goods and evils. Recall Paley's example from the previous section: that the pleasure of eating is gratuitous, whilst the pain of hunger is *necessary*. Note that Paley also believed that this 'single instance' would 'make all this clear'.[66] In order to be concise, let us take Paley at his word and offer a single parallel argument in favour of gratuitous evil. I propose that the evil-god challenger makes the following claim: that pleasures (such as those associated with eating) are necessary and sufficient in motivating creatures to survive, whilst pains (such as the pain of hunger) are *added* in order to further our suffering. In other words, god could have created a world in which the flavour of fruits, the serenity of sunbathing and the quench of satisfying our thirst were enough to pull us towards survival. Yet, the designer *chose* to add the additional pains, shivers and thirsts – namely, surplus evils – in order to guarantee our unhappiness. I take this argument to be sufficient for paralleling Paley's original observation. In reality, it is unlikely that either pain or pleasure is gratuitous: a creature who experiences the pain of hunger and the pleasure of eating is more likely to survive than their part-zombie counterpart. However, if one were to argue that neither pain nor pleasure is gratuitous, then this would not constitute a parallel argument for evil god (that is to say, an *indirect* attack against orthodox theism), but a *direct* criticism of both Paley's and the challenger's positions. Therefore, for the purposes of developing an evil-god challenge, the objector should claim that it is not certain goods that are gratuitous, but certain evils.

Finally, I turn to Swinburne's question of suicide and the intrinsic value of life. The question asked of the challenger is as follows: if the world's evils outweigh the world's goods, then why do so few people end their lives through suicide? In answering Swinburne, the challenger may be tempted to appeal, once more, to Hume's *Dialogues*, in which Philo asks, 'But if they were really as unhappy as they pretend, says my antagonist, why do they remain in life?' Hume's answer: 'This is the secret chain, say I, that holds us. We are terrified, not bribed, to the continuance of our existence.'[67] On this account, we do not hold on to life because we believe the world's goods exceed the world's evils: we choose not to end our lives because we are terrified to discover what (if anything) lies beyond our current lives. This is, I believe, the appropriate response from the evil-god challenger to the question of suicide. However, this response does *not* address Swinburne's fundamental claim, that life is intrinsically valuable – a great gift – which all creatures are reluctant to throw away. As I argue in the following section, it seems that Swinburne is right, for we *are* grateful for our lives. Our time on earth is precious to us, and we consider it a shame when somebody wastes their time in existence. Life is a great gift, which we encourage each other to spend wisely; as the sundial motto goes, 'Use the hour, it will not come again.'

We are now in a position to present the parallel argument from creation for evil god. Once more, I offer a simple version of the argument in order to accommodate further examples of evil to be found in the natural order of things:

1s. If the natural world contains a significant amount of evil, then it is reasonable to attribute evil to god through creation. (Premise)
2s. The natural world contains a significant amount of evil. (Premise)
3s. It is reasonable to attribute evil to god through creation. (Conclusion)

Following the argument presented, it would appear reasonable to invoke unorthodox creation theology to attribute 'evil' to god. This is close to what Philip Goff has in mind – in his book, *Why? The Purpose of the Universe* – when he describes the creation of our universe as 'a cosmic sin': that it would, claims Goff, be morally wrong for a maximally powerful being to create a world such as ours.[68, 69] This same sentiment was shared by Schopenhauer, who offers the following reflection: 'It appears as if the dear Lord created the world for the benefit of the Devil – in which event he would have done far better not to have created it at all.'[70] Although I believe that these positions are reasonable – that is to say, I believe the challenger can make a strong case for (1r) and (2r) –

I maintain that there are several asymmetries that can be identified in relation to (2r). In short, I maintain that the world contains more intrinsic goodness than intrinsic evil. I explore these asymmetries in Sections 3.5–3.7.

3.5 To be, or not to be

In Section 3.3, I referred to several intrinsic goods that are to be found in the natural order of things; the examples I wish to focus on include existence, life, consciousness, free will and beauty. I maintain that each of these values constitutes an asymmetry favouring the attribution of goodness (over evil) to god. In each case, the argument states that if these concepts refer to intrinsic goods, then it is more likely that the world was created by a good god than an evil god – for a good god, and not an evil god, would be motivated (or disposed) to create a world for our benefit. In this section, I begin by discussing the intrinsic value of existence, life and consciousness. To be concise, I group together existence, life and consciousness throughout this section – as is common in the literature – and use these terms interchangeably. In doing so, we should recognize that existence is an all-encompassing category, containing everything that does (or will ever) exist. Therefore, if existence is intrinsically good, and not intrinsically evil, then it is likely that the value of existence constitutes a significant asymmetry in favour of good god.

As we have seen, proponents of traditional theism, such as Swinburne, identify existence as an intrinsic good.[71] To remind ourselves, and to emphasize the motivation for thinking that existence is an intrinsic good, consider the following thought experiment. Suppose you were able to step outside of yourself – into a twisted version of John Rawls's original position[72] – and were made ignorant of all the world's goods and evils. In this scenario, you know nothing about the pleasure, pain, happiness or suffering that any living thing will endure in its earthly existence. Now, suppose you were forced to make the following decision: do you want to bring living, conscious creatures into existence, or leave the universe empty and lifeless? The intuitive value judgement seems to be that the world would be better *with* living, conscious entities than without them. It seems that, as Gregory Miller has put it, 'Without consciousness, the world would be an empty, meaningless wasteland.'[73] In other words, when we consider the intrinsic value of life, existence and consciousness, we believe that it is greater, and more meaningful, to be than not to be.

Recently, discussion of this position has appeared in the evil-god literature. For example, Lancaster-Thomas – in her paper 'The Evil-god Hypothesis and the Argument from Mal-design' – has argued that the challenger can mirror Swinburne's belief in the intrinsic value of existence.[74] The parallel, asserted by the challenger, states that it is just as reasonable to believe that existence is intrinsically evil as it is to believe that existence is intrinsically good. 'Consequently', says Lancaster-Thomas, 'bringing a sentient being into existence, no matter the quality of its life, causes it harm'.[75] If this parallel were successful, then it is no less reasonable to ground evil god's moral character in the intrinsic *evil* of life, than it is to ground good god's character in the intrinsic *goodness* of life.

Ultimately, I believe that this response is unsuccessful. In her paper, Lancaster-Thomas relies exclusively on an appeal to Benatar's anti-natalism. This same appeal to Benatar is also made by Lancaster-Thomas in reference to perfect-being theology (recall the principle of the inferiority of existence),[76] and by Chris Byron in his own discussion of the evil-god challenge.[77] To understand why we should reject the anti-natalist parallel, it is important to be clear on the specifics of Benatar's view. In his book, *Better Never to Have Been* – the text referenced by Lancaster-Thomas and Byron – Benatar accepts that anti-natalism is both 'unpopular' and 'counter-intuitive'.[78] One might think that the contentious nature of anti-natalism (when compared to intuitive natalism) tips the weight of evidence in favour of good god; however, there is a more substantial problem with the challenger's appeal to Benatar. Simply put, Benatar argues that everybody *within* life will (inevitably) suffer. Therefore, says Benatar, it would be better if we chose not to bring conscious creatures into existence in the first place. More precisely, Benatar's argument relies on an asymmetry between pleasure and suffering: that the absence of suffering is good (so the denial of life is good), whereas the absence of pleasure cannot be bad (so the denial of life cannot be bad). Benatar summarizes his 'master' argument as follows:[79]

> The reason why we think that there is a duty not to bring suffering people into existence is that the presence of this suffering would be bad (for the sufferers) and the absence of the suffering is good (even though there is nobody to enjoy the absence of suffering). In contrast to this, we think that there is no duty to bring happy people into existence because while their pleasure would be good for them, its absence would not be bad for them (given that there would be nobody who would be deprived of it).[80]

As we see, Benatar's pessimism is not based on the intrinsic negative value of existence. Instead, his argument rests on the nature of extrinsic evils. For Benatar, life is bad because of the things that exist (or do not exist) within life. However, what Benatar does *not* claim is that life *itself* is bad. It is for this reason that the challenger's appeal to Benatar (that life is intrinsically bad) is ineffective.[81] In other words, Lancaster-Thomas and Byron's 'parallel argument' is not, in fact, a parallel argument.[82, 83] Therefore, I maintain that the challenger should abandon their appeal to Benatar's anti-natalism.

Rather than appealing to Benatar, the challenger may still want to claim that life is intrinsically evil. However, when we run Pike's (and our Rawlsian) thought experiment, the reasonable conclusion to draw is that existence is something we value (rather than disvalue) for the sake of itself. Furthermore, following Swinburne, this is a principle for which we also have *a posteriori* evidence. People typically consider life to be a gift, which we have a moral obligation to create, sustain and spend wisely. Even when people's lives are filled with boredom or suffering, they may still believe that life is worth holding on to – that it is a shame that their life (an intrinsic good) has been contaminated by suffering (an extrinsic evil). This same evidence is not available to the challenger, and, therefore, constitutes a notable asymmetry favouring the attribution of goodness (over evil) to god.

Before proceeding to discuss the intrinsic value of free will, it is worth mentioning that – elsewhere in Benatar's work – the challenger may find a more promising objection to the argument from the intrinsic value of existence. Offering his thoughts on the world's collective sum of intrinsic goods, Benatar argues that the total value of the world's extrinsic evils *outweighs* the total value of the world's goods (extrinsic *and* intrinsic): 'Even the intrinsic pleasures of existing do not constitute a net benefit over never existing. Once alive, it is good to have them, but they are purchased at the cost of life's misfortune – a cost that is quite considerable.'[84] As stated, this is a separate argument to that of Lancaster-Thomas and Byron. Rather than being a parallel of the argument from intrinsic values, Benatar's response is an argument from the total value of goods and evils (intrinsic and extrinsic). As we shall see, the argument for grounding evil god in the *totality* of the world's evils is also used by evil-god challengers, most notably Law.[85] I concede that this is a promising solution to the argument from the world's intrinsic goods; we shall return to this argument in Section 3.8.

3.6 Freedom over slavery

In this section, I discuss the intrinsic value of free will. If free will is an intrinsic good, and if we assume that all human beings and many of our non-human counterparts are free, then we have a significant amount of goodness in nature that favours the attribution of goodness (over evil) to god. I begin by outlining the motivation for believing that free will is an intrinsic good, before offering (and responding to) several objections on behalf of the challenger.

Amongst orthodox theists, belief that free will is an intrinsic good is widespread. For example, Augustine thought that it was better to sin – and seek god's forgiveness afterwards – than to lack the ability to do wrong. Augustine writes:

> A runaway horse is better than a stone which does not run away because it lacks self-movement and sense perception, so the creature is more excellent which sins by free will than that which does not sin only because it has no free will.[86]

As we can see, for Augustine, a world with free will and its negative consequences is greater than a world of automata who are only capable of doing good. To take a more recent example, Plantinga has also argued that free will is a tremendous good, in and of itself: 'A world containing creatures who are significantly free … is more valuable, all else being equal, than a world containing no free creatures at all.'[87]

To understand why Augustine and Plantinga believe free will is an intrinsic good, let us consult our thought experiments from the previous sections. Playing Pike's game, it would be preferable to choose the 'free' door over the 'not free' door. Similarly, in the original position – in which we're forced to decide whether to create a world of free beings or a world of automata – we would opt for a world of free beings. According to the good-god defender, we would make these decisions simply because the world would be *better* if it contained free beings than not. The challenger may be tempted to claim that free will is an intrinsic evil; namely, something that we disvalue rather than value. One way of motivating this view would be to say that people would prefer to live in a world without responsibility than with responsibility – a world free of the guilt and shame that shadows our actions. However, such an argument appeals to the emotions free will causes (extrinsic evils) rather than the value of free will in and of itself. In contrast, the thought experiments that I have cited – and the many wars fought in defence of people's freedoms – demonstrate our belief that (all else being equal) we would rather be free than not. (If the reader is still not convinced, I encourage them to consider the price of their own free will. I expect the price will be high.)

Law – in his flagship paper 'The evil-god challenge' – offers three reasons for rejecting the argument from the intrinsic value of free will. Later in this section, I respond to each of Law's arguments. I claim that two of Law's arguments can be easily overcome, whereas his argument from the totality of evils (the same argument we saw from Benatar in Section 3.5) is more difficult. Before I discuss Law's arguments, I begin by outlining and evaluating two objections from an earlier proponent of the evil-god challenge: Stein. I reject both of Stein's objections, arguing that neither objection can be used to establish a symmetry between our two competing hypotheses. I conclude that – with the exception of Law's argument from the totality of evils – the arguments against grounding god's goodness in the intrinsic value of free will are unsuccessful.

Let us begin with two of Stein's arguments. First, in an earlier version of the evil-god challenge, Stein attempts to avoid the intrinsic free-will asymmetry by arguing that free will is not, in fact, an intrinsic good.[88] According to this objection, because free will is not an intrinsic good, the value of free will does not constitute evidence in favour of the good-god hypothesis. We should acknowledge that the denial of free will's value cannot be used to form an argument for evil god; instead, what Stein offers is a *direct* attack against traditional theism, which asserts that the beliefs of good-god believers are unreasonable. With this in mind, the traditional theist may offer the following response. By attacking the underlying assumptions of traditional theism directly, Stein moves away from the evil-god challenge *simpliciter* (which aims to reject belief in good god indirectly), and, therefore, Stein sacrifices the central virtues of the evil-god challenge: that is, to be 'as metaphysically and epistemically sympathetic as possible' in order to undermine traditional theism without engaging in contentious debates.[89] Therefore, when we place this argument in the wider context of the challenge, we see that it should be rejected.

Second, Stein proposes that free will may not be an 'all or nothing' phenomenon.[90] According to this view, free will comes in degrees (some agents are freer than others), and, therefore, this constitutes an injustice on god's part. (After all, if god were good, then why would god not provide everybody with the highest degree of freedom?) According to Stein, it follows that this injustice favours the evil-god hypothesis over the good-god hypothesis. Stein summarizes his position in the following extract:

> Fortunately, I think that there is a better way to preserve the isomorphism. Underlying this argument against the invertibility of the free will theodicy is the assumption that free will must be all or nothing. But I think this is false. ... I think the isomorphism can be saved, because while the demonist ([evil-god believer)] may have to explain why the demon [(evil god)] granted people some amount of free will, the theist will have the opposite problem: why did God not grant people complete free will or at least make them freer than he actually did?[91]

Unlike Stein's first argument, this argument attempts to develop a positive case for evil god. However, once more, there is a straightforward response available to the good-god defender. Free will may not be an 'all or nothing' phenomenon, says the traditional theist, but there will be a threshold at which we can describe an entity as 'free' or 'not free'. Consider, for example, the entities spread across the great chain of being. Rocks and waterfalls are not free – and it is unlikely that dragonflies and ladybugs are free either – but humans (if we entertain the theist's underlying metaphysics) certainly are. Given that humans are endowed with free will, which is intrinsically good, we are justified in attributing goodness to god as he is the benefactor of such gifts. Furthermore, Stein may be right in claiming that some people are freer than other, but this would not justify the attribution of evil to god – instead, Stein's argument challenges good god's compatibility with the available evidence. To understand why, let us consider the proposition at hand: that 'god has blessed everybody with the gift of free will, but this gift varies in degrees'. I maintain that it would be reasonable to attribute goodness to an agent who distributes varying gifts, but it would not be reasonable to attribute evil to this same gift giver. To understand why, consider the following example. Suppose that every Christmas, an omniscient, omnipotent Santa Claus delivers gifts to all of the earth's children. Moreover, suppose that many of these gifts vary in their monetary and sentimental values. From this information alone, it would be unreasonable to think that 'Santa Claus is evil', but significantly more reasonable to think that 'Santa Claus is good'. Therefore, I claim that the question of why some people are freer than others (or why Santa distributes varying gifts) is a question of god's (and Santa's) compatibility with the available evidence ('why did god or Santa give us *this* gift?'), rather than a reason to attribute evil to god (or Santa).

Having rejected Stein's arguments against the grounding of god's goodness in the intrinsic value of free will, I now turn my attention to Law's objections. Before we engage with Law's rebuttals, it is important to note that in each of his arguments, Law (unlike Stein) does not contest the view that free will is an intrinsic good. Moreover, all three of Law's arguments can be applied to *any* argument that claims god's goodness can be grounded in the world's intrinsic goods – including existence (see Section 3.5) and beauty (see Section 3.7). In his first response, Law argues that the asymmetry (free will as an intrinsic good) may be neutralized by appealing to intrinsic evils. Law puts forward three candidates for the roles of intrinsic evils, stating that 'it is no less plausible that *pain, suffering* and *death* are intrinsic evils'.[92] If pain, suffering and death are intrinsic evils, the argument goes, then perhaps it is roughly as reasonable to attribute evil to god (through intrinsic evils) as it is to attribute goodness to god (through intrinsic goods). Rather than attacking Law's argument directly, let us give him the benefit of the doubt and say that pain, suffering and death *are* intrinsic evils. The problem with this response is that it overlooks the sheer quantity of intrinsic goods that are available to the orthodox theist. As we have seen, in addition to pleasure, happiness and life (the counterparts to Law's intrinsic evils, 'pain, suffering and death'), the good god believer also claims that existence, consciousness, beauty and free will are intrinsic goods. From these examples alone, it does not appear that, as Law claims, 'the two asymmetries balance out'.[93] In response, the challenger may wish to bolster Law's argument by adding to his list of intrinsic evils. As G. E. Moore argued in *Principia Ethica*, other intrinsic evils may include such things as 'cruelty' and 'lasciviousness'.[94] However, these evils also have their counterparts – kindness and love – and the additional intrinsic goods (again, existence, consciousness, beauty and free will) keep the evidence weighted in favour of good god. Therefore, in order for their response to be successful, the challenger must also explain why we should think that the total *amount* of intrinsic evil corresponds to the total amount of intrinsic good. For the reasons outlined in Section 3.5–3.7, I expect that such an argument is not available to the challenger, and, therefore, I maintain that we reject Law's first rebuttal.

Second, Law argues that the asymmetry arising from intrinsic goods (and a lack of intrinsic evils) may be 'counterbalanced or outweighed by other asymmetries favouring the evil-god hypothesis'.[95] In other words, according to this position, whilst the intrinsic value of free will constitutes an asymmetry favouring good god, this asymmetry does not justify the attribution of goodness (over evil) to god. On behalf of the good-god defender, I offer the following response. Throughout this book, I identify several reasons for attributing goodness (and not evil) to god, and many of these arguments appear to be significant – see Reformed epistemology (Section 3.9) and arguments from revelation theology (Chapter Four). However, contrary to Law, my analysis does not reveal a single argument that favours the attribution of evil (over goodness) to god. With these considerations in mind, I believe we should be sceptical of the challenger's speculation that they will succeed in their quest for further asymmetries.

Finally, Law claims that even if the world's intrinsic goods outweigh the world's intrinsic evils, intrinsic goods can be counterbalanced by the world's significant amount of *extrinsic* evils. (This is the same response we saw from Benatar at the end of the previous section.) I discuss this objection at length in

Section 3.8. However, for now, it is worth noting that Law and Benatar are right in at least one important aspect: there must be a limit to the explanatory power of the world's intrinsic goods. In other words, there must be a point at which the orthodox theist accepts that intrinsic goods have come at too high a price. Consider the following extract from Swinburne – taken from his popular book, *Is There a God?* – in which he discusses the explanatory limits of free will:

> A parent may allow an elder child to have the power to do some harm to a younger child for the sake of the responsibility given to the elder child; but there are limits. And there are limits even to the moral right of God, our creator and sustainer. ... Limits there must be to God's rights to allow humans to hurt each other; and limits there are in the world to the extent to which they can hurt each other, provided above all by the short finite life enjoyed by humans and other creatures. ... Unending unchosen suffering would indeed to my mind provide a very strong argument against the existence of God.[96]

For Swinburne, nothing in the material world has met this limit: not all of the world's wars, not all of the world's genocides and not all of the bloodshed that is inherent to the system of natural selection.[97] If Swinburne is right, then it is reasonable to ground god's goodness in the world's intrinsic goods; however, if Swinburne is wrong, then, given the totality of goods and evils in the natural world, it is not reasonable to ground good god (rather than evil god) in creation. We shall return to this point after we have considered the argument from aesthetic value.

3.7 All things bright and beautiful

In this section, I consider the argument from intrinsic beauty, also known as 'the aesthetic argument' or 'the argument from beauty'. According to this argument, beauty is an intrinsic good, and the natural world is more beautiful than it is ugly. A predominantly beautiful world is better than a predominantly ugly world, and, therefore – because good god (and not evil god) must create the best of all possible worlds – it is significantly more reasonable to attribute goodness to god than it is to attribute evil to god. The argument from beauty is a popular one, with different versions appearing in the works of F. R. Tennant,[98] Forrest[99] and Swinburne.[100] Although some traditional theists offer the argument as part of a cumulative case for god's goodness, others believe that the world's beauty may be sufficient for attributing goodness to god. In fact, Forrest considers this to be the best argument for good god's existence, writing: 'If I had to choose one feature of the universe that most clearly supports theism, it would be the beauty of things rather than the suitability of the universe for life.'[101] Each view – that the argument from beauty needs to be supported by further arguments, or that the argument is independently sufficient for attributing goodness to god – is compatible with the conclusion of my wider project, which consists of the claim that there are several powerful reasons for favouring the good-god hypothesis over the evil-god hypothesis.

Let us explore the argument from beauty in more detail. In *The Existence of God*, Swinburne offers the following explanation:

> Whatever God creates will be a good product; and so any physical universe that he creates will be beautiful, as are humans and animals. ... Even if no one apart from God himself sees such a world, it is good that it exists.[102] He would seem to have overriding reason not to make a basically ugly world beyond the powers of creatures to improve. Hence, if there is a God there is more reason to expect a basically beautiful world than a basically ugly one. ... A priori, however, there is no particular reason for expecting a basically beautiful rather than a basically ugly world. In consequence, if the world is beautiful, that fact would be evidence for God's existence.[103]

As the extract shows, Swinburne believes that if the world is basically beautiful, then we have more reason to believe that god is good than evil.[104] There are at least two ways of motivating the belief that the world is beautiful. First, one might claim that *instances* of beauty outweigh instances of ugliness – that is to say, there are more (or greater) beautiful parts of the universe than there are ugly parts. Second, it may be argued that the world is *on the whole* beautiful (and not, on the whole, ugly) – in other words, it is reasonable to believe that when we take a step back and consider the big picture, we will see that the ugly parts of the universe actually contribute to a beautiful (rather than an ugly) whole. In this section, I consider both versions of the argument. My analysis reveals that both reasons for believing the world is beautiful are more reasonable than their parallels (which say that the world is ugly), and, therefore, favour the attribution of goodness (over evil) to god.

As I explained in Section 1.4, the evil-god challenger should accept the underlying metaphysical and epistemic framework of the good god defender before they seek to develop parallel arguments in favour of evil god. Therefore, let us assume that beautiful experiences are pleasurable experiences and that ugly experiences are unpleasurable experiences. Moreover, let us assume that the natural world is somehow responsible for our experiences of it, that god caused the natural world to exist and that we can reasonably attribute moral character to the universe's cause (god) through its effects (the natural world's aesthetic values).

Now, let us explore the first argument for motivating the view that we live in a basically beautiful world: that there are more beautiful *parts* in the natural world than there are ugly parts. In considering this view, I encourage the reader to reflect on their own aesthetic experiences of nature. In our everyday lives, when we look to nature, it appears to stimulate experiences of awe, beauty and gratitude far more than it stimulates experiences of disdain, ugliness and resentment. We *want* to experience landscapes (mountain-top views), different species (the smells of flowers, the sounds of birds, the sightings of foxes) and the movements of planets, moons and stars (consider one's feeling of awe when the moon eclipses the sun). As Swinburne puts it:

> Consider the stars and planets moving in orderly ways, and plants growing from seed into colourful flowers and reproducing themselves. ... The universe is beautiful in the plants, rocks and rivers, and animal and human bodies on earth, and also in the swirl of galaxies and the birth and death of stars.[105]

This assessment of nature is not unique to theism, for many atheists believe that the world contains more beautiful parts than ugly parts. In fact, even good god's most outspoken opponents, such as Dawkins, defend such a position. Consider the following extract from Dawkins:

> I think that when you consider the beauty of the world and you wonder how it came to be what it is, you are naturally overwhelmed with a feeling of awe, a feeling of admiration and you almost feel a desire to worship something. I feel this, I recognize that other scientists such as Carl Sagan feel this, Einstein felt it. We, all of us, share a kind of religious reverence for the beauties of the universe, for the complexity of life – for the sheer magnitude of the cosmos, the sheer magnitude of geological time.[106]

This asymmetry is also defended by environmental aestheticians, such as Allen Carlson. According to Carlson, who studies the aesthetic value of the natural world independently of debates in philosophy of religion, the world contains more beauty than it does ugliness. As Carlson puts it: 'The natural environment, insofar as it is untouched by man, has mainly positive aesthetic qualities; it is, for example, graceful, delicate, intense, unified and orderly, rather than bland, dull, insipid, incoherent and chaotic.'[107] In summary, for Tennant, Forrest, Swinburne, Dawkins and Carlson: beauty is the rule and ugliness the exception.

Of course, according to the challenger, there is also ugliness to be found in nature. This ugliness – whether it be parasites burrowing into the eyes of children or cheetahs devouring the organs of antelope – generates negative aesthetic experiences. According to Emily Brady, negative aesthetic experiences typically involve 'qualities like deformity, decay, disease, disfigurement, disorder, messiness, distortion, odd proportions, mutilation, grating sounds, being defiled, spoiled, defaced, brutal, wounded, dirty, muddy, slimy, greasy, foul, putrid and so on'.[108] That is to say, in short, experiences with negative aesthetic qualities repulse us. The literature on nature's aesthetic values contains an enormous number of experiences whose character is negative. I provide one such example below:

> Take the aye-aye, for instance, a nocturnal lemur found in Madagascar. It is all out of proportion: small eyes, huge large ears, a rather bald and fleshy looking body, and sharp razor-like incisor teeth. We learn that it gets much of its food by tapping tree trunks and then scooping out grubs from inside the tree, using its teeth and a long, narrow, creepy middle finger. The more knowledge one has, perhaps the more one reacts with mild revulsion. Of course, it may be that this reaction also involves fascination, but this does not discount, in itself, the negative reaction connected to the very odd features of the animal.[109]

With this example in mind, rather than examining a catalogue of examples and evaluations, let us accept that the natural world contains a large number of ugly parts. The crucial question is whether instances of ugliness in the natural world counterbalance (or outweigh) instances of beauty – for if they do, then it is no more reasonable to attribute goodness to god through the world's beauty than it is to attribute evil to god through the world's ugliness.

When answering this question, the traditional theist should acknowledge that aesthetic judgements are private mental events, and, therefore, encourage the challenger to approach this question in good faith. For, if the challenger were to make honest assessments of nature's aesthetic value, then I believe that they too shall conclude that the natural world is more beautiful than it is ugly. To understand why, let us consider four reasons for thinking that nature contains more instances of beauty than ugliness. First, I wish to reiterate that our everyday aesthetic experiences are more positive than they are negative; that is, we find ourselves enjoying our experiences of nature far more than we find ourselves detesting them. Second, as we have already seen, this appears to be the predominant view of environmental aestheticians – an evaluation that should not be taken lightly. (As Carlson puts it, the natural world has '*mainly*' positive qualities.[110]) Third, we also find that those who study nature – outside of philosophy – share this same sentiment. Consider the following extract from David Attenborough, who has spent the best part of six decades observing the natural world:

> It seems to me that the natural world is the greatest source of excitement; the greatest source of visual beauty; the greatest source of intellectual interest. It is the greatest source of so much in life that makes life worth living.[111]

If the world did not contain more beauty than ugliness, then the assessments of biologists such as Attenborough – who claim that nature is 'the *greatest* source of excitement', 'the *greatest* source of visual beauty' and what '*makes life worth living*' – would strike us as unreasonable: but, on the contrary, they strike us as more reasonable than not. This leads us to our fourth consideration. When making their case for the planet's conservation, environmentalists often appeal to nature's beauty. When we look to the actions of the wider public, we see that people take this conviction seriously: for people act on their beliefs that it is wrong to discard litter in a woodland, that it would be wrong to replace the nation's fields with shopping centres and that it would be wrong to paint Mount Everest green – not only because of the creatures who depend on these environments, but because we value nature for its aesthetic properties. If the challenger were to claim that the environment is uglier than it is beautiful, then this would decrease the overall value of nature. However, the consequences of this pessimistic parallel principle would contrast so strongly with our ordinary value judgements that, in my view, it is not worth defending. It is with these considerations in mind that I claim it is more reasonable to believe that the natural world contains more instances of beauty than ugliness. We are now in a position to formulate the argument from 'natural instances of aesthetic value'. I present the argument as follows:

1t. If the natural world contains significantly more instances of beauty than instances of ugliness, then it is more reasonable to attribute goodness to god than it is to attribute evil to god through creation's aesthetic value. (Premise)
2t. The natural world contains significantly more instances of beauty than instances of ugliness. (Premise)
3t. It is more reasonable to attribute goodness to god than it is to attribute evil to god through creation's aesthetic value. (Conclusion)

I now discuss the attribution of beauty to the *whole* of creation. The argument states that if the world is *overall* beautiful, and not overall ugly, then we have another reason to attribute goodness (and not evil) to god. The argument presented is taken from Alexander Pruss, who uses this argument as part of his response to the atheistic argument from evil (and ugliness).[112] However, as we shall see, the asymmetry can be imported into the evil-god challenge. I begin by outlining the structure of Pruss's argument, before presenting and rejecting three objections (to both arguments from beauty) on behalf of the challenger. I conclude that it is more reasonable to attribute beauty to nature as a whole, than it is to attribute ugliness to nature as a whole.

According to Pruss, when we identify an object as ugly – such as the hands in Claude Monet's *Woman with a Parasol* (see Figure 2) – we often do so when the part is isolated from their whole.[113]

However, to consider an instance of ugliness in isolation from the whole is (more often than not) a mistake, for when we zoom out – says Pruss – we discover,

Figure 2 The Woman's Hand – A Section of Claude Monet's *Woman with a Parasol*. Public Domain via Wikimedia Commons.

more frequently than not, that an instance of ugliness forms an important part of a beautiful whole (see Figure 3).

For Pruss, it is reasonable to believe that instances of ugliness (can) form part of a beautiful artwork. In other words, in the light of the whole piece, instances of ugliness are likely to be unimportant or even beneficial to an overall beautiful artwork. (In this case, the undeveloped hands draw our attention elsewhere – towards the woman, her son and the wind – which adds to, rather than detracts

Figure 3 Claude Monet, *Woman with a Parasol*. Public Domain via Wikimedia Commons.[114]

from, the artwork's overall beauty.)[115] The same is true of individual instances of beauty. When we see a beautiful part of an artwork – such as Thomas and James in Leonardo da Vinci's *The Last Supper* (see Figure 4) – it is reasonable to infer that the larger artwork will also be beautiful (see Figure 5).

Figure 4 Thomas (left) and James (right) – A Section of Leonardo da Vinci's *The Last Supper (restored)*. Public Domain via Wikimedia Commons.

Figure 5 Leonardo da Vinci, *The Last Supper (restored)*.[116] Public Domain via Wikimedia Commons.

For Pruss, then, it seems reasonable that from both ugly and beautiful parts, we can sensibly infer that the overall artwork is going to be beautiful. However – and here comes the asymmetry – the parallel case is not as effective. According to Pruss, it is not as reasonable to claim that an artwork is overall *ugly* from both beautiful and ugly parts. In other words, based on an artwork's beautiful and ugly parts, it is much more difficult to judge that the overall artwork will be ugly than it is to infer that the overall artwork will be beautiful. As Pruss puts it, 'It is riskier to judge an artist untalented on the basis of a small part than to judge an artist talented on the basis of small part';[117] therefore, he says, 'positive judgments can be confidently made based on a small part, but negative ones not so much.'[118] If Pruss is right, then it seems more reasonable to infer that the natural world is, on the whole, beautiful – based on its beautiful and ugly parts – than it is to say the natural world is, on the whole, ugly.

If the argument stands – and it is more reasonable to believe that the overall natural world is beautiful than ugly, then – as good god would (and evil god would not) create a beautiful world, it is more reasonable to attribute goodness (than evil) to god. I summarize the asymmetry argument from the world's overall aesthetic value as follows:

1u. If it is more reasonable to believe that the natural world is overall beautiful than it is to believe that the natural world is overall ugly, then it is more reasonable to attribute goodness to god than it is to attribute evil to god through creation's overall aesthetic value. (Premise)
2u. If the natural world contains instances of both beauty and ugliness, then it is more reasonable to believe that the natural world is overall beautiful than it is to believe that the natural world is overall ugly. (Premise)
3u. The natural world contains instances of both beauty and ugliness. (Premise)
4u. It is more reasonable to believe that the natural world is overall beautiful than it is to believe that the natural world is overall ugly. (2–3u)
5u. It is more reasonable to attribute goodness to god than it is to attribute evil to god through creation's overall aesthetic value. (Conclusion)

In an attempt to overcome both arguments from the intrinsic value of beauty (1–3t and 1–5u), I shall now construct and respond to three objections on behalf of the evil-god challenger. First, the challenger may attempt to reject Pruss's argument for the world's overall beauty. The counterargument I shall propose relies on a distinction between artistic values (such as a skilful brush stroke or the harmony between an artwork's parts) and aesthetic values (such as beauty or ugliness). Pruss's examples, says the objector, reveal something about the whole–part relationship of artistic values, but nothing about the whole–part relationship of aesthetic values. Based on an *artistically* positive part of an artwork (such as the faces of Thomas and James in Figure 4), judgements about the overall artistic value of an artwork can be made with confidence (see Figure 5). However, based on an *aesthetic* part of an artwork, judgements about the overall aesthetic value of an artwork cannot be made confidently. The challenger insists that it is reasonable to infer from beautiful parts (see Figure 6) that they form part of ugly artworks (see Figure 7), and it is reasonable to infer from ugly parts (see Figure 8) they form part of beautiful artworks (see Figure 9). Therefore, as demonstrated by Figures 6–9, we cannot – contrary to Pruss – draw reasonable conclusions about the overall aesthetic qualities of artworks from their isolated parts. If this objection were successful, then it is no more reasonable to attribute beauty to the (overall) natural world from its beautiful and ugly parts, than it is to attribute ugliness to the (overall) natural world from its beautiful and ugly parts, and, therefore, this counterargument undermines Pruss's asymmetry that was said to favour good god.

Figure 6 Beautiful Embroidery – A Section of Quentin Massys's *An Old Woman (The Ugly Duchess)*. Public Domain via Wikimedia Commons.

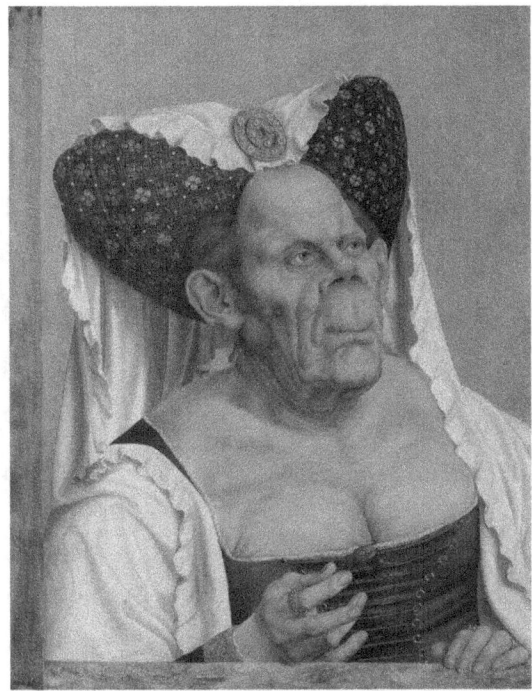

Figure 7 Quentin Massys, *An Old Woman (The Ugly Duchess)*.[119] Public Domain via Wikimedia Commons.

Figure 8 Torture in Hell – A Section of Fra Angelico's *The Last Judgement*. Public Domain via Wikimedia Commons.

Figure 9 Fra Angelico, *The Last Judgement*.[120] Public Domain via Wikimedia Commons.

I shall now respond to this counterargument on behalf of the traditional theist. First, we should acknowledge that the underlying assumption of the argument proposed – that artistic value can be separated from aesthetic value – is highly contentious. However, such a debate goes beyond the limits of our inquiry, and we may – with little cost to the good-god defender – leave such debates to the aestheticians. For our current purposes, it suffices to say the following. On the one hand, if it turns out that artistic values cannot be separated from aesthetic values, then we have a powerful asymmetry in favour of good god: a non-parallelable observation that beauty outweighs ugliness (1–3t) and a non-parallelable method of moving from beautiful and ugly parts to an overall beautiful whole (1–5u). On the other hand, suppose that artistic values *can* be separated from aesthetic values, and, therefore, that the challenger can successfully respond to Pruss's argument. Even if this were the case, the response would have little (to no) impact on our original asymmetry – that the amount of beautiful instances (and the lack of ugly instances) constitutes powerful evidence for favouring the attribution of goodness (over evil) to god. It follows that when we consider the totality of the available possibilities, the balance of evidence favours good god over evil god.

Second, the challenger may offer a response to our first argument (1–3t) from instances of beauty. The objection begins by asserting that there is a *necessary* relationship between moral properties and aesthetic properties. (In other words, the challenger may claim that all worldly instances of moral properties are beautiful and that all worldly instances of immoral properties are ugly.) The response proceeds to appeal to the significant amount of evil that is to be found in the natural order of things. (To illustrate the argument, I apply Nagasawa's concept of systemic evil.) Suppose that 'the entire biological system on which nature is based is fundamentally evil'.[121] Accordingly, when we scratch beneath the surface of our seemingly beautiful world, we find that the underpainting is basically evil, and, therefore – following our assumption – basically ugly. As we saw in Sections 3.3 and 3.4, and as we shall see again in Section 3.8, it appears no more reasonable to attribute goodness to god on the basis of the world's total sum of good than it is to attribute evil to god on the basis of the world's total sum of evil. Therefore, when we recognize the aesthetic properties of these goods and evils, so says the challenger, we see that the world is no more beautiful than it is ugly. This, says the challenger, overcomes the purported asymmetry from instances of intrinsic beauty.

I offer two responses to this objection. First, it is important that we acknowledge the unlikelihood of the central proposition at hand – that all worldly instances of immoral properties possess negative aesthetic qualities (i.e. appear to us as ugly). Consider, for example, aesthetically pleasing immoral protagonists (such as *Breaking Bad*'s Walter White[122]) and immoral artworks (such as Vladimir Nabokov's *Lolita*[123]).[124] Conversely, we may find moral characters aesthetically *dis*pleasing (such as Millard Coody's portrayal of Jesus in the *The Lawton Story of 'The Prince of Peace'*[125]) or aesthetically displeasing artworks as morally praiseworthy (such as Laurence Tureaud hip-hop album, *Mr. T's Commandments*[126]). Second, even if we give the evil-god challenger the benefit of the doubt – and accept that immoral qualities cannot be separated from negative aesthetic qualities – then this would not allow the challenger to respond to Pruss's asymmetry argument (1–5u), for it appears more reasonable to infer that the whole painting (and underpainting) is beautiful from its individual parts than it is to believe that the whole painting is ugly from its individual parts. Thus, on the one hand, if moral properties do not necessarily have aesthetic properties, then we have an asymmetry favouring good god (1–3t). Moreover, in contrast, if all moral properties have aesthetic properties, then we have another asymmetry favouring good god (1–6u).

Finally, the challenger may claim that evil god is compatible with the existence of a beautiful world. According to this argument, there are knowable reasons for why evil god would allow the world to contain a significant amount of beauty, and, therefore, neither argument from beauty constitutes a reason for favouring the good-god hypothesis over the evil-god hypothesis. Law offers the following explanation:

> Why, then, does an evil god create natural beauty? To provide some contrast. To make what is ugly seem even more so. If everything were uniformly, maximally ugly, we wouldn't be tormented by the ugliness half as much as if it was peppered with some beauty.[127]

Rather than being a parallel argument for why it is reasonable to attribute evil to god, Law's argument aims to show that evil god is compatible with the available evidence. For this reason, it does not constitute a parallel of either argument presented throughout this section (1–3t, 1–6u). When the traditional theist appeals to beauty in the natural world, they do so to *attribute* certain qualities to god – that is, to *establish* god's moral character. However, when the challenger claims that evil god has reasons for allowing beauty to exist, they overlook the need to attribute evil to god. For this reason – and given the asymmetries presented throughout this section – I take this rebuttal to be unsuccessful.

In summary, it appears that aesthetic arguments favour the attribution of goodness (over evil) to god. Therefore, in combination with the natural world's other intrinsic goods – such as existence, life, consciousness and free will – the traditional theist can present a strong cumulative case in support of the attribution of goodness (rather than evil) to god. I present the argument as follows:

1v. If the natural world contains significantly more intrinsic goodness than intrinsic evil, then it is more reasonable to attribute goodness to god than it is to attribute evil to god through creation's intrinsic values. (Premise)

2v. The natural world contains significantly more intrinsic goodness than intrinsic evil. (Premise)

3v. It is more reasonable to attribute goodness to god than it is to attribute evil to god through creation's intrinsic values. (Conclusion)

In the following section, I respond to this argument on behalf of the challenger.

3.8 The totality of good and evil

In this section, I discuss the argument for attributing goodness (and evil) to god – not through individual teleological arguments (such as the arguments presented from the world's intrinsic goods) but – through the *totality* of the world's goods and evils. According to Lancaster-Thomas, 'for *each* of the forms of the teleological argument, a similarly strong parallel argument for the existence of evil god can be constructed that satisfactorily mimics it'.[128] However, with the asymmetries I have developed in mind (Sections 3.5–3.7), I claim that we have sufficient reason to reject this conclusion: each version of the design argument does not have their satisfactory parallel. However, as I have suggested throughout this chapter, there is a more promising view – from Benatar and Law – which claims that the totality of the world's extrinsic and intrinsic goods (including existence, life, consciousness, free will and beauty) is neutralized – or outweighed – by the world's extrinsic evils. This is a broader claim, one that argues that the combined set of creation arguments for god's benevolence are roughly as reasonable as the combined set of creation arguments for god's malevolence. Thus, in response to the asymmetry argument from the world's intrinsic goods (1–3v), the challenger may present the following argument:

1w. If the totality of good in the natural world (extrinsic and intrinsic) does not outweigh the totality of evil in the natural world (extrinsic and intrinsic), then it is no more reasonable to attribute goodness to god than it is to attribute evil to god through creation. (Premise)

2w. The natural world contains significantly more intrinsic goodness than intrinsic evil. (Premise)

3w. The natural world contains significantly more extrinsic evil than extrinsic goodness, which successfully counterbalances the natural world's intrinsic goodness. (Premise)

4w. The totality of good in the natural world (extrinsic and intrinsic) does not outweigh the totality of evil in the natural world (extrinsic and intrinsic). (2–3w)

5w. It is no more reasonable to attribute goodness to god than it is to attribute evil to god through creation. (Conclusion)

In the light of this argument, the evil-god challenger can state the problem as follows: why is the belief that *the world's intrinsic and extrinsic goods outweigh the world's intrinsic and extrinsic evils* significantly more reasonable than the belief that *the world's intrinsic and extrinsic evils counterbalance (or outweigh) the world's intrinsic and extrinsic goods*?

Given the inaccuracies that are inherent to the weighing up of the world's goods and evils, I expect that any answer to this version of the challenge will be deeply contentious. Therefore, I claim that instead of grounding god's goodness in (solely) the world's goods and evils, the orthodox believer should present their argument from creation in conjunction with Reformed epistemology (see

Section 3.9), perfect-being theology (see Chapter Two) or revelation theology (see Chapter Four). It is in these areas that the grounding of good god is significantly more reasonable than the grounding of evil god. This is not a major concession, however, for if the good-god defender postulates that one cannot ground god in (exclusively) creation theology, then – as we saw in Section 1.4 – the evil-god defender must follow suit. It is worth noting that many orthodox theists have accused evil-god challengers of limiting their argument to creation – for example, see Bergmann and Brower,[129] Glenn Peoples[130] and Craig[131] – whilst ignoring the other branches of theology. Moreover, these same orthodox theists have conceded that one cannot overcome the atheist's objection that the world contains more evil than good. Take, for example, the following statement from Craig in which he rejects the argument from evil (that the world's evils are sufficient for ruling out the existence of good god): 'These kinds of speculations – about how much good and evil is in the world – are beyond our ability to make with any real confidence.'[132] As we cannot calculate the amount of good and evil in the world, says Craig, he maintains that the problem of evil is not a persuasive reason for rejecting good god's existence. Notably, this also commits Craig to the view that the world's goods do not constitute a solid, intellectual reason for thinking that god is good. In fact, this is precisely Craig's response to the evil-god challenge:

> Christians don't believe in the goodness of God because of an inductive survey of the world – that, seeing all of the good things that happen, we therefore conclude, 'Wow, God must be really good!' I agree with Stephen [Law] entirely: you could not refute the existence of an evil god by pointing to all the good things that happen. ... In reality, Christians attribute goodness to God – not because the world is good, but – because of facts relating to objective moral values and what it means to be 'God'.[133]

Bergmann and Brower take this a step further. Not only do they argue that theists should avoid grounding god's goodness in creation (like Craig), but they claim that no traditional theist (to their knowledge) has ever committed themselves to such a view. In their own words:

> In any case, no traditional theists we know of have ever argued for God's perfect goodness by appealing to a stipulative definition or by simply inferring it from the existence of some good in the world.[134]

As we saw in Section 3.3, Paley is an obvious candidate of a traditional theist who does, contrary to Bergmann and Brower, infer god's goodness from 'some good in the world'. Nevertheless, if Bergmann, Brower, Craig and Law are right – that, in the words of Law, '[a]ppeals to subjective estimations can carry little weight'[135] – then the orthodox theist has two options. First, the good-god defender may choose to abandon creation theology in order to avoid the possibility of the challenger grounding evil god in creation. Such a solution, however, not only appears *ad hoc*, but removes the possibility of attributing any property to god through creation – a consequence that not only seems *un*natural, but which many orthodox theists will want to resist. Second, the orthodox theist may present creation theology in conjunction with some other framework – such as perfect-being theology, Reformed epistemology (an approach which is, arguably, creation-based in nature) or revelation theology. This is the preferable method, for – as we saw in Section 1.3 – our concern is the *broad* evil-god challenge, which states that the symmetry thesis must hold across *all* of the various aspects of classical monotheism. With this in mind, if it is significantly more reasonable to attribute goodness (and not evil) to god across the various branches of theology, then the orthodox theist can afford to grant the evil-god hypothesis a modest degree of probability (through creation theology) in order to attribute some properties to god through creation. In other words, if the good-god hypothesis is significantly more reasonable than the evil-god hypothesis, then the claim that 'evil god can be grounded in creation' constitutes a minor (and not a major) symmetry. I expect that this is a price worth paying if the theist wishes to describe god as the 'creator' and 'designer' of the universe – although, such descriptions of god may also be available through revelation theology.

Before proceeding, it is also worth noting that, as we saw in Section 3.6, the good-god defender identifies a limit to the amount of evil with which good god can be said to be compatible. Therefore, in order to parallel the orthodox design argument, the challenger must also recognize a limit to the amount of goodness with which evil god would be compatible. For example, if, as Swinburne suggests, 'unending unchosen suffering' would falsify the good-god hypothesis, then the challenger must concede that 'unending unchosen *happiness*' would falsify the evil-god hypothesis.[136] It is at this point that apologists on both sides of the debate dig in their heels and claim that the world exhibits the perfect (or close to perfect) balance of good and evil – exploiting Hume's insight that it is impossible to 'compute, estimate and compare all the pains and all the pleasures in the lives of all men and of all animals'.[137] Here we find ourselves at philosophy's great impasse: debating whether or not the world's evils rule out the existence of good god (and, conversely, whether the world's goods rule out the existence of evil god). According to Hill, over 3,600 articles and books were written on the problem of evil between 1960 and 1998 alone, placing the question of whether the world's goods exceed the world's evils beyond the scope of any sensible inquiry.[138] As we have seen, the good god theist's inability to accurately measure the world's goods and evils serves only to benefit the challenger, who trades on the imprecision that is inherent to such a task, before claiming to have a powerful reason for grounding evil god in nature. In the following section, I present an argument for grounding good god that cannot be paralleled by the argument from the totality of good and evil.

3.9 Reformed epistemology

One method of supplementing the attribution of goodness to god through creation theology is by appealing to Reformed epistemology. I begin this section with a brief account of Reformed epistemology before discussing the implications for the evil-god challenge. I conclude that Reformed epistemology offers another asymmetry that favours the grounding of good god over evil god.

Plantinga has argued that knowledge of god is revealed to us through everyday experiences in the form of 'properly basic beliefs'.[139] Properly basic beliefs are not the products of inductive or deductive reasoning. Rather, as Plantinga puts it, it is 'rational, reasonable and proper' to hold properly basic beliefs '*without any evidence or argument*'.[140] In other words, there are some beliefs that are reasonable to hold on the basis of our sensory modalities, on the proviso that our senses are functioning properly. To take an example, with my brain and eyesight functioning properly, suppose I were enjoying a stroll around my local park. During my walk, it would be reasonable for me to believe that 'the sky is blue' and that 'the squirrel is grey' without needing any arguments or reasons to support my beliefs. As Plantinga writes, 'experience is what justifies me in holding [these beliefs]; this is the *ground* of my justification, and, by extension, the ground of the belief itself'.[141] Originating with John Calvin, Plantinga says that – in the same way my knowledge of the sky and the squirrel can be arrived at through my eyesight – knowledge of god is produced through our god-given faculty, the *sensus divinitatis*.[142] Calvin offers the following description:

> There is within the human mind, and indeed by natural instinct, an awareness of divinity. This we take to be beyond controversy. To prevent anyone from taking refuge in the pretense of ignorance, God himself has implanted in all men a certain understanding of his divine majesty. Ever renewing its memory, he repeatedly sheds fresh drops.[143]

These 'fresh drops' or 'basic beliefs' can be articulated in the form of propositions, such as 'god is watching me', 'god loves me unconditionally' and 'god forgives me for what I have done'.[144] From these propositions, says the Reformed epistemologist, we can construct a description of god's nature – such as the description that 'god is good' and 'god is not evil'.

If the *sensus divinitatis* exists, then we would expect humans to be naturally disposed towards belief in good god.[145] Several large-scale studies have found this to be the case. To take one example, the University of Oxford's 'Cognition, Religion and Theology' Project – a £1.9-million endeavour involving fifty-seven researchers and forty separate studies across twenty different countries – found that humans are predisposed towards belief in a god or gods.[146] In the words of Roger Trigg and Justin Barrett, the project's leads, theism is 'the default option for humans. Atheism is not our natural state',[147] and the theism we are typically inclined towards involves belief in a good god. Whilst some of the gods in these studies were not maximally good – some have limited moral characters, others mixed moral characters and many form part of a polytheism – no psychological or anthropological study to date has found a culture who have been disposed to believe in a monotheistic evil god.

Herein lies another asymmetry between our two hypotheses. Whereas a predisposition to believe in good god is seemingly widespread (evidence of the *sensus divinitatis*), there is no predisposition towards belief in evil god, and, therefore, no evidence of a 'sense of divine-malice'. In other words, there exist properly basic beliefs favouring good god, but no (or very few) properly basic beliefs favouring evil god, and, therefore, Reformed epistemology favours the grounding of good god over evil god. I present the argument as follows:

1x. If the *sensus divinitatis* produces a significant number of properly basic beliefs that indicate god is good and does not produce a significant number of properly basic beliefs that indicate god is evil, then it is more reasonable to attribute goodness to god than it is to attribute evil to god through Reformed epistemology. (Premise)
2x. The *sensus divinitatis* produces a significant number of properly basic beliefs that indicate god is good and does not produce a significant number of properly basic beliefs that indicate god is evil. (Premise)
3x. It is more reasonable to attribute goodness to god than it is to attribute evil to god through Reformed epistemology. (Conclusion)

(Note that as well as constituting a strong argument against the symmetry thesis, the case from Reformed epistemology also provides a reason to reject

Lancaster-Thomas's analysis of the evil-god challenge, in which she concludes that the good god hypothesizer's 'belief-wall can be reduced to intuitions'.[148] I present further examples against Lancaster-Thomas's thesis in Chapter Four.)

On behalf of the evil-god challenger, I now offer three arguments in response to the case for grounding god's goodness in Reformed epistemology – I claim that none of these rebuttals overcome the proposed asymmetry (1–3x). First, the challenger may contend that the argument presented confuses the *epistemological* claims of Reformed epistemology with the *popularity* of belief in good god. The essence of this reply is that neither argument affects the plausibility of the other. For example, it could be argued that the prevalence of theism has no impact on the plausibility of Reformed epistemology; similarly, one may argue that the plausibility of Reformed epistemology has no impact on the popularity of religious belief. I respond to both of these points as follows. Like many Reformed epistemologists, I appeal to the popularity of traditional religious belief only to illustrate the likelihood that other people may possess the *sensus divinitatis*. Nevertheless, I concede that this is not a necessary feature of the argument. According to Reformed epistemology, to be rational and justified in favouring the good-god hypothesis over the evil-god hypothesis, all that one requires is a properly basic belief involving good god and not evil god. In short, the anthropological discussion helps illustrate the argument, but it is not necessary to it.

Second, the challenger may claim that the *logical possibility* of a properly basic belief indicating that god is evil suffices to show that it is no more reasonable to ground good god in Reformed epistemology than it is to ground evil god in Reformed epistemology. We saw a similar tactic from the challenger in the case of perfect-being theology (hypothetical intuitions), and the same response will rear its head again in the case of religious experience (Sections 4.7–4.9) and miracles (Sections 4.10–4.13). This response is similar to the *reductio* objections that are typically presented against Reformed epistemology in the literature, all of which state that if belief in good god is properly basic, then some other absurd belief – such as belief in Superman or the Flying Spaghetti Monster[149, 150] – may be considered properly basic too. One version, introduced by Plantinga himself, considers Charles Schulz's comic book character Linus, who holds the belief 'that the Great Pumpkin returns every Halloween'.[151] Plantinga rejects Linus's belief in the Great Pumpkin, stating that 'the Reformed epistemologist may concur with Calvin in holding that God has implanted in us a natural tendency to see his hand in the world around us; the same cannot be said for the Great Pumpkin, there being no Great Pumpkin and no natural tendency to accept beliefs about the Great Pumpkin'.¹⁵² In short, to borrow from Law, 'imaginary evidence isn't really evidence',¹⁵³ and, therefore, given that there is no natural tendency to believe in the Great Pumpkin – and no natural tendency to believe in evil god – we should rule out the possibility that belief in evil god might be considered a properly basic belief.

Third, the challenger may be tempted to argue that evil god would have reasons for instilling the false belief that he is good and not evil. We saw this same response proposed by Lancaster-Thomas in relation to positive intuitions – such as the belief that god would want to deceive us into thinking that goodness is a great-making property (see Section 2.4). It is worth emphasizing that this is a popular response amongst proponents of the evil-god challenge. In his own defence of the evil-god challenge, Murphree summarizes the objection as follows:

> And such seems to be the nature of each empirical fact advanced as evidence of theism: religious experiences, answered prayers, miracles, sacred literature, fulfilled prophesies, ecclesiastical traditions and *even 'properly basic' beliefs* in God are all things that might be expected from anti-God ([evil god)] as well as from God. Indeed, such even seems to be the case for every possible empirical fact: nothing empirical can conceivably count as evidence against the claim that it will be anti-God, rather than God, whom creatures will face come Judgment Day.¹⁵⁴

In summary, following Lancaster-Thomas and Murphree, the challenger may claim that evil god would *not* be motivated to give humans a sense of divine-malice – after all, he wants to remain hidden – and, therefore, we should not expect humans to form properly basic beliefs that attribute evil to god. Instead, evil god chooses to give us a *sensus divinitatis* in order to deceive us of his true nature and intentions. This deception – says the challenger – is an intrinsic evil and, moreover, allows evil god to bring about higher-order extrinsic evils. To take one example, suppose that evil god causes humans to believe in good god (an intrinsic evil), but humans choose to sin despite of this knowledge (a higher-order extrinsic evil). After all, the sin of the misinformed good-god theist is worse than a sin committed by an atheist or evil-god believer; the former involves turning one's back on a (reputedly) all-loving parent, the latter an absent parent or an abusive parent. It follows that, according to the objection, evil god has well-defined reasons for giving humans a *sensus divinitatis*, and, therefore, evil god is compatible with the evidence cited. I respond to this objection as follows. As I outlined in Section 1.7, this is an argument for evil god's compatibility with the evidence (a compatibility argument) rather than a case for attributing evil to god (a grounding argument). The good-god defender can concede that both hypotheses are compatible with the available evidence, but we should strongly prefer – all other consideration pertinent to the reasonableness of our two hypotheses being equal – a grounded hypothesis over a non-grounded hypothesis. The argument from Reformed epistemology, as I have presented it, offers reasons for grounding good god (attributing goodness to god through properly basic beliefs) over evil god. That is to say, it would be unreasonable to conclude that 'god is evil' solely from a collection of propositions that suggest 'god is good'.

Finally, the evil-god defender may insist that many people do, in fact, have properly basic beliefs that imply god is evil. For example, when a natural disaster strikes, the *sensus divinitatis* might produce beliefs such as 'god is angry' or 'god is punishing me'. From these propositions, says the challenger, it is reasonable to attribute evil (rather than goodness) to god. In response, the traditional theist should explain that the examples cited say nothing about whether or not god is justified (or unjustified) in his anger or punishments. In reality, it is significantly more likely that these beliefs are formed within a framework that supports good-god theism over evil-god theism – that is to say, the *sensus divinitatis* will reveal that 'god exists' and that 'god is good', and then, at some later point, beliefs such as 'god is punishing me' will be brought into this pre-existing framework. Therefore, to amend our previous examples, the *sensus divinitatis* will produce belief such as 'god is *justifiably* angry' or 'god is *justifiably* punishing me', but not that 'god is *un*justifiably angry' or that 'god is *un*justifiably punishing me'. It seems that these latter beliefs are (very rare, if not) non-existent.[155]

The argument for grounding god's goodness in Reformed epistemology does not appeal to the natural world's goods and evils (extrinsic or intrinsic) and, therefore, the case for grounding good god in Reformed epistemology cannot be neutralized (or outweighed) by the grounding argument constructed in Section 3.8 (1–3x) – namely, that it is no more reasonable to ground good god in the totality of the world's goods than it is to ground evil god in the totality of the world's evils. Although, it is worth noting – as Plantinga recognizes himself[156] – that properly basic beliefs are open to defeat, and, therefore, the traditional argument from evil may be employed as a potential reason for rejecting the properly basic belief that 'god is good'. This, however, is an argument against good god's *compatibility* with the available evidence rather than an argument for *grounding* evil god. With these considerations in mind, I maintain that it is more reasonable to ground good god (and not evil god) in Reformed epistemology.

Table 4 An Analysis of Grounding God's Moral Character through Creation Theology. © Jack Symes

	Extrinsic good/evil	Intrinsic good/evil	Totality of good/evil	Reformed epistemology
Attribute goodness to god	✓	✓	✓	✓
Attribute evil to god	✓	✗	✓	✗

3.10 Conclusion

In this chapter, I developed arguments for grounding good god and evil god in creation. First, I outlined an account of maximal moral character. Although the action-based account of moral character was lacking, we saw that an (essentially) action-based view followed from a motivation-based or disposition-based account of moral character. Second, I considered the central motivations for orthodox creation theology, claiming that extrinsic and intrinsic goods in nature support the grounding of good god's moral character. Third, I offered a parallel account – an unorthodox creation theology – on behalf of the evil-god challenger, in which I argued that extrinsic evils in nature support the grounding of evil god. Fourth, I identified several asymmetries from the world's intrinsic values, claiming that it is highly unlikely that the evil-god challenger can parallel arguments from intrinsic goods – such as those from the value of existence, life, consciousness, free will and beauty. Towards the end of this chapter, I accepted that one argument for evil god – namely, that the totality of the world's evils (extrinsic and intrinsic) counterbalance (or outweigh) the totality of the world's goods (extrinsic and intrinsic) – may constitute a powerful argument for the attribution of evil to god. Finally, I went on to develop an argument for grounding good god in Reformed epistemology. I claimed that people form properly basic beliefs from which they can reasonably attribute goodness to god, however, they do not (or are highly unlikely to) form properly basic beliefs from which they can reasonably attribute malevolence to god. I also claimed that the argument for grounding evil god in the totality of the world's evils cannot be used to counterbalance the argument for grounding good god in Reformed epistemology. For these reasons, I conclude that it is more reasonable to attribute goodness to god than evil to god through creation. My analysis is illustrated in Table 4.

In Chapter Four, our final chapter, I discuss the possibility of grounding god's moral character in revelation theology. I outline several asymmetries between the two hypotheses and claim that the arguments for grounding good god are stronger than those for grounding evil god.

Chapter Four

God Revealed

Though sceptic storms may blast and blow
 Our ship adrift, off course,
The crow's nest calls out, 'Miracle!'
 Revealing good god's force.

4.1 Introduction

In Chapter Two, we identified our first important asymmetry in favour of orthodox theism. We saw that it is more reasonable to attribute goodness to god through perfect-being theology than it is to attribute evil to god. In Chapter Three, we identified several more asymmetries and concluded, in the case of intrinsic goods and Reformed epistemology, that it was more reasonable to attribute goodness to god than evil. In this chapter, I offer a third set of asymmetries in favour of orthodox theism by considering the grounding of both hypotheses in relation to revelation theology. My analysis reveals several unparallelizable arguments for the attribution of goodness (and not evil) to god.

According to revelation theology, knowledge of god can be accessed through divine intervention.[1] In this chapter, I discuss three types of divine intervention: scripture, religious experience and miracles. There is a long tradition of revelation theology in which orthodox theists have attempted to ground god's goodness. However, there is no long-standing tradition of 'unorthodox revelation theology' – the project of attributing evil to god – as genuine monotheistic belief in evil god is (essentially) non-existent.[2] Therefore, in keeping with the spirit of the evil-god challenge, as defined in Section 1.4, I attempt to ground evil god's moral character within the same epistemic framework as the orthodox theologian. In each case, however, I argue that when the evidence is properly contextualized, the parallel arguments (as regards revelation theology) for evil god are shown to be less effective than their orthodox counterparts.

This chapter has the following structure. I begin, in Section 4.2, by outlining an argument for grounding evil god in the Christian Scriptures; I do so by appealing to god's (seemingly) evil actions in the Old Testament.[3] In Section 4.3, I reject the argument for grounding evil god in the Christian Scriptures by offering asymmetries – most notably, drawing from Scripture's *explicit* claims about god's goodness – in favour of good god. In the light of this response, I argue that the argument from god's evil actions in Scripture ought to be recast as a compatibility objection against god's benevolence (rather than as an argument for grounding evil god). In Section 4.4, I argue that in responding to this compatibility objection, the good-god defender should avoid appealing to sceptical theism, as to do so would significantly decrease the plausibility of grounding good god (over evil god) in Scripture. I proceed, in Section 4.5, to outline an argument for grounding evil god in the nature and distribution of the world's contradictory scriptures. In this same section, I respond to this argument by contextualizing the competing claims of scripture in terms of their explicit claims about god's goodness. In Section 4.6, I introduce the argument for grounding god's moral character in religious experience and, in Section 4.7, provide a detailed account of a popular negative religious experience – demonic possession – which is said to offer evidence in favour of the attribution of evil to god. I argue, however, that unlike positive experiences – in which subjects report good god to be the apparent object of their experience – demonic possessions, asymmetrically, display god's malice through the actions of lesser beings. I go on to claim, in Section 4.8, that the same is true of other negative experiences, such as quasi-sensory and numinous experiences. In Section 4.9, I outline (and respond to) an argument for the unjust distribution of religious experiences, in which I argue that the distribution of religious experiences (both positive and negative) does not offer a reason for the grounding of evil god over good god. In Section 4.10, I introduce the argument from miracles. I offer definitions of 'positive miracles' and 'negative miracles' and acknowledge that many orthodox believers reject the existence of the latter. I contest this claim, in Section 4.11, by outlining a number of negative miracles – such as those performed by witches, the devil and other lesser beings – before explaining why some challengers believe that these constitute evidence for evil god. In Section 4.12, I respond to the argument from negative miracles by invoking two arguments that were developed earlier in the chapter: the first contextualizes scriptural negative miracles by considering them in relation to Scripture's explicit claims about god's goodness, and the second states that positive miracles (unlike negative miracles) are performed by god. In Section 4.13, I construct a final argument for evil god, in which I argue that the distribution of miracles is unjust, and, therefore, constitutes evidence in favour of evil god; I explain that this objection constitutes a direct attack (a compatibility objection) against good god, rather than a parallel argument for the grounding of evil god. I conclude in Section 4.14.

4.2 Drunk with blood

One popular argument against belief in god's goodness focuses on the actions of god in the Christian Scriptures. The argument maintains that because the god of the Bible performs a significant amount of malevolent actions, it is more reasonable to attribute evil to god than it is to attribute goodness to god. This argument was popularized by the new atheist movement at the beginning of the twenty-first century,[4] most recently reappearing in Dawkins's *Outgrowing God* (2020). Dawkins introduces the argument as follows:

> Whether or not we think God is an entirely fictional character, we can still judge whether he is good or bad, just as we might judge Lord Voldemort or Darth Vader or Long John Silver or Professor Moriarty or Goldfinger or Cruella de Vil. So ... when I say 'God did so-and-so' I mean 'the Bible says that God did so-and-so', and from these accounts we can judge if the God character is a nice character, whether the stories about him are fact or fiction.[5]

Dawkins goes on to provide several reasons for why he thinks the god of the Bible is evil and not good.[6] This same approach is used by several proponents of the evil-god challenge, most notably Millican, who claims that god's actions in Scripture provide evidence for believing that god is evil. God's actions in Scripture, says Millican, involve 'precisely the sort of thing that one would expect to be inspired by Antigod ([evil god]), but certainly not by God!'[7] Millican continues, 'Many people have believed in a being much like Antigod, so anyone who argues that the beliefs of billions must have some truth may be unwittingly committed to antitheism!'[8] Here, I follow the new atheists' and evil-god challengers' suggestion by offering a case for grounding evil god's moral character in Scripture.

In building our parallel case, let us recognize that in Scripture, god is responsible for the creation of good and evil: 'I form the light, and create darkness: I make peace, and create evil: I the Lord do all these things.'[9] In other words, the biblical god makes good and evil actions possible. Having created the opportunity to do good and evil, god himself then chooses – says the challenger – to perform a significant number of evil actions.

In his book *Drunk with Blood*, Steve Wells calculates that the biblical god is directly responsible for at least 2,821,364 killings.[10] This is a conservative estimate, as in most cases, the Bible does not provide specific numbers. In truth, god's total body count, says Wells, may be as high as twenty-five million, the majority of which are attributed to the Noachian flood.[11] I wish to note that many atheists appeal to god's killing in the Noachian flood in building their case against god's goodness; however, we should be sceptical of this appeal for the following reason. Citing Wells, Steven Pinker has claimed that 'Biblical literalists date the flood to around 2300 BCE',[12] at which time – according to estimates from Colin McEvedy and Richard Jones (whose data is used by both Pinker and Wells)[13, 14] – the world population was approximately twenty million.[15] However, Pinker and Wells's methodology appeals to a literal interpretation of the Bible (dating the flood to 2300 BCE), while basing the age and population of the earth on a *non-biblical* source (namely, McEvedy and Jones's population history). This approach is inconsistent. An appropriate methodology would assume the biblical date of the flood alongside the biblical age of the earth. Therefore, given the significant variation between estimates of pre-flood populations – for example, Tom Pickett believes the population was seventeen billion,[16] whilst Bodie Hodge places flood victims in the hundreds of thousands[17] – let us, for our current purposes, omit deaths caused by the Noachian flood and accept Wells's tally (2,821,364) of the numbers specified in the Bible.

In addition to god's direct killings, there are numerous examples in which god inflicts suffering on his people, or chooses to kill them indirectly (i.e. orders killings on his behalf). Raymund Schwager counts 'one hundred verses in which Yahweh himself appears the direct executioner of violent punishments' and 'in over one hundred other passages Yahweh expressly gives the command to kill people'.[18] Scripture also represents a god that acts out of jealousy (a negative emotion) and who wishes humans to suffer because of his jealousy. Consider the following extract from the Old Testament:

> Thus shall mine anger be accomplished, and I will cause my fury to rest upon them, and I will be comforted: and they shall know that I the Lord have spoken it in my zeal, when I have accomplished my fury in them. ... I shall execute judgments in thee in anger and in fury and in furious rebukes. I the Lord have spoken it. When I shall send upon them the evil arrows of famine, which shall be for their destruction, and which I will send to destroy you: and I will increase the famine upon you, and will break your staff of bread: So will I send upon you famine and evil beasts, and they shall bereave thee: and pestilence and blood shall pass through thee; and I will bring the sword upon thee. I the Lord have spoken it.[19]

As the passage states, god is motivated to send famine and evil beasts, so the people will know that *he alone* is the lord. Finally, in addition to god's killings, mistreatments and dubious motives, god also intends to bring about sin – as argued by Schwager and Matthew Hart & Hill.[20, 21] Hart and Hill offer a number of examples, including god's hardening of the Pharaoh's heart 'so that he will *not* let the people go'.[22] In this case, we see that god's motivation for keeping the Israelites in slavery was to justify inflicting plagues seven through ten, to 'show you my power, so that my name may be proclaimed in all the earth'.[23] This, says the challenger, appears to be the will of an evil god rather than a good god. With these seemingly evil actions in mind, we are now in a position to outline an argument for evil god from Scripture. I present the argument as follows:

1y. If god performs a significant amount of evil actions in Scripture, then it is reasonable to attribute evil to god through Scripture. (Premise)
2y. God performs a significant amount of evil actions in Scripture. (Premise)
3y. It is reasonable to attribute evil to god through Scripture. (Conclusion)

In summary, the god of Scripture is responsible for millions of (direct and indirect) killings, untold amounts of suffering and the sin of humankind. To return to Dawkins, this makes god 'arguably the most unpleasant character in all fiction'; a god who is 'jealous and proud of it; a petty, unjust, unforgiving control-freak; a vindictive, bloodthirsty ethnic cleanser; a misogynistic, homophobic, racist, infanticidal, genocidal, filicidal, pestilential, megalomaniacal, sadomasochistic, capriciously malevolent bully'.[24] In other words, the god of the Bible, says the challenger, is an evil god.

4.3 Drunk with love

In this section, I argue that it is more reasonable to attribute goodness (than it is to attribute evil) to god through Scripture. There are three reasons for this. First, let us recognize that the case for god's purported malice (1–3y) rests on god's *actions* in Scripture. However, as well as performing a (seemingly) significant amount of evil actions, god also performs a significant amount of good actions. The god of Scripture brings all creatures into existence,[25] produces an enormous amount of happiness,[26] has praiseworthy motives[27] and causes humans to do good.[28] Therefore, as god's (seemingly) evil actions do not significantly outweigh god's good actions, one may also ground god's goodness in Scripture. The argument has the following structure:

1z. If god performs a significant number of good actions in Scripture, then it is reasonable to attribute goodness to god through Scripture. (Premise)
2z. God performs a significant number of good actions in Scripture. (Premise)
3z. It is reasonable to attribute goodness to god through Scripture. (Conclusion)

Second, the orthodox theist may tip the scales in favour of good god by appealing to Scripture's *explicit* claims about god's nature and *teleological* claims about the purposes of god's actions. Explicit statements are direct claims about god's moral character (as opposed to being inferred by the reader through god's actions) and teleological statements are those which make direct claims about the *purpose* of god's actions (as opposed to the reader assuming god's final intentions). Scripture's explicit claims are clear on the matter of god's moral attributes. We are told, 'No one is good except God alone',[29] and 'Good and upright is the Lord'.[30] In the same vein, Scripture's teleological claims speak of god's promise that good will ultimately triumph over evil – an end at which, in the fullness of time, goodness and the true prophet (Christ) will defeat evil and the false prophet (the Antichrist),[31] and all people will receive what is good and just.[32] As god tells us himself, 'For I know the plans I have for you ... *plans to prosper you and not to harm you*, plans to give you hope and a future.'[33] This appeal to Scripture's explicit claims and teleological claims cannot be paralleled by the evil-god defender, and, therefore, this argument places the weight of evidence firmly in good god's favour. The argument from explicit and teleological claims can be stated as follows:

1aa. If scripture states that god is good and does not state that god is evil, then it is more reasonable to attribute goodness (than evil) to god through Scripture. (Premise)
2aa. Scripture states that god is good and does not state that god is evil. (Premise)
3aa. It is more reasonable to attribute goodness (than evil) to god through Scripture. (Conclusion)

Third, god's seemingly evil actions may be contextualized in the light of Scripture's explicit and teleological claims (from hereon, 'explicit claims'). For example, Joseph's sale into slavery may be accounted for by Joseph's successful navigation of the famine,[34] god's hardening of the Pharaoh's heart may be explained by god not wanting the Pharaoh to act out of the wrong motivation, or to display god's power over wrongdoers,[35] and – ultimately – all of god's killings and punishments may be justified by god's promise of eternal life and divine justice.[36] As the Bible says explicitly that god is good and not evil, god's killings, punishments, motives and 'sins' – when properly contextualized – may be considered moral rather than immoral. Significantly, this same hermeneutical approach is not available to the evil-god challenger, who can only attempt to *infer* god's moral character by appealing to god's actions; in contrast, the theist can appeal to god's actions *as well as* explicit statements about god's goodness. The resulting view is that it is significantly more reasonable to ground god's benevolence (than it is to ground god's malevolence) in Scripture.

4.4 Sceptical theism

Before proceeding, I wish to acknowledge that the argument for grounding evil god in Scripture may be recast as an argument against good god's compatibility with the available evidence. The argument questions whether it is reasonable to believe that god is good given that god performs such a significant amount of (seemingly) immoral actions in Scripture. In this section, I recommend that the orthodox believer does *not* respond to this objection by appealing to 'sceptical theism'. If one does appeal to sceptical theism, then – following Law and Erik Wielenberg[37, 38] – the good-god defender will lose their advantage over the challenger (1–3aa) and undermine their case against grounding evil god in Scripture.

According to sceptical theism, an omniscient god has knowledge of specific goods that are epistemically unavailable to human beings, and, therefore, we should be doubtful of our ability to understand the motivations or dispositions behind god's actions. In his paper, 'Sceptical theism and a lying God', Law describes this position as follows:

> According to sceptical theism, those goods, evils and entailment relations between them that we know of may, for all we know, constitute the unrepresentative tip of a vast, largely hidden iceberg of goods, evils, and entailment relations. ... [Thus] if sceptical theism is true, then the fact that we cannot think of any God-justifying reason for his permitting some evil does not justify us in concluding that no such reason exists.[39]

In the light of god's seemingly evil actions in Scripture, the good-god defender may wish to appeal to sceptical theism and claim that god has unknowable (but good) reasons for performing them. I now explain – again, following Law – why this would be a mistake.

If the traditional theist were to invoke sceptical theism to solve the problem of why god performs (seemingly) evil actions, then Scriptural claims about god's character – such as the explicit and teleological claims outlined in the previous section – are no more likely to be divine truths than divine lies.[40] In other words, if god's motivations are unknowable, then why think god's motives are good ('god reveals truths') rather than evil ('god reveals lies')? The same applies to god's actions. Ordinarily, the orthodox theist applies scepticism to god's seemingly evil actions, but the same approach also applies to god's seemingly good actions. When god performs a seemingly *immoral* act, the theist questions one's ability to determine the act's moral value; however, when god performs seemingly *moral* acts, we should apply this same reasoning. The resulting view is that when the evidence is based solely on divinely revealed (or divinely inspired) Scripture, and we cast doubt on our ability to know god's motives, we cannot say whether god is revealing truths or falsehoods; and, therefore, we cannot say whether Scripture favours good god over evil god.

For these reasons, rather than resurrecting the evil-god challenger's argument from Scripture, I recommend that the good-god theist provides *knowable* reasons for why god performs (seemingly) immoral actions in Scripture. It follows that if the traditional theist can provide knowable reasons for god's actions – and we saw some examples in the previous section – then one can maintain the Scriptural asymmetries presented in Section 4.3.

4.5 War, huh (*good god*) – what is it good for?

A second popular argument for evil god concentrates on the nature and distribution of the world's scriptures (universal revelation). In contrast to restricted revelation – which focuses on a specific set of Scriptures (such as the Christian Scriptures) – universal revelation assesses god's moral character in relation to *all* scriptures. I begin this section by developing an argument for attributing evil to god through universal revelation; I end this section by rejecting this same argument in favour of traditional theism. I conclude by recasting the argument from contradictory scriptures as a compatibility objection against god's goodness, before offering a solution on behalf of the good-god defender.

According to several proponents of the evil-god challenge – including Millican,[41] Law[42] and Lancaster-Thomas[43] – the conflicting messages of the world's scriptures give us reason to favour the evil-god hypothesis over the good-god hypothesis. As evil god (but not good god) would have reasons to deceive and harm his creations, so says the argument, it is more likely that god is evil than it is that god is good. Law summarizes the problem as follows:

> Suppose that the evil-god hypothesis is true. This malignant being may not want us to know of his existence. In fact, it may help him maximize evil if he deceives us about his true character. ... Taking on a 'good' guise, he might appear in one corner of the world. ... He might then do the same in another part of the globe, with the exception that the instructions he leaves regarding what should be believed contradict what he has said elsewhere. Our evil being could then stand back and watch the inevitable conflict develop.[44]

As the extract suggests, Law's argument consists of at least two claims: first, that the world's scriptures contradict one another and, second, that evil god would aim to distribute conflicting messages to sow division and generate conflict. Let us consider each in turn. First, in order to be concise, I focus on contradictions between the New Testament and the Qur'an, limiting myself to a clear and unambiguous case: those relating to the life and person of Jesus of Nazareth. In the Christian Scriptures, Jesus is described as god incarnate,[45] as one person of the trinity,[46] with ultimate authority over heaven and earth.[47] These claims contradict those of Jesus in the Qur'an, where he is identified as a prophet rather than a god. Consider the following passage:

> When God says, 'Jesus, son of Mary, did you say to the people, "Take me and my mother as two gods alongside God"?' he will say, 'May You be exalted! *I would never say what I had no right to say* ... I was a witness over them during my time among them.'[48]

Here, we see Jesus describing himself as a 'witness' to god rather than god's equal. This should not be understated: the Christian Scriptures reveal a god who is expressed as three metaphysically distinct (and arguably consubstantial) persons, whilst the Qur'an rejects this outright. I cite a second example:

> People of the Book, do not go to excess in your religion, and do not say anything about God except the truth: the Messiah, *Jesus, son of Mary, was nothing more than a messenger of God*, His word directed to Mary and a spirit from Him. So believe in God and His messengers and do not speak of a 'Trinity' – stop [this], that is better for you – God is only one God, He is far above having a son, everything in the heavens and earth belongs to Him and He is the best one to trust.[49]

The Qur'an also rejects key events in Jesus's life, as described in the New Testament, such as those relating to Jesus's crucifixion and earthly resurrection.[50, 51]

> They did *not* kill him, nor did they crucify him ... God raised him up to Himself. God is almighty and wise.[52]

With these examples in mind, let us accept Law's claim that there are significant contradictions between the scriptures. Therefore, so says the challenger, at least one of the world's scriptures constitutes a deception on god's part. (Of course, as we shall see, such an argument relies on the asymmetrical assumption that all scriptures are divinely revealed.)

Second, Law argues that contradictions between the world's scriptures create division and conflict. This is obviously true – the significance of Jerusalem in the Jewish and Islamic scriptures (and the ensuing conflict) is a clear case in point. However, it is worth keeping in mind that the extent to which scriptures can be held responsible for conflicts – including mental, social and physical conflicts – is difficult to examine. For example, it is unlikely that the causes of many conflicts, including those described as 'holy wars' and acts of 'religious extremism', are fundamentally scriptural. Even followers of the pacifist scriptures instigate conflicts involving physical violence, as Damien Keown explains in his discussion of Buddhist ethics: 'On the one hand, the classical sources teach strict pacifism, while on the other Buddhist states have not been averse to the use of force and have frequently invoked religion as a justification for military campaigns.'[53] My claim here is not that contradictory scriptures do not cause division and conflict, but that it is difficult to determine how *much* division and conflict they cause. However, with this qualification in mind, let us proceed by accepting Law's claim – that contradictions between scriptures cause conflict – without specifying the amount of conflict that they have caused. This concession will come at little cost to the challenger's argument, which claims that as evil god (and not good god) would be motivated or disposed to generate division and conflict, any amount of gratuitous deception and division that is caused by god will favour the evil-god hypothesis over the good-god hypothesis. Thus, Law concludes:

> When we consider the spread of evidence supplied by the miracles, religious experiences, and also the historical evidence associated with the various different faiths, it is at least arguable that the pattern we find fits the evil-god hypothesis better than the good.[54]

On behalf of the traditional theist, I now offer two responses to the argument from contradictory scriptures. (I maintain that both of my responses apply to all forms of the argument from contradictory scriptures in the evil-god literature – including those from Millican, Lancaster-Thomas and Law.) My first argument relies on the same asymmetry we saw in Section 4.3: namely, that god's benevolence can be grounded through revelation's *explicit* claims about god's character. As we have seen, the good-god defender has unparallelizable reasons for attributing goodness (and not evil) to god through Scripture: explicit statements revealing god's goodness. Significantly, we also find explicit statements about god's goodness across the other scriptural traditions, and, therefore, this same response is available to the traditional theist in the context of universal revelation. To take three examples, the Qur'an speaks of a god who 'loves the doers of good',[55] the *Guru Granth Sahib* identifies 'One God' who 'is without hate'[56] and, in the writings of *Bahá'u'lláh*, god declares, 'I knew my love for thee; therefore I created thee … and revealed to thee My beauty.'[57] The orthodox revelation theologian may claim that god's goodness can be grounded in these verses, yet the same move cannot be paralleled by the evil-god defender. Therefore, in the light of this consideration, we must ask whether it is reasonable to attribute evil to god through scriptures which (explicitly) state that god is good. I propose that it would *not* be reasonable to move from the claim that 'all scriptures reveal that god is good, but between the scriptures there are metaphysical and historical contradictions' to the view that 'god is evil'. By analogy, consider a parent who tells each of their children that they love them, but contradicts themself when they teach their different children about the world's history and metaphysics. It appears more reasonable to take the parent at their word (see the principles of testimony and credulity in the following section) than it does to attribute malevolence to the parent's character. That is not to say, however, that the challenger's argument does not constitute an argument against good god's compatibility with the available evidence. When recast as a compatibility objection against good god, the argument states that if god *were* good, then he would avoid deceiving his creations and stirring up conflict.[58] The argument can be presented as follows:

1bb. If god deceives people and causes conflict, then it is unlikely that god is good. (Premise)
2bb. God deceives people and causes conflict. (Premise)
3bb. It is unlikely that god is good. (Conclusion)

I doubt that Millican, Lancaster-Thomas and Law would reject this re-description of the problem. After all, in Law's own explanation of the argument, he begins by assuming that evil god can be grounded – '*suppose* that the evil-god hypothesis is true'[59] – before attributing contradictory scriptures to evil god. Although a response to the compatibility objection from contradictory scriptures goes beyond the limits of my inquiry, I accept that if the argument were successful, it might show that it is unreasonable to ground god's goodness in scripture. Note, however, that this does not mean it would be reasonable to ground evil god in scripture either; at best, the compatibility objection would show that neither hypothesis can be grounded in scripture.

This leads us to my second response, which applies to both arguments from contradictory scriptures: grounding and compatibility. I begin by acknowledging that both arguments from contradictory scriptures rely on the assumption that *all* scripture is valid. However, the good-god hypothesizer is likely to (and, in my view, should) reject the legitimacy of other scriptural traditions in order to evade the challenger's objections. For example, persuaded by the evidence of Jesus's earthly resurrection, Christians may offer reasons for rejecting the Qur'anic verses which deny the Trinitarian doctrine. (For our purposes, it suffices to say that theologies to this end have been offered by the likes of Craig and Swinburne.[60, 61]) Now, in the context of the argument for grounding evil god in scripture, recall that (as we saw in Section 1.4) the evil-god defender should attempt to accept the underlying framework of orthodox theism and then build their parallel arguments upon this same framework. If the underlying framework is maintained by the challenger, then we may say (following Craig and Swinburne) that only the Christian Scriptures are valid – therefore undermining both arguments from contradictory scriptures. Alternatively, the challenger may choose to amend the underlying premise that 'only Christian Scriptures are revealed by god' and replace this with an alternative principle, that 'all scriptures are revealed by god'. As I have noted, however, Christian theologians offer reasons for rejecting such a claim, and, therefore, the evil-god defender must develop a similarly reasonable case for the legitimacy of all scriptures. As Miller has put it, 'if the evil-god theorist wants to argue that the Christian is being unreasonable, they will have to actually argue that other religions are equally plausible. And it is difficult to see how they could do so'.[62] I anticipate that if the challenger were to develop such an argument, then their universal theology would be less reasonable than the Christian's restricted theology, for – as we have seen – it will contain significantly more contradictions (historical and metaphysical) than restricted theology.[63] Out of our competing theologies – 'Christian theology' and 'global theology' – we should favour (as the more likely to be legitimate) that which contains fewer contradictions. Therefore, it appears that a Christian theology should be preferred over a global theology, which means that, once more, good god should be preferred over evil god.

As we have seen, the popular arguments from scripture cannot be used to form a (similarly reasonable) parallel argument for evil god. In the proceeding sections, I draw the same conclusion in relation to religious experience and miracles.

4.6 Religious experience

In one of the earliest versions of the evil-god challenge, Madden argues that evil god's moral character can be grounded in religious experience.[64] Madden's discussion of evil god and religious experience was later developed by New and Law,[65, 66] and has since been discussed at length by Lancaster-Thomas.[67] All of these challengers maintain that arguments from religious experience constitute reasons for believing that the evil-god hypothesis is roughly as reasonable (or is more reasonable than) the good-god hypothesis. However, my analysis reveals that this conclusion should be rejected. In making my case, during this section, I begin by providing an overview of Swinburne's framework for understanding religious experience, as well as Swinburne's view that religious experiences are largely positive in nature. In Section 4.7, I outline a case for a popular religious experience – demonic possessions – which are said to constitute evidence in favour of evil god. (In this same section, I reject Swinburne's view that religious experiences are largely positive.) In Section 4.8, I consider two other types of religious experience – quasi-sensory and numinous – that are said to constitute evidence favouring evil god. However, unlike positive religious experiences, in which subjects report good god to be the apparent object of their experiences, the challenger, appealing to negative religious experiences, infers god's malice through the actions of *lesser* evil beings (such as Satan and his minions). In the light of these considerations, I conclude that it is more reasonable to attribute goodness to god than it is to attribute evil to god.

The argument for grounding evil god in religious experience begins by granting the orthodox theist the assumption that religious experiences are valid and reveal god's goodness ('positive experiences'), before recognizing the existence of alternative experiences: those that *purportedly* reveal that god is evil ('negative experiences').[68] If we accept the validity of positive experiences, and we apply orthodox theism's underlying epistemological principles consistently, then we should also accept the validity of negative experiences. It follows, says the challenger, that if it is reasonable to derive god's benevolence from reports of positive experiences, then it is similarly as reasonable to derive god's malevolence from reports of negative experiences. Before I outline (and analyse) this parallel argument in more detail, it is important that we get clear on the specifics of the orthodox argument for good god.

As Lancaster-Thomas explains, the validity of religious experiences can be built upon Swinburne's principles of credulity and testimony.[69] According to the principle of credulity:

> In the absence of special considerations, all religious experiences ought to be taken by their subjects as genuine, and hence as substantial grounds for belief in the existence of their apparent object – God, or Mary, or Ultimate Reality, or Poseidon.[70]

On this account, if positive or negative experiences occur, then one should accept them as reasonable grounds for believing that their *apparent objects* (good god or evil god) exist. Therefore, in order to attribute evil to god, as the orthodox theist attributes goodness to god, the challenger ought to identify negative experiences in which evil god is the apparent object. Swinburne's second principle is the principle of testimony: 'The principle that (in the absence of special considerations) the experiences of others are (probably) as they report them.'[71] In other words, if a person reports a positive experience or a negative experience, we should assume that they are trustworthy eyewitnesses unless we have compelling evidence to the contrary. When these principles are combined, the resulting view is as follows: if a person reports a religious experience (positive or negative), then we should consider these reports to be reliable evidence for the existence of the objects witnessed – the key caveats being that we have no substantial reasons for believing that the subject was lying, or that their experience has no credible naturalistic explanation (e.g. that the subject was intoxicated during the experience).

It is important to acknowledge that there are a significant number of positive experiences in which eyewitnesses have claimed to have directly encountered good god. The reader will be familiar with such cases. To take some examples, god appears to numerous witnesses throughout the Abrahamic scriptures: he walks with Adam and Eve in the Garden of Eden,[72] speaks to John and Jesus on the banks of the River Jordan[73] and bargains with Muhammad in the Kingdom of Heaven.[74] Contemporary examples are no less common. As Rodney Stark and Charles Glock point out in their book, *American Piety*, the majority of American

Christians claim to have perceived good god as part of a religious experience.[75] Here, I provide three concise examples from William James's *The Varieties of Religious Experience*:

> God surrounds me like the physical atmosphere. He is closer to me than my own breath.[76]
>
> God is quite real to me. I talk to him and often get answers.[77]
>
> God was present, though invisible; he fell under no one of my senses, yet my consciousness perceived him. ... I asked myself if it were possible that Moses on Sinai could have had a more intimate communication with God.[78]

With these examples in mind, let us accept that there are, to quote Jerome Gellman, 'a large number of instances in which mere finite mortals *have* experienced God'.[79] We are now in a position to present the orthodox argument from religious experience. I construct the argument as follows:

1cc. Religious experiences should be believed by subjects who experience them (in the absence of special considerations to the contrary). (Premise)
2cc. Subjects who report religious experiences should be believed (in the absence of special considerations to the contrary). (Premise)
3cc. Subjects experience religious experiences of good god. (Premise)
4cc. Subjects report religious experiences of good god. (Premise)
5cc. Religious experiences of good god should be believed. (1–4cc)
6cc. It is reasonable to attribute goodness to god through religious experience. (Conclusion)[80]

If negative experiences of evil god are widely reported, then this would constitute a problem for the good-god defender – for the evil-god challenger may replace the word 'good' in 3–5cc with word 'evil', and, therefore, arrive at the conclusion that one can attribute evil to god through religious experience. Swinburne recognizes the power of this objection himself:

> It does follow that, if there were a substantial number of religious experiences [of evil god] that entailed the non-existence of a particular supernatural being [(good god)], that would cast significant doubt on the credibility of claims to have perceived that being [(good god)].[81]

However, in seeking to avoid this problem, Swinburne denies that many people report experiences of evil god: 'If there were vastly many experiences apparently of an omnipotent Devil [(evil god)], then that sort of evidence would exist; but there are no such experiences.'[82] As I argue in Section 4.8, I believe that this is a reasonable conclusion to draw. However, Swinburne makes an additional claim regarding the experiences of other evil agents. As with experiences of evil god, Swinburne also argues that there is little evidence for lesser (evil) deities:

> That leaves us to look for a personal explanation of the occurrence of violations or quasi-violations—by the agency either of God or of some lesser spirit (ghost, poltergeist, demon, or whatever). ... There is quite of bit of evidence that counts far more strongly for the existence of God than for the existence of lesser spirits. ... Hence, in the absence of positive evidence for the existence of lesser spirits whose action does not depend on the permission of God, the most probable explanation of any violation or quasi-violation is that it was brought about by or with the permission of God.[83]

For this reason, Swinburne claims that there is no need to postulate lesser deities such as the Devil and his demons.[84] I reject this view in Section 4.7, in which I claim that there are a significant number of reports involving experiences of evil deities. Moreover, I claim that if the traditional theist does not attribute negative experiences to lesser deities, then they face a (potentially) forceful compatibility objection against god's goodness: if god is good, then why does he cause so many negative experiences? I discuss this further in the following section, before outlining (and rejecting) Lancaster-Thomas's 'parallel argument' from religious experience in Section 4.8.

4.7 Demonic possession

There is a vast literature encompassing a wide range of religious experiences, many of which vary in popularity and type. Therefore, I limit myself to three categories of negative experiences: demonic possession, quasi-sensory negative experiences and numinous negative experiences.* Each of these categories of negative experiences has been used by Lancaster-Thomas as part of her parallel case for attributing evil to god through religious experience. In this section, I focus on demonic possession – I go on to explore quasi-sensory and numinous experiences in Section 4.8. Demonic possession occurs when a non-physical evil spirit enters the body of a physical creature. The spirit typically manifests itself by causing the creature mental or physical harm. In this section, I discuss

---

* Many religious experiences are described as 'miracles', and many miracles are described as 'religious experiences'. If the reader were to re-organize the cited examples in good faith, I expect that my analysis would still reveal strong asymmetries favouring the attribution of goodness to god.

biblical accounts, outline the findings of various anthropological studies and offer several modern examples of demonic possession. The conclusion I seek to establish is that (contrary to Swinburne) negative experiences (per Madden and Lancaster-Thomas) are widespread. However, the reader should note that none of these experiences identify evil god as their apparent object – an asymmetry which we shall return to in Section 4.8.

A literal reading of the Christian Scriptures reveals a number of negative experiences, the most common of which is demonic possession. The first biblical reference to demonic possession appears in 1 Samuel, which tells of King Saul's possession.[85] In the New Testament, Luke speaks of 'a woman which had a spirit of infirmity eighteen years, and was bowed together, and could in no wise lift up herself'.[86] The woman crippled by an evil spirit in Luke is one of the many victims of demonic possession throughout the New Testament.[87] There are at least ten significant exorcisms that are performed by Jesus in the Synoptic Gospels. In some cases, the number of exorcisms is provided – for example, in Matthew, Jesus heals one boy possessed by a demon[88] – and sometimes, multiple exorcisms are performed simultaneously: 'Now when Jesus was risen early the first day of the week, he appeared first to Mary Magdalene, out of whom he had cast seven devils.'[89] Elsewhere, the number of exorcisms is not given. For example, in Matthew, 'They brought unto him many that were possessed with devils: and he cast out the spirits with his word, and healed all that were sick.'[90] The effects of these demonic possessions were detrimental to the victims. For example, spirits made their hosts blind and mute,[91] caused them severe fits[92] and forced them to commit disturbing acts of self-harm.[93] In short, the predominant view amongst historians and theologians is that belief in demonic possession was widespread at the time of the biblical writers.[94, 95, 96, 97, 98]

Beyond the ancient Judaic and Christian civilizations, belief in demonic possession has continued to be popular. T. K. Oesterreich identifies hundreds of possession accounts, spanning from the ancients to the twentieth century, 'in all countries of the inhabited globe'.[99] Similarly, drawing from a sample of 488 societies, anthropologist Erika Bourguignon 'found that beliefs in spirit possession were present in 74 per cent of ... sample of societies, that is, in 360 of our 488 societies'.[100] Such beliefs persist today. For example, in 2013 a YouGov poll found that 18 per cent of Brits and 51 per cent of Americans believe that 'someone can be possessed by the devil or some evil spirit',[101, 102] and Bourguignon notes a significant increase of exorcism reports at the end of the twentieth century.[103] Descriptions of these experiences are incredibly similar to those found in the Synoptic Gospels. In fact, Oesterreich describes a 'perfect similarity of the facts', arguing that the biblical accounts 'coincide so exactly with what we know of these states from the point of present-day psychology, that it is impossible to avoid the impression that we are dealing with a tradition which is veracious'.[104]

Merete Jakobsen – cited heavily by Lancaster-Thomas – in her survey of data collected by the Alister Hardy Religious Experience Research Centre ('AHRC'), highlights approximately 200 examples of modern-day negative experiences, many of which involve demonic possession.[105] Consider the following example:

> For about nine months I lived in intense misery, and it seemed as if someone was presenting my whole life to me, and only one action at a time. Clairaudiently a voice spoke and said, 'This is hell', and although before this breakdown I had thought of myself as a reasonable good living woman I now saw myself as black and evil. ... During this nine-month period it seemed as if I was possessed by evil and for most of the time I raved.[106]

Such accounts give a vivid and distressing insight into the reality of modern demonic possessions.

In the light of these considerations, I believe that Swinburne ought to accept that reports of demonic possessions are popular. Doing so would put Swinburne in good company – for Nagasawa claims that 'exorcism is practised in nearly all major religious traditions',[107] and in his discussion of natural evil, Plantinga introduces the possibility that 'Satan rebelled against God and has since been wreaking whatever havoc he can'.[108, 109] Even critics of the evil-god challenge have acknowledged the existence of these beliefs. For example, in her reply to Law, Scrutton cites a number of disturbing instances of purported demonic possession, arguing that 'belief in demons and evil spirits is common in a wide range of religious traditions, including various forms of Christianity and Judaism'.[110] However, in an attempt to maintain the asymmetry between positive experiences and negative experiences, Swinburne may be tempted to offer the following rebuttal: that when the number of reports involving demonic possession are compared to the number of reports of positive experiences, demonic possession turns out to be a part of an insignificant minority. In other words, on the whole, there are far more positive experiences than there are negative experiences.

In rejecting Swinburne's conclusion, let us analyse this claim – that there is not significant evidence of negative experiences performed by lesser deities – in more detail. Jakobsen, analysing 4,000 of the AHRC's 6,000 first-hand accounts, found that 4–5 per cent of reported religious experiences could be described as 'negative' or 'evil'.[111] I believe that there are (at least) seven reasons for thinking that, in reality, the actual number of negative experiences is considerably higher. First, we should keep in mind that the number of reported negative experiences does not reflect the number of actual negative experiences – one reason for which is the social stigma that is associated with negative experiences. Illustrating this same point, Lancaster-Thomas cites the following evaluation from Jakobsen:

> Try to express your belief ... immediately you are aware that you are considered a crank by some, a servant of the non-existent devil by others, and a source of embarrassment to your family. So what does one do? In most cases the answer would appear to be, maintain strict silence about one's private revelations for fear of being considered a fool, or worse. I wonder just how many people alive today are doing just that ... staying silent is the safest approach.[112, 113]

Furthermore, Lancaster-Thomas suggests that human beings are cognitively disposed to interpret religious experiences as positive rather than negative – the leading causes being confirmation bias, societal pressures and the favourability of positive experiences due to their pragmatic benefits (such as increased well-being).[114] Given the empirical limitations in drawing comparisons between the prevalence of withheld positive experiences and withheld negative experiences, I do not claim that unreported negative experiences outweigh unreported positive experiences. My point is simply this: in the first instance, we should be sceptical of those who draw conclusions about negative experiences from the AHRC's data. Second, beyond scepticism, we should acknowledge the AHRC's limited sample size, the archive of which contains approximately 6,000 accounts. Based on such a small data set, we should challenge any attempt to generalize the AHRC's findings to the 107 billion people who have existed.[115] The third limitation concerns the scope of the data: namely, that all of the accounts were collected after 1969. In contrast, concluding his study of demonic activity, Oesterreich argues that prior to the Age of Enlightenment, 'It may be said without exaggeration that the whole of the preceding centuries theoretically regarded the air as filled with demons, peopled with spirits of all sorts.'[116] (As a missionary visiting nineteenth-century China wrote, 'Possession is here in the country a daily occurrence which attracts no attention.'[117]) Fourth, the criteria of what should be described as a 'religious experience' is somewhat vague, and, therefore, it is difficult to know how many negative experiences are left out of the AHRC's data pool. (For example, should ghost sightings and alien abductions be considered *religious* experiences?) As Stark and Glock point out, 'It ought to be made clear that various events or feelings are only religious experiences if a person *defines* them as such.'[118] Fifth, as we have already seen (per Oesterreich and Bourguignon), other studies have found that negative experiences are significantly more common. For example, in 1987, David Hay and Gordon Heald claimed that 12 per cent of reported religious experiences were negative, a statistic that increased to 25 per cent in the BBC's Soul of Britain survey conducted in 2000.[119] Elsewhere, such as in Glock and Stark's *Religion and Society in Tension*, it is claimed that 'Historically, "evil" and "good" supernatural forces have been about equally common', and that 'there seem to be reasonable grounds to assert that diabolical contacts have played nearly as important a role as the divine in Western religious life'.[120] Sixth, we have strong reason to challenge the nature of the AHRC's research. As Meg Maxwell and Verena Tschudin have pointed out: 'In the archives of the AHRC are only a small number of experiences of evil. It may be that this represents an idiosyncrasy in that requests and questionnaires did not ask for this type of experience.'[121] Notably, Tschudin and Maxwell's scepticism that the AHRC's data should be seen as representative of negative experiences more generally is shared by Sir Alister Hardy himself. The following passage is taken from Hardy's *The Spiritual Nature of Man*:

> It seems likely that the proportion of people who have such experiences may be much greater than our figures would suggest, *for our appeal was for records of religious or spiritual experience rather than those of an evil nature* ... It must remain for future random surveys to give us more information on the proportion of the population who either believe in 'the Devil' or feel themselves in the presence of evil powers.[122]

Hardy recognized that the AHRC's survey did not ask for accounts of negative experiences and, therefore, it is likely that the proportion of negative experiences is significantly higher than the 4.5 per cent cited by Jakobsen. Finally, it is also worth noting that the majority of these reports come from good-god believers, which are often interpreted within the context of good-god theism.

Leaving these problems aside, let us grant the good-god defender the (*very generous*) benefit of the doubt and disregard all of the religious experiences outside of the 4,000 AHRC accounts analysed by Jakobsen. Even on this conservative estimate, the number of people who claim to have had negative experiences is still significant. To understand this number, consider the amount of people who have claimed to have undergone religious experiences. John Hick, for example, cites the aforementioned BBC national survey (which claims that 76 per cent of people claim to have had a religious experience) and church surveys (in which 53 per cent of church members report religious experiences).[123] Based on these data, let us *modestly* assume that 40 per cent of people in the UK have had a spiritual or religious experience. With approximately 66.8 million people in the UK (2019),[124] according to our estimate (40 per cent), 26.7 million members of the British population have had a religious experience. (Applied worldwide, this would be at least 3 billion people.) From here, we can say that if the AHRC's database were reflective of the UK population (4.5 per cent of religious experiences are negative), then following our estimate, roughly 1.2 million members of the British population have had a negative religious experience (and 135 million people worldwide). Based on this estimate (135 million), the number of worldwide negative experiencers is enormous, outweighing the world's combined population of Sikhs (26 million), Jews (14.7 million), Jains (4.2 million), Zoroastrians (2.6 million) and Rastafarians (0.6 million).[125] In the light of the relevant data sets, it appears that Swinburne's claim that there is an 'absence of positive evidence for the existence of lesser spirits', especially evil spirits, is unreasonable.[126]

Given the strong evidence in favour of negative experiences, it appears that the traditional theist ought to postulate the existence of lesser (evil) deities whose actions are not determined by god. I maintain that if the orthodox theist does not attribute negative experiences to lesser deities, then these experiences must be attributed directly to god. This unlocks a potentially damaging parallel argument for evil god, that – as I argue in the following section – the good-god defender should (and can) avoid.

4.8 Experiencing evil god?

In the previous sections (4.6–4.7), I proposed that if it is reasonable to believe that positive experiences exist, then it is reasonable to believe that negative experiences exist. I proceeded to argue that positive experiences do not significantly outweigh negative experiences. However, in this section, I argue that negative experiences such as demonic possessions do not constitute similarly reasonable evidence for evil god (as positive experiences do good god) because (unlike many positive experiences) negative experiences do not typically identify god as their apparent object. Nevertheless, Lancaster-Thomas has argued that 'people *have* had direct religious experiences of evil god'.[127] Therefore, I begin this section by attempting to strengthen Lancaster-Thomas's case by discussing two of (what I take to be) the most plausible (but still insufficient) categories of negative experiences: quasi-sensory negative experiences and numinous negative experiences. I provide several examples, before claiming that none of these examples motivates a reasonable parallel argument for evil god.

In our first example, the victim describes a frequently occurring negative quasi-sensory visual experience. The event is said to take place in the victim's house:

> I can remember coming out of my bedroom door, switching on the landing light so I was not in the dark, and to my right in just ... the edge of my vision ... about six feet away from me ... I could see the Devil. Now, I don't really know how to say this, because I knew perfectly well that there was a figure there, and he literally had cloven hooves, shaggy hides and horns – I mean he was literally this romantic Victorian image, as it were, of how the Devil was drawn, or even earlier, even sixteenth or seventeenth century. And I was very, very, very afraid.[128]

For the victims, these experiences are evidently terrifying. The same is true of experiences with a negative quasi-sensory auditory aspect, as shown by the following example:

> Then a little figure manifested itself. It was like a sitting dog with a curly tail, large ears up pointed, a man's face and had horns curling forward. It spoke to me in a high-pitched unpleasant voice saying 'You are afraid of us but you cannot get rid of us. We are going to stay with you and we can come nearer.'[129]

Finally, to take a third example of a quasi-sensory experience, victims also report negative tactile experiences:

> Suddenly I saw Satan. He was a brownish-black demon with close-set beady black eyes, pointed ears and forked tail. In his right hand he carried a three-pronged fork: in his left hand he carried a long pair of pincers. He was surrounded by rat-like devils. Satan caused the room to become icy cold. ... Satan gripped my toes in his pincers causing excruciating pain.[130]

As we saw with demonic possession, quasi-sensory experiences typically have an immediate and disturbing impact on their victims. As Jakobsen concludes, encounters with evil often involve 'ice cold shivers, tingling scalp[s], sweating with terror, paralysed lips, vomiting from fear, shaking ... [and] being unable to speak or move'.[131] However, also like demonic possession, none of these experiences report an encounter with evil god. In fact, the same is true for all of those cited by Lancaster-Thomas under the categories of 'quasi-sensory', 'revelatory' and 'regenerative' negative experiences.

The closest Jakobsen and Lancaster-Thomas get to an experience of evil god are those which involve an ambiguous 'power',[132] 'atmosphere',[133] 'feeling'[134] or 'presence' of evil,[135] which are commonly reported under the category of 'numinous' negative experiences. Lancaster-Thomas offers three examples that involve an evil presence. I cite the strongest candidate below:

> I was out one night in Sussex ... when I came to a ruined building, I felt the presence of something evil, which made me feel extremely uncomfortable and frightened ... On no other occasion in my life have I had such an overpowering feeling of the presence of evil which invoked such fear in myself.[136]

Again, evil god is not identified (explicitly) as the apparent object of the negative experience. However, the challenger may argue that it is, nonetheless, reasonable to attribute this experience to god. In response, I recommend that the good-god defender states the following: that it is no more reasonable to attribute a 'presence of evil' with the Devil or other lesser (evil) deities than it is to attribute a 'presence of evil' to god. In contrast, it is significantly more reasonable to attribute positive experiences in which good god is the apparent object to good god, than it is to attribute experiences of good god to lesser deities. It follows that many *positive* experiences provide an *unambiguous* case for god's goodness, whilst *negative* experiences are no more (or more) likely to be the work of lesser deities than god.

Lancaster-Thomas does not discuss this objection, including under her subheading, 'Experiences of evil are encounters with the devil'.[137] Instead, she responds to the claim that the Devil performs negative experiences by including 'theistic dualism in the evil-god hypothesis by speculating the existence of a lesser, benevolent god (or perhaps a fallen demon) that co-exists with evil god'.[138] As the reader can infer, this is a separate objection, one that relies on a pre-established symmetry between (the grounding of) evil god and good god. In other words, like many of the arguments discussed in the previous chapters, Lancaster-Thomas's response assumes that it is reasonable to attribute evil to god – overlooking the need to ground evil god – before proceeding to argue for evil god's compatibility with positive experiences.

In order to be clear on this matter, consider Lancaster-Thomas's argument for evil god from religious experience. The following is taken directly from Lancaster-Thomas's paper:

1dd. Religious experiences should be believed by subjects who experience them (in the absence of special considerations). (Premise)
2dd. Subjects who report religious experiences should be believed (in the absence of special considerations). (Premise)
3dd. Subjects experience religious experiences. (Premise)
4dd. Subjects report religious experiences. (Premise)

5dd. Religious experiences exist. (Conclusion 1)
6dd. Evil god exists. (Conclusion 2)[139]

Now, compare this argument (1–6dd) with Swinburne's orthodox argument from religious experience (1–6cc). Significantly, premises 3–4cc state that there are religious experiences 'of good god'. However, in the parallel case (3–4dd), Lancaster-Thomas makes no mention of the *objects* of religious experiences. This analysis reveals that 1–6dd does not constitute a parallel argument; as Lancaster-Thomas acknowledges herself, 'With regard to analogous logical form, it seems imperative that successful [parallel arguments] retain the same logical form as their corresponding [target arguments]. If the logical form differs, then the parallel argument should not be considered a parallel *whatsoever*.'[140, 141] In order to offer a sufficiently powerful version of Swinburne's argument, the challenger must make a case for the following:

1ee. Religious experiences should be believed by subjects who experience them (in the absence of special considerations to the contrary). (Premise)
2ee. Subjects who report religious experiences should be believed (in the absence of special considerations to the contrary). (Premise)
3ee. Subjects experience religious experiences *of evil god*. (Premise)
4ee. Subjects report religious experiences *of evil god*. (Premise)
5ee. Religious experiences *of evil god* should be believed. (Conclusion 1)
6ee. Evil god exists. (Conclusion 2)

As we have seen, the problem with this argument lies in premises 3–4ee: subjects do not report to have undergone religious experiences of evil god.[142] Therefore, we have a strong reason to favour the orthodox argument from religious experience (1–6cc) over its parallel (1–6ee).

Before proceeding, let us consider two responses on behalf of the challenger. One solution, which I take from Lancaster-Thomas's paper, is to insist that evil god can be understood as the cause of negative experiences. As Lancaster-Thomas puts it, although these experiences 'are not attributed to evil god in name, they could certainly be interpreted as experiential evidence for the existence of an evil supernatural being'.[143] In other words, the challenger may claim that it does not matter if subjects of negative experiences report an encounter with evil god; all that matters is that they can be understood as such. As I have stated, however, the problem with this response is that it is no more reasonable to attribute negative experiences to a lesser evil 'supernatural being' than it is to attribute them to evil god. On the other hand, it is more reasonable to attribute positive experiences to good god than to lesser deities because good god is the apparent object of a significant number of positive experiences. Therefore, on the balance of evidence – even if religious experiences could be attributed to objects beyond those that appear within the experiences themselves – it will be more reasonable to attribute positive experiences to good god than negative experiences to evil god. At this point, the challenger may push back, claiming that it is no more reasonable to believe that all religious experiences (positive and negative) can be attributed to good god than evil god. After all, evil god has knowable reasons for disguising himself and appearing to his creations as good. However, as we have seen in previous cases, this argument overlooks the need to attribute evil to god. Once more, in the case of religious experience (see 1–3ff), we have stronger reasons for attributing goodness to god than evil to god.

A second potential solution is to identify the Devil not as a lesser being, but as a manifestation of evil god. In motivating such an argument, the challenger may argue that negative experiences of Satan (a lesser being) are, in fact, those of the Antichrist (one aspect of evil god). Despite cultural depictions of Satan as a demonic creature with 'two horns like a lamb', the Christian Scriptures typically reserve this description for the Antichrist,[144] and this creature bears a strong resemblance to the entity that is described in our earlier examples. For the evil-god challenger, the Antichrist may be to evil god what Christ is to good god: one member of the (un)holy trinity. Thus, the evil-god hypothesizer may be tempted to propose that if it is reasonable to infer the existence of Jesus (and therefore good god) via positive experiences of Christ, then it is also reasonable to infer the existence of the Antichrist (and evil god) via negative experiences of the Antichrist. There are two problems with this approach. First, unlike Jesus – who is the incarnation of maximal goodness – the Antichrist is not *maximally* evil, omnipotent and omniscient. Moreover, according to Christian theology, the Antichrist is under the control of good god, which rules out a potential symmetry between Christ and the Antichrist. Furthermore, the challenger cannot make the *ad hoc* claim that the Antichrist fulfils the criterion of being 'maximal evil incarnate' either. Instead, the challenger must ground Antichrist's character – attributing omnipotence, omniscience and maximal malevolence to the Antichrist – by paralleling the orthodox theist's grounds for establishing Jesus's nature (that is to say, through eyewitness accounts and Scripture). As the Christian Scriptures describe Jesus and not the Antichrist as the incarnation of god, we must conclude that a similarly reasonable parallel argument is not possible. Second, even if the Antichrist's maximal malevolence (and other properties) could be grounded, the challenger would still lack negative experiences of evil god *the father*, which – given reports of positive experiences with good god *the father* – tips the balance of evidence in favour of grounding good god over evil god.

I therefore claim that negative experiences do not provide a similarly reasonable case for attributing evil to god as positive experiences do for attributing goodness to god.[145] The argument for this conclusion can be presented as follows:

1ff. If good god is the apparent object of a significant number of religious experiences and evil god is not the apparent object of a significant number of religious experiences, then it is more reasonable to attribute goodness to god than it is to attribute evil to god through religious experience. (Premise)

2ff. Good god is the apparent object of a significant number of religious experiences and evil god is not the apparent object of a significant number of religious experiences. (Premise)

3ff. It is more reasonable to attribute goodness to god than it is to attribute evil to god through religious experience. (Conclusion)

Although negative experiences do not allow for the attribution of evil to god, they may be used to form an objection to good god's compatibility with the available evidence. I present the argument as follows:

1gg. If god allows a significant number of negative experiences to occur, then it is unlikely that god is good. (Premise)

2gg. God allows a significant number of negative experiences to occur. (Premise)

3gg. It is unlikely that god is good. (Conclusion)

Here we see the significance of allowing for the existence of lesser (evil) deities. If the traditional theist claims that negative experiences are the free actions of lesser deities (that is to say, if god has justified reasons for allowing negative experiences to occur), then the good-god defender can offer a powerful response to the compatibility argument from negative experiences (1–3gg). However, if the theist does not postulate the existence of lesser deities, then the likelihood of the conclusion (3gg) increases significantly. For these reasons, in order to maintain the asymmetry argument from religious experience (1–3ff), I maintain that the theist attributes all negative experiences to lesser deities and (a significant number of) positive experiences to god.

4.9 Universal distribution

In this section, I outline (and reject) a final argument for attributing evil to god through religious experience. The argument presented focuses on the distribution of religious experiences – a distribution which, according to the challenger, is said to be unjust. I consider two arguments from evil-god challengers – the first from Law, the second from Lancaster-Thomas – which both claim that the distribution of religious experiences favours the evil-god hypothesis over the good-god hypothesis. However, my analysis reveals that when these arguments are placed within the context of grounding (see Section 1.7) and the apparent objects of religious experiences that are reported by witnesses (see Sections 4.7–4.8), it can be said that the argument for evil god from the universal distribution of religious experiences is unsuccessful.

Let us begin with Law. Although Law, unlike Lancaster-Thomas, does not defend the existence of negative experiences, he argues that in the case of positive experiences we 'should not ... rule out the possibility that ... the evil-god hypothesis is actually rather more reasonable than the good-god hypothesis'.[146] Law offers two reasons in support of his conclusion. First, given that evil god would want to deceive us about his true intentions, it seems likely that evil god would be motivated to bring about positive experiences (of which there are many) as 'it may help him maximize evil if he deceives us about his true character'.[147] Second, as we have already seen, Law argues that evil god (and not good god) would be motivated to create a 'recipe for ceaseless conflict, violence and suffering' by revealing contradictory messages to different groups across the globe, convincing them that 'the one true all-good god' is on their side.[148] Let us take each of Law's arguments in turn. First, the good-god defender should accept Law's account of evil god's intentions: evil god *would* have reasons to deceive his creations. However, the traditional theist should also argue that Law's claim relies on the assumption that the attribution of evil to god is as reasonable as the attribution of goodness to god. In other words, before the challenger asserts that evil god is compatible with the available evidence – if they wish to establish a strong symmetry between our competing hypotheses – then they should also provide reasons for thinking that the evil-god hypothesis can be grounded in religious experience (that religious experiences provide roughly as much reason to attribute evil to god than goodness to god). Therefore, given our grounding asymmetry favouring good god (1–3ff), the traditional theist may accept that evil-god is compatible with the available evidence, but argue that religious experience offers stronger reasons for attributing goodness to god over evil.

Second, as with the argument from contradictory revelations (see Section 4.5), the argument from contradictory religious experiences should be seen as a compatibility objection against god's goodness, rather than an argument for grounding evil god. In other words, Law's argument is not a parallel argument for the grounding of evil god, as it is not reasonable to move from the belief that 'there are historical and metaphysical contradictions between some religious experiences, but in all religious experiences god is good but not evil' to the conclusion that 'god is evil'. As we saw in Section 4.5, the traditional theist can also offer a reply to this compatibility objection, for the compatibility argument against good god from universal religious experience assumes that *all* religious experiences are valid. However, this is not an assumption that the good-god defender is likely to share. As it is not as reasonable to claim that all religious experiences are valid than it is to claim that only Christian religious experiences are valid (my assertion), we can draw the reasonable conclusion that Law's argument from universal distribution does not constitute a powerful reason for rejecting the argument for grounding good god in religious experience. On the other hand, the argument for grounding good god (and not evil god) in religious experience (1–3ff) constitutes a powerful asymmetry. Therefore, on the balance of evidence, it appears that – despite Law's objections – we should continue to favour the good-god hypothesis over the evil-god hypothesis.

Let us turn to our second set of objections. Lancaster-Thomas aims to strengthen Law's argument from the distribution of religious experiences by appealing to negative experiences (the evidence for which is presented in Sections 4.7–4.8). Like Law, Lancaster-Thomas maintains that religious experiences (positive and negative) are distributed unjustly, and, therefore, are more likely to be the work of evil god than good god. The conclusion is supported by two central claims: first, that injustice is an evil that evil god (but not good god) would seek to promote and, second, that both positive experiences and negative experiences are unjustly distributed. As we saw with Law's first claim, the good-god defender should accept that evil god would be motivated or disposed to promote injustice. This comes at no cost to the good-god defender, for our question is whether or not it is reasonable to attribute evil to god in the first place. Second, I believe the good-god defender should also accept that positive experiences and negative experiences appear to be distributed unfairly. However, this does not mean that the unjust distribution of religious experiences favours the evil-god hypothesis over the good-god hypothesis. There are two reasons for this. First, as we have seen, negative experiences are performed by lesser deities: they are not performed by god. Therefore, it is not god who unfairly distributes negative experiences but free, lesser (evil) deities – deities who are themselves hell-bent on promoting injustice. Moreover, the 'unjust' distribution of positive experiences cannot be used to attribute evil to god either, for it would be unreasonable to move from the claim that 'in all religious experiences god is good but not evil, but god only appears to some people and not others' to the conclusion that 'it is more reasonable to believe that god is evil than good'. The argument can, however, be reframed as an argument against good god's compatibility with the available evidence. If god is good, says the objector, then why does he appear to some people but not others? Again, arguments for compatibility are beyond our scope. (However, it is worth noting that there is a long history of apologetics that seeks to reconcile good god's existence with divine hiddenness. For example, in his book, *The Hiddenness of God*, Michael Rea has argued that 'the fact that God loves us perfectly provides, all by itself, no reason for thinking that God is so devoted to our wellbeing or to pursuing relationships with us as to prevent divine hiddenness altogether'.[149]) Given the vast literature on direct objections against good-god theism – such as the problem of evil and the problem of divine hiddenness – I concede that a successful compatibility argument may show that both hypotheses are equally unreasonable. (For what it's worth, I do not think any argument has shown this to date.) Nevertheless, my conclusion remains unaffected: we ought to conclude that it is more reasonable to attribute goodness to god than evil through religious experience.

In summary, it seems that religious experience offers a much stronger case for good god than for evil god. This may, in the view of several good-god defenders, be sufficient for undermining the symmetry thesis. As Lougheed writes, 'If it's true that religious experience makes Christianity more probable than an evil god, then the symmetry thesis is false.'[150] I do not go as far as Lougheed, for the argument from religious experience is rarely employed as a standalone argument for god's goodness and, instead, is offered by orthodox theists as part of a cumulative case. With that said, it is clearly more reasonable to attribute goodness than evil to god through religious experience and, when combined with further considerations – such as the arguments from perfect-being theology, moral action, Reformed epistemology, Scripture and miracles – appears to undermine the symmetry thesis in favour of good god.

4.10 Miracles

Having developed arguments for grounding god's goodness in scripture and religious experience, I now turn to the question of whether it is reasonable to attribute evil to god through miracles. Surprisingly, the literature contains little discussion of miracles in relation to the evil-god challenge – and, as we shall see, where there is discussion, the definitions and examples that have been offered are underdeveloped. Therefore, in order to establish a framework for future work on the topic, I begin my discussion by outlining the nature of positive miracles and negative miracles. In the following section (4.11), I offer several examples of negative miracles, before developing an argument that favours the attribution of goodness over evil to god in Section 4.12. I address some potential objections in Section 4.13.

Definitions of miracles are typically formed in relation to the good-god hypothesis. For example, take the following definition from Nagasawa:

> A miracle is a violation of the laws of nature that is caused by an intentional agent; and it has religious significance.[151]

In his discussion of the cited definition, Nagasawa claims that miracles – although having negative consequences for some people – '*must* have [overall] positive outcomes'.[152] This necessary condition is hidden in the definition itself, within the concept of being 'religious', which denotes belief in good god, good gods or some other higher being worthy of praise. Therefore, let us amend Nagasawa's definition in order to reflect its wider context:

> A *positive* miracle is a violation of the laws of nature that is caused by an intentional agent; and it has objectively *positive* significance or consequences.

I now turn to the question of what constitutes a 'negative miracle'. In his fictional encyclopaedia entry, New – one of the earliest proponents of the evil-god challenge – offers the following definition for what he calls an 'anti-miracle':

> Anti-miracles are harmful or evil events which cannot be explained scientifically. Such events are attributed by antitheists [(evil-god defenders)] to the supernatural agency of the Devil [(evil god)].[153]

This definition is yet to be contested in the literature; however, there are a number of problems with New's proposal. In the first line, New tells us that anti-miracles are negative events that cannot be explained 'scientifically'. Assuming New is referring to 'physical science', as popularly conceived, it is unclear whether he means explainable by *present* science or *future* science. However, on both accounts, the definition offered is insufficient, for there are many objects and events that fit New's definition that we (rightly) do not consider to be miracles. To take an example, at present, no (reasonable) philosopher or scientist believes that a complete explanation of *the conscious experience of pain* can be offered by (pure) physical science. However, on New's account, conscious experiences of pain would meet his definition of a '*harmful* event that cannot be explained scientifically', and, therefore, fulfil the criteria for being a negative miracle. Belief that future science may be able to explain consciousness does not alleviate the problem either. Consider another example: an evil spirit, in some non-physical realm, telling a malicious lie to another spirit. Again, this is an 'evil event which cannot be explained scientifically', but it should not count as a miracle. What is missing from New's definition is that miracles require a suspension of the natural order of things.[154] Therefore, instead of adopting New's definition, I recommend that the challenger adjusts Nagasawa's definition of miracles. In contrast to positive miracles, we should define negative miracles as follows:

> A *negative* miracle is a violation of the laws of nature that is caused by an intentional agent; and it has objectively *negative* significance or consequences.[155]

This definition avoids the stated problems, for a negative experience of pain does not violate the laws of nature. Furthermore, if the laws of nature hold that non-physical entities can interact with other non-physical entities, then one spirit lying to another does not violate the laws of nature. Our post-Newian definition also rules out examples of 'negative miracles' that have been, mistakenly, used by other evil-god challengers. To take one such case, Millican has argued that natural disasters constitute negative miracles and, from here, he draws the conclusion that miracles constitute stronger evidence for evil god than good god. Millican summarizes his argument as follows:

> [Considering miracles,] natural disasters are, as we have already observed, far more common than natural fortunes, and are typically of far greater significance. Manna might fall from the skies once in forty centuries; floods, famines, earthquakes and volcanoes are altogether more common, and far better substantiated. So if there is an omnipotent being up there, Antigod [(evil god)] is on this count a better candidate than God.[156]

The problem with Millican's examples is that they fail to identify violations of the laws of nature. If we can account for floods, famines, earthquakes and volcanic eruptions in terms of physical causes and effects (which we can), then there is no need to postulate a non-physical cause (such as an evil god). On behalf of the challenger, I offer a series of examples that meet our updated definition in Section 4.11.

Before proceeding, let us recognize that according to orthodox revelation theology, miracles are typically believed to constitute evidence in favour of god's goodness. Therefore, in developing a parallel argument for evil god, the challenger should argue that negative miracles constitute evidence for the attribution of evil to god. I note that many philosophers – including Law and Swinburne[157, 158] – reject the existence of negative miracles. Swinburne offers the following justification:

> I emphasize that the religious movement or moral or doctrinal teaching must already have some modest degree of probability; the detailed historical evidence for the miracle will then increase that probability. ... It is only in respect of movements or teachings that might well be good or true that we can attribute any apparently miraculous support to divine agency. A purported miracle in support of a movement of racial hatred, or confirming the goodness of child sacrifice, could not have been a real miracle – either it did not occur or it was not miraculous.[159]

Swinburne's denial of negative miracles stems from his claim that the evil-god hypothesis does not enjoy a 'modest degree of probability', and, therefore, there are no reasonable grounds for attributing negative miracles to a non-existent evil god. There are two points of tension between Swinburne's view and my own. First, throughout this book, I have argued that the evil-god hypothesis does enjoy a modest degree of probability, but that it is more reasonable to attribute goodness to god than evil. Therefore, I take negative miracles to provide (limited) evidence for the grounding of evil god. Second, I believe Swinburne underestimates the amount of evidence in favour of negative miracles (as he does negative experiences). Given the weight of evidence for negative miracles, I argue that if Swinburne were to apply his epistemic framework consistently, then he ought to accept the reality of negative miracles. I make this case in the following section, before offering a response (to the view that negative miracles can be used to attribute evil to god) in Section 4.12.

4.11 Miraculous malevolence

The Abrahamic scriptures offer numerous candidates for negative miracles. As we have seen, god's flooding of the earth – an account shared by each of Abrahamic traditions[160] – had devastating consequences. Likewise, god's plagues – boils,[161] thunderstorms[162] and locusts[163] – and god's massacring of Egypt's firstborn children also appear to fit our definition of negative miracles.[164] (In the latter case, the killing of firstborn children is not reserved for the Egyptian slaveowners but is inflicted on all of Egypt's mothers, 'even unto the firstborn of the maidservant that is behind the mill; and all the firstborn of beasts'.)[165]

Elsewhere, the Scriptures speak of negative miracles performed out of anger and malice – see god's wrath and the Antichrist[166, 167] – and Satan performs negative miracles with god's permission.[168] As the biblical scholar Erkki Koskenniemi has concluded, belief in negative miracles was pervasive throughout this period.[169]

Next, let us consider the grounding of evil god in post-biblical negative miracles. According to Faye Taylor, 27 per cent of Sainte Foy's miracles (third century) are described as 'negative'; 14 per cent involved physical harm and a further 10 per cent resulted in death.[170] Moving into the medieval period, the University of Sheffield's *Measuring the Miraculous?* database documents over 650 miracles that are said to have occurred between the third and twelfth centuries.[171] The database suggests that around 25 per cent of miracles that affected the upper classes were negative, with approximately 15 per cent of miracles amongst lower classes being negative. Examples include Satan crushing monks beneath walls, and nuns dying spontaneously from fatal diseases. Moving into the latter half of the second millennium, between the fifteenth and eighteenth centuries, belief in negative miracles was the dominant view amongst witch-believing Europeans. As Reginald Davies explains, throughout this period, belief in witches and their negative miracles was the predominant view amongst traditional theists. Amongst the most ruthless and determinate witch-hunters was Calvin and his followers – who, acknowledging their theological motivations,[172] were rivalled in their persecution of witches only by the Catholic Church. In the *Summis desiderantes affectibus*, Pope Innocent VIII offers the following insight:

> Many persons of both sexes, unmindful of their own salvation and straying from the Catholic Faith, have abandoned themselves to devils ... by their incantations, spells, conjurations and other accursed charms and crafts, enormities and horrid offences have slain unborn infants and the unborn offspring of cattle, have blasted the produce of the earth ... these wretches furthermore afflict and torment men and women ... with terrible and piteous pains.[173]

The 'confessions' of witches give us an idea of the negative miracles they were said to have performed. Witches typically confirmed that they had made deals with Satan and other evil spirits, instructed spirits to kill or inflict suffering on other humans and non-human animals, performed spells to kill or curse other humans and controlled the weather to destroy livestock and harvests.[174] It is not possible to determine the total number of witches who were executed by good-god believers throughout this period, but, as Davies puts it, 'It is nonetheless *certain* that many tens, if not hundreds, of thousands died at the stake.'[175] Given the scale and ruthlessness of the witch-hunters, it is reasonable to hold that belief in negative miracles was genuine and widespread. Given the limited number of studies and sample sizes, there is no obvious (reliable) method of determining the prevalence of belief in negative miracles amongst the wider population. Nevertheless, given the cited accounts, it is reasonable to conclude that belief in negative miracles has been accepted by a significant number of societies throughout history.

The traditional theist may accept the account provided but insist that this does not constitute a significant body of evidence in comparison to reports of positive miracles. Before we proceed, it is worth noting that the theist is right to claim that we can expect reports of positive miracles to outweigh reports of negative miracles; I end this section by outlining three of the reasons for this expected disparity. First, unlike positive miracles, we should recognize that there are no organized religions or organizations that are devoted to the identification and certification of negative miracles. Like Swinburne, the overwhelming majority of the world's population do not consider the evil-god hypothesis to be a reasonable hypothesis or, as Law argues, reject it out of hand as 'patently ridiculous'.[176] Second, given our cultural (shame) and cognitive (well-being) dispositions, people are likely to interpret negative (neutral, or even mixed miracles) to be positive ones. In other words, those who witness negative miracles are likely to interpret them within the context of beliefs held by wider society, such as within the framework of traditional theism. Third, when negative miracles do occur, it is unlikely that witnesses will describe them as 'miracles' because – as we have seen – the term 'miracle' denotes a positive, religious outcome. As David Basinger has pointed out, for the majority of the world, the term 'miracle' *necessarily* denotes a positive event[177] – that is to say, for some people, the idea of a 'negative miracle' is oxymoronic. In short, a negative miracle will be reported only if a witness considers the miracle to be negative, and it is unlikely that they will consider it as such. If we factor these limitations into the evidence cited in this section for negative miracles, it is, I maintain, reasonable to conclude that positive miracles do not (in reality) *significantly* outweigh negative miracles.[178]

Let us be clear on the argument at hand. The argument for attributing evil to god through negative miracles is a simple one: negative miracles are evil, god is responsible for negative miracles, and, therefore, it is reasonable to attribute evil to god. Once evil god has been grounded in negative miracles, the challenger may proceed to claim that evil god is compatible with positive miracles, for evil god would be motivated to create some higher-order evils (such as deceit and character destruction) for which he needs to bring about some goods.

Like many arguments for evil god, at face-value, the argument from negative miracles seems highly plausible. However, as I argue in the following section, once the argument is properly contextualized, we see that the argument from negative miracles is not as reasonable as its orthodox counterpart.

4.12 Miraculous benevolence

In this section, I discuss whether or not negative miracles constitute evidence for attributing evil to god. In my view, the challenger's weakness lies in the arguments inability to ground evil god in negative miracles. In short, I maintain that god is not responsible for negative miracles, but is responsible for positive miracles, and, therefore, it is more reasonable to attribute goodness to god than it is to attribute evil to god. Consequently, I propose that the argument from negative miracles is better recast as a direct argument against god's goodness, rather than an indirect parallel argument for evil god.

There are two aspects to my argument: both of which focus on contextualizing the examples of negative miracles from the previous section. First, let us consider the biblical examples cited at the beginning of Section 4.11. As we saw in Section 4.3, the orthodox theist can offer two responses to scriptural arguments for evil god. First, the good-god defender should appeal to the many positive miracles that are to be found in the Abrahamic scriptures. To take some well-known examples, consider god's bringing all creatures into existence,[179] Jesus's feeding of the 5,000[180] and Muhammad's 'healing of sick eyes, wounds, burnt skin, broken legs and muteness'.[181] These positive miracles, so claims the orthodox theist, would establish a provisional symmetry between our two hypotheses, as the challenger will appeal to negative scriptural miracles (see Section 4.2).

Second, one may tip the weight of evidence from Scriptural miracles in favour of good god by appealing to the explicit statements about god's character and intentions throughout the Scriptures. As the Scriptures reveal that god is good and not evil – and assuming the orthodox theist can offer specific, knowable and morally praiseworthy reasons for why god performs negative miracles – then it is more reasonable to attribute goodness and not evil to god through scriptural miracles. Therefore, as there are stronger scriptural reasons for thinking that god is good and not evil, god's seemingly evil miracles in Scripture ought to be presented as an argument against good god's compatibility with the available evidence ('why does good god perform so many negative miracles?') rather than a similarly reasonable argument for grounding evil god in Scripture.

Second, let us consider non-scriptural examples of negative miracles. Here, the good-god defender may appeal to an amended version of the argument presented in Section 4.8, in which I rejected the possibility of grounding evil god in negative religious experiences. Recall that it was more reasonable to attribute goodness (and not evil) to god through religious experience because positive experiences (but not negative experiences) identify god as the apparent object of such experiences. This is equally applicable to the argument from miracles. In the examples cited, we see free, evil agents (witches, demons and the like) perform negative miracles, but no negative miracles that are attributed directly to god. In contrast, there are numerous examples in which positive miracles are attributed to god. For instance, in his book *Healing Miracles*, Rex Gardener provides many examples of god's miraculous healings and earthly resurrections.[182] Moreover, traditional theists may also appeal to Jesus's (forty) positive miracles – which include his fighting off demons,[183] curing the sick,[184] healing the disabled[185] and resurrections of the dead[186] – as miracles 'performed by god'. A parallel argument of this type is not available to the evil-god defender, and, therefore, the argument from miracles favours the attribution of goodness to god (who is purported by those who experience positive miracles to be the apparent bestower) rather than the attribution of evil to god (who is rarely, if ever, purported to perform negative miracles). With these considerations in mind, I present the argument for grounding good god through miracles as follows:

1hh. If god performs a significant number of positive miracles and does not perform a significant number of negative miracles, then it is more reasonable to attribute goodness to god than it is to attribute evil to god through miracles. (Premise)
2hh. God performs a significant number of positive miracles and does not perform a significant number of negative miracles. (Premise)
3hh. It is more reasonable to attribute goodness to god than it is to attribute evil to god through miracles. (Conclusion)

As we saw in the case of negative experiences (Section 4.8), rather than being an argument for grounding evil god, the argument from negative miracles ought to be recast as a compatibility objection against good god's existence. In its simplest form, the argument has the following structure:

1ii. If god allows a significant number of negative miracles to occur, then it is unlikely that god is good. (Premise)
2ii. God allows a significant number of negative miracles to occur. (Premise)
3ii. It is unlikely that god is good. (Conclusion)

In responding to this argument (1–3ii), we see again the importance of postulating lesser deities within the framework of orthodox theism. In short, the good-god defender ought to follow a similar approach to that which I outlined at the end of Section 4.8. Whereas good god is responsible for positive miracles (as witnesses identify good god as the bestower of positive miracles), lesser evil spirits are to be held responsible for negative miracles (as witnesses identify evil spirits, and not evil god, as the bestower of negative miracles). For these reasons, it is more reasonable to attribute positive miracles (and goodness) to god than it is to attribute negative miracles (and evil) to god.

4.13 Immoral miracles

In this section, I develop a final argument in favour of the evil-god hypothesis. As we shall see, this argument is offered in the spirit of the earlier arguments from Millican, Law and Lancaster-Thomas. The argument claims that miracles are unjustly distributed and vary in their significance, and, therefore, miracles are more likely to be the work of evil god than good god because evil god (and not good god) would be motivated to promote injustice. I outline examples in this section of miracles that, challengers might claim, promote injustice. I then reject these examples as potential arguments for attributing evil to god and suggest that they are reformulated as compatibility objections.

Christine Overall has argued that given the nature and distribution of positive miracles, we have reason to believe that seemingly moral miracles are, in fact, immoral miracles.[187] Here, I give three examples of 'immoral miracles': seemingly positive miracles that turn out, upon further reflection – according to the objector – to be immoral. First, the objector may question why good god does not intervene more regularly. Given that good god always has the opportunity and ability to perform *more* positive miracles, why does he choose not to do so? (Note that this is, in essence, the traditional problem of evil.) The objection proceeds to claim that because god can, but does not, perform positive miracles more frequently, then this *lack* of positive miracles points towards immoral *in*action on god's part. Second, there is the problem of why good god chooses to save and assist some people but not others. As argued by James Keller, when good god chooses to save or assist one person and allows a second person to suffer or lose their life, the 'positive' miracle implies that good god has *picked* one person and has *not picked* another and this constitutes an unfair and immoral action on god's part.[188] Third, there is the problem of why good god chooses to perform insignificant miracles when he could perform significant miracles. For example, why does god intervene with the laws of nature to enable a donkey to talk,[189] or for a coin to appear in the mouth of a fish,[190] when he could put an end to famines and genocides? As Maurice Wiles writes, 'It would seem strange that no miraculous intervention prevented Auschwitz or Hiroshima, while the purposes apparently forwarded by some of the miracles acclaimed in traditional Christian faith seem trivial by comparison.'[191]

I end this section by placing the argument from immoral miracles in the context of the evil-god challenge. I argue that, like many of the arguments that we have seen for evil god, the argument from immoral miracles cannot be used to ground evil god's moral character. The argument does, however, constitute a direct attack against god's goodness.

In response to the argument from immoral miracles, I offer the following argument on behalf of traditional theism. First, to say that some evidence (such as immoral miracles) ought to be attributed to evil god over good god is to overlook the need for attributing evil to god. As I have argued throughout this book, however, it appears that we have stronger reasons for attributing goodness than evil to god. Second, I claim that it is *not* more reasonable to ground evil god through 'immoral miracles' than it is to ground good god in 'immoral miracles'. To understand why, note that all three examples of 'immoral miracles' appeal to the existence of positive miracles, before they claim that god should perform *more* (frequent or significant) positive miracles. Although such consideration may be used as part of an argument against god's goodness, it does not give us a reason to attribute evil to god. To understand why, consider the following analogy. It would be unreasonable to move from the proposition that 'god has created a very big universe but could have created a bigger universe' to the conclusion that 'god is weak'. However, one could move from the proposition that 'god has created a big universe but could have created an even bigger universe' to the conclusion that 'god is powerful'. Similarly, it is unreasonable to move from the proposition that 'god always performs positive miracles but could perform more (frequent or significant) positive miracles' to the conclusion that 'god is evil'. However, it may be reasonable to move from the proposition that 'god performs positive miracles but could perform more (frequent or significant) positive miracles' to the conclusion that 'god is good'. The objections stated – 'why did god not create a bigger universe?' and 'why does god not perform more positive miracles?' – should, therefore, be considered compatibility objections, which attack god's power and goodness directly, rather than arguments for postulating the existence of a weak or evil god. For our purposes, it suffices to say that *if* the argument from immoral miracles shows that belief in good god is unreasonable, then there is no need to develop an evil-god challenge. In contrast, if the argument from immoral miracles does not show that belief in good god is unreasonable, then we have another strong reason for favouring tradition theism – that is, that good god, but not evil god, can be grounded in miracles.

4.14 Conclusion

In this chapter, I overviewed the arguments for grounding god's moral character through revelation theology. First, I outlined the case for attributing evil to god through the (seemingly) malevolent actions of god in the Christian Scriptures. However, we saw that it was more reasonable to attribute goodness rather than evil to god when god's biblically benevolent actions are combined with Scripture's explicit claims about god's goodness. Second, I discussed the possibility of attributing evil to god through the contradictory claims of universal scriptures. I argued that because the world's scriptures also make explicit claims about god's goodness and that restricted revelation is more plausible than universal revelation, it would be unreasonable to attribute evil to god through positive (although contradictory) claims about god's nature. Third, I outlined and responded to arguments for attributing evil to god through religious experience. Although I defended the view that subjects of religious experience often report experiences that can be categorized as negative, I argued that witnesses of negative experiences rarely (if ever) identify god as the apparent object of such experiences. In contrast, I claimed that there are many positive experiences in which good god is identified as an apparent object, which therefore constitutes another asymmetry favouring good god. I proceeded to argue that although negative experiences cannot ground god's malevolence, they can be recast as a compatibility objection against god's goodness; I then offered a solution to this same compatibility objection by attributing negative experiences to lesser supernatural beings. Finally, I discussed the possibility of grounding god's moral character in miracles. I argued that as negative miracles rely on scriptural claims (which can be contextualized by Scripture's explicit statements revealing god's goodness) and the actions of lesser evil deities, the argument from negative miracles is not as powerful as the argument from positive miracles in which Scripture and witnesses frequently identify god as their direct cause. The last argument I developed suggested that the distribution of positive miracles constituted an injustice on god's part, and, therefore, should be attributed to evil

Table 5 An Analysis of Grounding God's Moral Character through Revelation Theology. © Jack Symes

	Actions in scripture	Explicit statements in scripture	Religious experience	Miracles
Attribute goodness to god	✓	✓	✓	✓
Attribute evil to god	✓	✗	✗	✗

god rather than good god. In response, I argued that this argument, like many arguments identified throughout this work, assumes that it is just as reasonable to attribute evil to god as it is to attribute goodness to God. Furthermore, I claimed that although the argument from immoral miracles may constitute a compatibility objection against good god, it is not reasonable to ground evil god in infrequent but always positive miracles. I present my analysis in Table 5.

On the basis of this analysis, I therefore conclude that it is more reasonable to ground good god in revelation theology than it is to ground evil god in revelation theology.

Conclusion

Why is belief in a maximally good god significantly more reasonable than belief in a maximally evil god? Because it is significantly more reasonable to attribute goodness to god than evil. I have argued for this conclusion in the following way.

First, I outlined the nature of the evil-god challenge. I explained that arguments for evil god must either be built upon the foundations of traditional theism or similarly reasonable parallel principles; this makes the evil-god challenge an *indirect* argument and not a *direct* argument against the existence of good god. I outlined several ways of constructing the challenge and argued in favour of 'the combined challenge'. The conclusion of the combined challenge maintains that the good-god hypothesis is absurd or ought not be considered true. In order to defeat the challenge, we saw that the orthodox theist must respond to the question of why the good-god hypothesis is significantly more reasonable than the evil-god hypothesis.

At the end of the first chapter, I drew a distinction between arguments for grounding (those that aim to establish god's moral character) and compatibility (those that aim to establish or defend god's existence). I described my response to the evil-god challenge as a cumulative asymmetry objection, which maintains that grounding arguments for good god are significantly stronger than grounding arguments for evil god. I went on to examine cases of grounding within the three main schools of philosophical theology: perfect-being theology, creation theology and revelation theology.

In the case of perfect-being theology, I claimed that it is more reasonable to attribute goodness to god than evil. First, I argued that it is more reasonable to believe that goodness (and not evil) is a great-making property; therefore, as god possesses all great-making properties to the optimal degree, it is more reasonable to attribute goodness to god. Second, I claimed that it is more reasonable to believe that Being Itself is good and not evil; as god *is* Being Itself, it is more likely that god is good than evil. Third, I argued that god is more likely to be motivated towards good actions and not evil actions, and, therefore, is again more likely that god is good and not evil.

I went on to discuss the arguments from creation theology. First, I developed a case for attributing goodness and evil to god through extrinsic goods and evils, in which I argued that the orthodox argument and its parallel were similarly reasonable. Second, I turned my attention to intrinsic goods and evils. I argued that there are significantly more intrinsic goods than there are intrinsic evils, and, therefore, intrinsic values favour the attribution of goodness to god over evil. Third, we saw how the challenger may argue that the totality of the world's evils (extrinsic and intrinsic) counterbalances the totality of the world's goods. Once more, I conceded that the orthodox argument and its parallel were similarly as reasonable. Fourth, I argued that good god's moral character, but not evil god's moral character, could be grounded in Reformed epistemology.

Finally, I examined several arguments for grounding god's moral character in revelation theology. First, in the light of Scriptures' explicit claims about god's goodness, I argued that it was more reasonable to attribute goodness to the god of Scripture. Second, in the case of religious experience, I defended the view that good god is often reported to be the apparent object of positive experiences – but that evil god is not reported to be the apparent object of negative experiences – and, therefore, it is more reasonable to ground good god (and not evil god) in religious experience. Third, I argued that good god is reported to be the bestower of positive miracles, but that evil god is not reported to be the bestower of negative miracles. Therefore, once again, I found it more reasonable to attribute goodness than evil to god.

In the light of these considerations, I conclude that it is significantly more reasonable to attribute goodness than evil to god through perfect-being theology, creation theology and revelation theology. I take this cumulative case to be simple and compelling. It is simple in the sense that it consists of reporting reasons as to why theists have traditionally attributed goodness to god; it is compelling because these reasons cannot be paralleled to support the concept of an evil god to the same level of efficacy. I present my analysis in Table 6.

As I have argued, there are strong reasons for favouring the good-god hypothesis over the evil-god hypothesis, and, therefore, the evil-god challenge has been defeated.

Table 6 An Analysis of Grounding God's Moral Character through Philosophical Theology (Conclusion). © Jack Symes

	Perfect-being theology			Creation theology				Revelation theology			
	Great-making properties	Privation theories	Moral motivation	Extrinsic good/evil	Intrinsic good/evil	Totality of good/evil	Reformed epistemology	Actions in scripture	Explicit statements in scripture	Religious experience	Miracles
Attribute goodness to god	✓	✓	✓	✓	✓	✓	✓	✓	✓	✓	✓
Attribute evil to god	✗	✗	✗	✓	✗	✓	✗	✓	✗	✗	✗

Notes

Preface

1. This is a simplified explanation. As we shall see, contemporary evil-god challengers also put forward independent arguments for evil god that do not parallel arguments for good god. Furthermore, some evil-god challengers do not intend to undermine traditional theism; instead, they use the challenge to gain a deeper understanding of theism's core beliefs.
2. Harper Lee, *To Kill a Mockingbird* (London: Arrow Books, 2010), 33.
3. *Philosophers on God: Talking about Existence*, ed. Jack Symes (London: Bloomsbury, 2024).

Introduction

1. Stephen Law, 'The Evil-God Challenge', *Religious Studies*, vol. 46 (3) (2010): 353–73.
2. 'The evil-god challenge: information', *Religious Studies*, February 2019, http://www.cambridge.org/core/journals/religious-studies/article/evilgod – challenge/E925DF20AF17F3C87B9449B25F649F27#fndtn-information. Download data confirmed by a source at the journal *Religious Studies*.
3. Law, 'Evil-God Challenge', 359.

Chapter One

1. The book's epigraphs were generously composed by Manish Popat-Szabries. The poem is original to this work and is included with permission from the author.
2. I follow tradition in using masculine pronouns for both good god and evil god; however, I do not maintain that either good god or evil god is male. I also follow Law in referring to 'good god' and 'evil god' in the lowercase, as well as hyphenating 'good god' and 'evil god' only when they are used in conjunction with a further concept such as 'evil-god challenge', 'good-god hypothesizer' and so forth.
3. Law, 'Evil-God Challenge', 360.

4   Different versions of the challenge use different terminology. For example, the evil-god hypothesis has also been described as 'antitheism' (New in 'Antitheism'), 'demonism' (Cahn in 'Cacodaemony') and 'diabolism' (Collins in 'Extended and Defended').
5   Law, 'Evil-God Challenge', 360.
6   Edward Madden and Peter Hare, *Evil and the Concept of God* (Springfield, IL: Charles C. Thomas, 1968), 32–4.
7   Lancaster-Thomas makes this same claim. See Asha Lancaster-Thomas, *An Exploration of the Evil-god Challenge* (University of Birmingham: PhD Thesis, 2020c), 10.
8   Edward Madden, 'The Many Faces of Evil', *Philosophy and Phenomenological Research*, vol. 24 (4) (1964): 481–92.
9   René Descartes, *Meditations on First Philosophy with Selections from the Objections and Replies*, ed. John Cottingham, 2nd edition (Cambridge: Cambridge University Press, 2017), 19 (22).
10 David Hume, *Dialogues and Natural History of Religion*, ed. J. C. A Gaskin (Oxford: Oxford University Press, 2008), 114.
11 William Paley, *Natural Theology: Or Evidence of the Existence and Attributes of the Deity, Collected from the Appearances of Nature*, ed. Matthew D. Eddy and David Knight (Oxford: Oxford University Press, 2008), 242.
12 Max Andrews, 'A Response to the Problem of an "Evil God" as raised by Stephen Law', *Sententias: Meaning, Purpose, and a Way of Thinking*, January 2012, https://maxandrews.wordpress.com/2012/01/20/a-response-to-the-problem-of-an-evil-god-as-raised-by-stephen-law.
13 Wallace Murphree, 'Natural Theology: Theism or Antitheism?', *Sophia*, vol. 36 (10) (1997), 75.
14 Angus Ritchie, *From Morality to Metaphysics: The Theistic Implications of Our Ethical Commitments* (Oxford: Oxford University Press, 2012), 165.
15 David Haight and Marjorie Haight, 'An Ontological Argument for the Devil', *The Monist*, vol. 54 (2) (1970): 218–20.
16 Steven Cahn, 'Cacodaemony', *Analysis*, vol. 37 (2) (1977): 69–73.
17 Peter Millican, 'The Devil's Advocate', *Cogito*, vol. 3 (3) (1989): 193–207.
18 Edward Stein, 'God, the Demon, and the Status of Theodicies', *American Philosophical Quarterly*, vol. 27 (2) (1990): 163–7.
19 Christopher New, 'Antitheism: A Reflection', *Ratio*, vol. 6 (1) (1993): 36–43.
20 Thomas S. Vernon, *The Complete Secularist* (Fayetteville, AR: M & M Press, 1994).
21 Murphree, 'Natural Theology'.
22 Wes Morriston, 'The Evidential Argument from Goodness', *The Southern Journal of Philosophy*, vol. 42 (1) (2004): 87–101.
23 Stephen Law, 'The God of Eth', *Think*, vol. 3 (9) (2005), 18.
24 Law, 'Evil-God Challenge'.

25 Stephen Law, *Believing Bullshit: How Not to Get Sucked into an Intellectual Black Hole* (New York: Prometheus Books, 2011a), 20–9.
26 Stephen Law, 'Introduction to the Evil God Challenge', *Think*, vol. 18 (51) (2019): 5–9.
27 Stephen Law, 'The Evil-God Challenge', in Philosophers on God: Talking about Existence, ed. Jack Symes (London: Bloomsbury, 2024), 113–8.
28 John Zande, *The Owner of All Infernal Names: An Introductory Treatise on the Existence, Nature & Government of Our Omnimalevolent Creator* (Great Britain: CreateSpace Independent Publishing, 2015).
29 Raphael Lataster, 'The Problem of Alternative Monotheisms: Another Serious Challenge to Theism', *European Journal for Philosophy of Religion*, vol. 10 (1) (2018): 31–51.
30 Asha Lancaster-Thomas, 'The Evil-god Challenge Part I: History and Recent Developments', *Philosophy Compass*, vol. 13 (7) (2018a): 1–8.
31 Asha Lancaster-Thomas, 'The Evil-God Challenge Part II: Objections and Responses', *Philosophy Compass*, vol. 13 (8) (2018b): 1–10.
32 Asha Lancaster-Thomas, 'The Evil-god Hypothesis and the Argument from Mal-design', *Dialogue: The Phi Sigma Tau Honor Society*, vol. 60 (1) (2018c): 101–10.
33 Asha Lancaster-Thomas, 'The Possibility of an Evil-God: A Response to Ward', *Think*, vol. 18 (51) (2019): 37–46.
34 Asha Lancaster-Thomas, 'Encountering Evil: The Evil-god Challenge from Religious Experience', *European Journal for Philosophy of Religion*, vol. 12 (3) (2020a): 137–61.
35 Asha Lancaster-Thomas, 'Truth, Consequences, and the Evil-god Challenge: A response to Anastasia Scrutton', *Religious Studies*, vol. 56 (3) (2020b): 447–54.
36 Lancaster-Thomas, *An Exploration*.
37 John Collins, 'The Evil-god Challenge: Extended and Defend', *Religious Studies*, vol. 55 (1) (2019): 85–109.
38 Lancaster-Thomas, 'History', 2.
39 Ibid.
40 Law, 'Evil-God Challenge', 353–6.
41 Chad V. Meister, *Evil: A Guide for the Perplexed*, 2nd edition (London: Bloomsbury, 2018), 6.
42 For the purposes of simplicity, I set aside several qualities frequently attributed to good god, such as incorporeality, immutability, impassibility and changelessness. See Yujin Nagasawa, *Maximal God: A New Defence of Perfect Being Theism* (Oxford: Oxford University Press, 2017a), 30.
43 One of the most common questions I am asked is whether I think it is more reasonable to believe in a morally apathetic god or a morally-mixed god than

a good god or an evil god; if it is, proposes my interrogator, then we should be running an 'apathetic-god challenge' or a 'mixed-god challenge' rather than an 'evil-god challenge'. First, I suspect that an apathetic god is less reasonable than the competing hypotheses for, according to the traditional theist, there appear to be objective moral values in the world, which an apathetic god would have no reason to bring about. Second, I expect that the conclusions I draw in the following chapters apply just as much to a mixed-god as they do to an evil-god – that is to say, in Table 6, we can simply switch 'attribute evil to god' for 'attribute good and evil to god'. For these reasons, I stay true to the existing literature throughout my thesis.

44 Following Murphree ('Natural Theology', 76), I think that a version of the evil-god challenge can also be presented against deists and panentheists. Moreover, I also think the problem arises for gods of limited character, polytheisms, pantheisms, Taoism, Confucianism, Buddhism, existential optimism, existential pessimism, earthly creatures (including humans) and so forth. In short, wherever one entity claims to know another's moral character, their claim can be challenged (granted, to limited degrees of success).

45 Lancaster-Thomas, 'History', 2.
46 Lancaster-Thomas, 'Truth', 452.
47 Lancaster-Thomas, 'History', 2.
48 I have recently learnt of an unpublished piece that defends the weak evil-god challenge over its counterparts: Dale Glover, *Answering the Evil God Challenge* (Ryerson University: MA Dissertation, 2022), 4. Glover argues that the weak evil-god challenge should be preferred over strong evil-god challenges because its conclusion is more modest. However, I maintain that the premises of what I call the strong 'combined challenge' – which I discuss at the end of Section 1.2 – are no less plausible than those of the weak evil-god challenge. Therefore, if Glover wishes to advocate for the weak evil-god challenge, then he must explain why the premises of the combined evil-god challenge are less plausible than those of the weak evil-god challenge.
49 Lancaster-Thomas, 'Truth', 448.
50 Madden, 'Many Faces'.
51 Cahn, 'Cacodaemony'.
52 Millican, 'Devil's Advocate'.
53 Morriston, 'Evidential Argument from Goodness'.
54 Law, 'Introduction to the Evil God Challenge', 7–9.
55 Lancaster-Thomas, 'History', 2.
56 Lancaster-Thomas, 'History' and 'Truth'.
57 Millican, 'Devil's Advocate'.
58 Kirk Lougheed, 'Religious Disagreement, Religious Experience, and the Evil God Hypothesis', *European Journal for Philosophy of Religion*, vol. 12 (1) (2020), 184–8.

59 In fact, Lougheed claims that 'This response goes a step further in suggesting that it's possible that both the evil-God and good God can co-exist. If this is right, then the evil-God challenge doesn't undermine the good God hypothesis at all.' (Ibid., 186.) Lougheed's claim is mistaken for two reasons. First, the evil-god literature focuses on comparing two competing monotheisms; switching to polytheism does not solve the original problem. Second, evil-god challenges can also be constructed against Lougheed's dualistic polytheism. I present the challenge as follows: why is belief in [good god and evil god] significantly more reasonable than belief in [a morally-mixed god] / [good god and good god] / [evil god and evil god]? Similar arguments are developed by Raphael Lataser and Herman Philipse in their paper 'The Problem of Polytheisms: A Serious Challenge to Theism', *International Journal for Philosophy of Religion,* vol. 81 (3) (2017): 233–46.

60 Peter Forrest, 'God, Anti-God and the Emotions: A Response to Murphree', *Sophia,* vol. 37 (1) (1998), 154.

61 Andrews, 'A Response to the Problem'.

62 Charles Daniels, 'God, Demon, Good, Evil', *Journal of Value Inquiry,* vol. 31 (2) (1997): 177–81.

63 Edward Feser, 'Law's "evil-god challenge"', *EdwardFeser.blogspot,* October 2010, www.edwardfeser.blogspot.com/2010/10/laws-evilgod-challenge.html.

64 Edward Feser, 'Broken Law', *EdwardFeser.blogspot,* November 2011, https://edwardfeser.blogspot.com/2011/11/broken-law.html.

65 Keith Ward, 'The Evil God Challenge – A Response', *Think,* vol. 14 (40) (2015): 43–9.

66 Christopher Weaver, 'Evilism, Moral Rationalism, and Reasons Internalism', *International Journal for Philosophy of Religion,* vol. 77 (1) (2015): 3–24.

67 Law, 'Introduction to the Evil God Challenge', 7.

68 See Section 3.3.

69 I am not committed to the view that intuitive absurdity is a separate *type* of absurdity than *a priori* or *a posteriori* absurdity.

70 Lancaster-Thomas, *An Exploration,* 120.

71 Law, 'Introduction to the Evil God Challenge', 7.

72 Lancaster-Thomas, 'Objections', 3.

73 Law, 'Introduction to the Evil God Challenge', 9.

74 Ben Page and Baker-Hytch make a similar point in their paper 'Meeting the Evil God Challenge', *Pacific Philosophical Quarterly,* vol. 101 (3) (2020), 493.

75 Otherwise put, it would be more reasonable to ground good god (than evil god) in creation. In Chapter Three, I discuss this argument in detail.

76 Law, 'Evil-God Challenge', 370.

77 Ibid., 353, 370.

78 Ibid., 357–8.

79   Ibid.
80   These examples are used by Law. See Ibid.
81   Perry Hendricks, 'Sceptical Theism and the Evil-god Challenge', *Religious Studies*, vol. 54 (4) (2018), 549.
82   Law, 'Evil-God Challenge', 353.
83   William Lane Craig, 'Reasonable Faith', in *Philosophers on God: Talking about Existence*, ed. Jack Symes (London: Bloomsbury, 2024), 37–9.
84   Hendricks, 'Sceptical Theism', 552.
85   Page and Baker-Hytch, 'Meeting the Evil God Challenge', 493.
86   Law, 'Evil-God Challenge', *Philosophers on God*, 109.
87   See Richard Lee, *The Dobe Ju/'hoansi (Case Studies in Cultural Anthropology)*, 4th edition (Belmont, CA: Wadsworth Publishing, 2013), 141.
88   See George Hart, *The Routledge Dictionary of Egyptian Gods and Goddesses*, 2nd edition (London: Routledge, 2005), 31–2.
89   See 'Marcionism', *Columbia Electronic Encyclopedia*, 6th edition, Columbia University (2021).
90   Yujin Nagasawa, 'The Problem of Evil for Atheists', in *The Problem of Evil: Eight Views in Dialogue*, ed. N. N. Trakakis (Oxford: Oxford University Press, 2018), 152.
91   Michael Carrithers, *Buddha: A Very Short Introduction* (Oxford: Oxford University Press, 2001), 55.
92   Arthur Schopenhauer, *Der handschriftliche Nachlass*, ed. Arthur Hübscher (Frankfurt: Kramer, 1966–75), IV/1, 96. Quoted in Michael Hauskeller, *The Meaning of Life and Death: Ten Classic Thinkers on the Ultimate Question* (London: Bloomsbury, 2020), 5–6.
93   Mark Hobart, 'Is God Evil?', in *The Anthropology of Evil*, ed. David Parkin (Oxford: Basil Blackwell, 1985), 188.
94   Hendricks, 'Sceptical Theism', 552.
95   The conclusion of the exclusivity challenge is that the good-god hypothesis ought not to be considered true. Here, I use the word 'absurd' rather than 'not to be considered true' for the purpose of keeping the flowchart clear.
96   Law, 'Evil-God Challenge', 359, 361.
97   Hume, *Dialogues*, 114.
98   Madden and Hare, *Evil and the Concept of God*, 32–4.
99   Haight and Haight, 'An Ontological Argument'.
100 Cahn, 'Cacodaemony'.
101 Stein, 'God, the Demon'.
102 Law, 'Evil-God Challenge', 360–1.
103 Hume, *Dialogues*, 114.
104 Madden and Hare, *Evil and the Concept of God*, 32–4.
105 Haight and Haight, 'An Ontological Argument'.

106 Stein, 'God, the Demon', 164–5.
107 Cahn, 'Cacodaemony'.
108 Law, 'Evil-God Challenge', 360.
109 Ibid., 368–70.
110 Ward, 'A Response'.
111 This is only an example. In reality, I think that this argument can be paralleled. In fact, as I argue throughout this thesis, I do not think there are any arguments for attributing evil (rather than goodness) to god that do not have symmetrical counterparts. In contrast, I propose that there are several arguments (for attributing goodness to god) that cannot be paralleled by the challenger.
112 Lancaster-Thomas, 'Objections', 2.
113 Nagasawa, *Maximal God*, 159.
114 Ibid., 134.
115 William Lane Craig, *Reasonable Faith: Christian Truth and Apologetics*, 3rd edition (Wheaton, IL: Crossway Books, 2008), 111.
116 Murphree articulates this principle in his own presentation of the challenge. See Murphree, 'Natural Theology', 76.
117 In a trivial sense, all of the underlying principles of orthodox theism may be replaced by atheistic principles which – one may claim – are roughly as reasonable as their theistic counterparts. However, if the underlying principles do not allow the challenger to construct parallel arguments for evil god, then we no longer have an evil-god challenge but a direct attack (for non-theism) against traditional theism.
118 Collins, 'Extended and Defended', 91–4.
119 Gottfried Wilhelm Leibniz, *Theodicy: Essays on the Goodness of God, the Freedom of Man and the Origin of Evil*, ed. Austin Farrer, trans. E. M. Huggard (Charleston, SC: BiblioBazaar, 2007), 232.
120 Murphree alludes to a similar parallel argument in his paper 'Natural Theology', 80.
121 There is a danger when using parallel arguments that they might appear, as Madden and Hare put it, 'whimsical' or unserious (*Evil and the Concept of God*, 32). My discussion assumes that parallel arguments are, on the contrary, serious and effective; however, this is not universally accepted. As Lancaster-Thomas points out (*An Exploration*, 40), 'Many scholars have attempted to specify exactly which elements of the [parallel augment] determine how effective the argument is; but disagreement between these scholars is rife.'
122 Lancaster-Thomas, 'Objections', 2.
123 Peter Millican, 'The One Fatal Flaw in Anselm's Argument', *Mind*, vol. 113 (451) (2004), 441.
124 Anselm of Canterbury, *Monologion and Proslogion: With the Replies of Gaunilo and Anselm*, ed. Thomas Williams (Indianapolis: Hackett Publishing, 1995), 29.

125 I discuss the plausibility of these suggestions in Chapter Two.
126 Craig, *Reasonable Faith*, 172.
127 This is only an example. In presenting the nature of the challenge, one need not commit themself to the view that the orthodox moral argument and its unorthodox counterpart are roughly as reasonable. However, some challengers defend this view. For example, see Lancaster-Thomas's 'History', 7 and Lancaster-Thomas's *An Exploration*, 195–201.
128 Lancaster-Thomas, 'Objections', 2–8.
129 Paley, *Natural Theology*, 237–76.
130 John King-Farlow, 'Cacodaemony and Devilish Isomorphism', *Analysis*, vol. 38 (1) (1978): 59–61.
131 Michael Bergmann and Jeffrey Brower, 'The God of Eth and the God of Earth', *Think*, vol. 5 (14) (2007): 33–8.
132 William Lane Craig, '#238 The "Evil god" Objection', *Reasonable Faith*, November 2011, www.reasonablefaith.org/writings/question-answer/the-evilgod-objection/#_edn2.
133 Craig, 'Reasonable Faith', *Philosophers on God*, 37–9.
134 Peter Forrest, 'Replying to the Anti-God Challenge: A God Without Moral Character Acts Well', *Religious Studies*, vol. 48 (1) (2012): 35–43.
135 Justin Brierley, Stephen Law and Glenn Peoples, 'Revisiting the evil God challenge – Law vs Peoples', *Unbelievable?* (Podcast), December 2011, www.premierchristianradio.com/Shows/Saturday/Unbelievable/Episodes/Unbelievable-10 December 2011-Revisiting-the-evil-God-challenge-Law-vs-Peoples.
136 Ritchie, *Morality to Metaphysics*, 161–77.
137 Nagasawa, *Maximal God*, 152–79.
138 Hendricks, 'Sceptical Theism'.
139 Perry Hendricks, 'The Proper Basicality of Belief in God and the Evil-god Challenge', *Religious Studies*, vol. 59 (1) (2023): 55–62.
140 B. Kyle Keltz, 'A Thomistic Answer to the Evil-God Challenge', *The Heythrop Journal*, vol. 60 (5) (2019): 689–98.
141 Kirk Lougheed, 'Religious Disagreement'.
142 Page and Baker-Hytch, 'Meeting the Evil God Challenge'.
143 Calum Miller, 'Why God Is Probably Good: A Response to the Evil-god Challenge', *Religious Studies*, vol. 57 (3) (2021): 448–65.
144 Carlo Alvaro, 'The Evil God Challenge: Two Significant Asymmetries', *The Heythrop Journal*, vol. 63 (5) (2022): 869–85.
145 Lancaster-Thomas, 'Objections', 5.
146 Daniels, 'God, Demon, Good, Evil'.
147 Feser, 'Law's "evil-god challenge"'.
148 Feser, 'Broken Law'.

149 Andrews, 'A Response'.
150 Ward, 'A Response'.
151 Weaver, 'Evilism'.
152 Feser, 'Broken Law'.
153 Law, 'Evil-God Challenge', 372.
154 Stephen Law, 'Fumbling Feser', *StephenLaw.blogspot*, November 2011b, www.stephenlaw.blogspot.com/2011/11/fumbling-feser.html.
155 Morriston, 'Evidential Argument from Goodness', 88.
156 Page and Baker-Hytch have called this the 'bracketing move'. See, 'Meeting the Evil God Challenge', 300.
157 Richard Swinburne, *Providence and the Problem of Evil* (Oxford: Oxford University Press, 1998), 247.
158 Paley, *Natural Theology*, 241.
159 Ibid., 255.
160 Lancaster-Thomas, *An Exploration*, 101.
161 Joshua Mugg, 'The Quietest Challenge to the Axiology of God: A Cognitive Approach to Counterpossibles', *Faith and Philosophy: Journal of the Society of Christian Philosophers*, vol. 33 (4) (2016): 441–60.
162 Alan M. Leslie, 'Pretense and Representation: The Origins of "Theory of Mind"', *Psychological Review*, vol. 94 (4) (1987): 412–26.
163 Mugg, 'Quietest Challenge', 447.
164 The example of a unicorn is Lancaster-Thomas's; the example of a banana-phone is Mugg's.
165 Mugg, 'Quietest Challenge', 447.
166 Page and Baker-Hytch make this same claim ('Meeting the Evil God Challenge', 303). In response to those who claim that the concept of evil god is an incoherent one, they write, 'We find this a stretch, and so here, we will defend only the more modest claim that certain metaphysical theses about goodness that are incompatible with evil god are fairly plausible and hence have a moderately high epistemic probability.' I endorse this view throughout my thesis.
167 King-Farlow, 'Cacodaemony'.
168 Forrest, 'A response to Murphree'.
169 Lancaster-Thomas, 'Objections', 8.
170 Ibid., 4–5.
171 Anastasia Scrutton, 'Why Not Believe in an Evil God? Pragmatic Encroachment and Some Implications for Philosophy of Religion', *Religious Studies*, vol. 52 (3) (2016), 359.
172 This is slightly contentious. As Hendricks argues in 'Sceptical Theism' (556), 'The popularity of the argument is irrelevant: all that matters is that the good-god theist accepts it, for that would give them reason to reject the symmetry thesis.' The motivation for my view, however, is as follows: we should offer solutions for as many traditional theists as possible.

173   Lee, *The Dobe Ju/'hoansi*, 119.
174   Lancaster-Thomas, 'Truth', 451–3.
175   Scholars vary as to which arguments they include within the categories of 'perfect-being theology', 'creation theology' and 'revelation theology'. Therefore, I expect that some readers will be displeased to learn that I have placed 'arguments from moral motivation' in the category of perfect-being theology and 'Reformed epistemology' in the category of creation theology. I am happy for these to be moved, as my analysis focuses on rejecting the broad symmetry thesis rather than the narrow symmetry thesis. That is, I argue that once all of the available evidence that is pertinent to the attribution of good or evil to god has been considered, it is more reasonable to attribute goodness to god than evil. (In other words, it does not matter which arguments fall into which category, all that matters is that the collective sum of these arguments favours the good-god hypothesis over the evil-god hypothesis.)
176   Thomas V. Morris, *Our Idea of God: An Introduction to Philosophical Theology* (Downers Grove, IL: InterVarsity Press, 1991), 12.

Chapter Two

1   Nagasawa, *Maximal God*, 25.
2   A number of other attributes are offered by perfect-being theologians. For examples, see Daniel Hill, *Divinity and Maximal Greatness* (London: Routledge, 2005), 9–18.
3   Lancaster-Thomas, *An Exploration*, 202–22.
4   Nagasawa, *Maximal God*, 2.
5   Note that the maximal-god thesis pre-dates Nagasawa's work (2017). For examples, see Alvin Plantinga, *The Nature of Necessity* (New York: Oxford University Press, 1974), 218 and Hill, *Divinity*, 1–5.
6   Nagasawa, *Maximal God*, 93.
7   Ibid., 82–8.
8   Ibid., 90–4.
9   Ibid., 92. (My emphasis.)
10 Ibid., 116.
11 Nagasawa's name for this view ('the maximal-god thesis') is somewhat misleading, as omni-god theists also consider themselves to be maximal-god theists – that is, they believe that God is maximally great. In fact, in his book *Divinity and Maximal Greatness*, Hill argues that these two theses are equivalent. I have adopted Nagasawa's labels in keeping with the evil-god literature.

12 The majority of traditional theists – including the majority referenced throughout this work (examples include Craig, Hill, Swinburne and Plantinga) – believe the omni-god thesis can be successfully defended.
13 Lancaster-Thomas, *An Exploration*, 216–8.
14 Ibid., 218.
15 Nagasawa, *Maximal God*, 9.
16 Ibid., 53–4.
17 Ibid., 53.
18 Hill, *Divinity*, 9.
19 Ibid., 13–8.
20 Nelson Pike, *God and Timelessness* (London: Routledge, 1970), 135–49.
21 William Lane Craig, 'How Does One Determine What a Great Making Property Is?', April 2015, *YouTube: 'Drcraigvideos'* (original footage produced by Reasonable Faith), www.youtube.com/watch?v=bcklaS61cbk, 1:40–2:55.
22 Morris, *Our Idea of God*, 38–40.
23 Pike, *God and Timelessness*, 135.
24 Hill, *Divinity*, 125.
25 Pike, *God and Timelessness*, 137.
26 Morris, *Our Idea of God*, 40.
27 Augustine of Hippo, *On the Free Choice of the Will, on Grace and Free Choice, and Other Writings*, ed. Peter King (Cambridge: Cambridge University Press, 2010), 3.5.15.56.
28 Examples include several traditional theists discussed throughout this work – such as Anselm, Augustine, Craig, Hill, Nagasawa and Plantinga.
29 J. L. Schellenberg, *The Hiddenness Argument: Philosophy's New Challenge to Belief in God* (Oxford: Oxford University Press, 2015), 98. (My emphasis.)
30 Nagasawa, *Maximal God*, 7.
31 Anselm, 'Proslogion', in *The Major Works* (Oxford: Oxford University Press, 1998), 88–9.
32 Descartes, *Meditations*, 52.
33 William Lane Craig, *A Reasonable Response: Answers to Tough Questions on God, Christianity and the Bible* (Chicago, IL: Moody Publishers, 2013), 169–72.
34 Hill, *Divinity*, 1.
35 Alvin Plantinga, *God, Freedom, and Evil* (Grand Rapids, MI: William B. Eerdmans Publishing Company, 1974), 111–2.
36 Nagasawa, *Maximal God*, 7–27.
37 Descartes, *Meditations*, 52.
38 Gottfried Wilhelm Leibniz, *Philosophical Papers and Letters*, ed. Leroy E. Loemker, 2nd edition (Dordrecht, Holland: Kluwer Academic Publishers, 1969), 386.
39 Moses Mendelssohn, 'On Evidence in Metaphysical Sciences', in *Philosophical Writings*, ed. Daniel O. Dahlstrom (Cambridge: Cambridge University Press, 1997), 282–3.

40 William Lane Craig, 'The Ontological Argument', in *To Everyone an Answer: A Case for the Christian Worldview*, ed. Francis J. Beckwith, William Lane Craig and J. P. Moreland (Downers Grove, IL: InterVarsity Press, 2004), 124–38.
41 Jordan Howard Sobel, 'Gödel's Ontological Proof', in *On Being and Saying: Essays for Richard Cartwright*, ed. Judith Jarvis Thomson (London: MIT Press, 1987), 241–61.
42 Charles Hartshorne, 'The Logic of the Ontological Argument', *Journal of Philosophy*, vol. 58 (17) (1961): 471–3.
43 Norman Malcolm, 'Anselm's Ontological Argument', *Philosophical Review*, vol. 69 (1) (1960): 41–62.
44 Nagasawa, *Maximal God*, 180–205.
45 Plantinga, *God, Freedom, and Evil*, 112.
46 Anselm, 'Proslogion', 87–8.
47 Ibid., 89.
48 Robert J. Richman, 'The Ontological Proof of the Devil', *Philosophical Studies*, vol. 9 (4) (1958): 63–4.
49 Haight and Haight, 'Ontological Argument', 218–20.
50 Millican, 'Devil's Advocate', 197–8.
51 New, 'Antitheism', 37.
52 Murphree, 'Natural Theology', 77–8.
53 Timothy Chambers, 'On Behalf of the Devil – A Parody of Anselm Revisited', *Proceedings of the Aristotelian Society*, vol. 100 (1) (2000): 93–113.
54 Law, 'Evil-God Challenge', 371.
55 Zande, *Infernal Names*, 15.
56 Lancaster-Thomas, 'History', 6.
57 Millican, 'Devil's Advocate', 197.
58 Law, 'Evil-God Challenge', 371.
59 Ibid., 356. (My emphasis.)
60 Anselm, 'Proslogion', 87.
61 Mohammad Saleh Zarepour, *Necessary Existence and Monotheism* (Cambridge: Cambridge University Press, 2022), 5.
62 Haight and Haight, 'Ontological Argument', 218–20.
63 Millican, 'Devil's Advocate', 196.
64 New, 'Antitheism', 37.
65 Murphree, 'Natural Theology', 77–8.
66 Law, 'Evil-God Challenge', 371.
67 Zande, *Infernal Names*, 15.
68 Lancaster-Thomas, 'History', 6.
69 Nagasawa makes use of a similar objection in response to Millican's devil parody of the ontological argument. See Yujin Nagasawa, 'The Ontological Argument and the Devil', *The Philosophical Quarterly*, vol. 60 (238) (2010), 82.

70. I think this is what Bergmann and Brower had in mind in their own response to the evil-god challenge. They write, 'no traditional theists we know of have ever argued for God's perfect goodness by appealing to a stipulative definition'. ('The God of Eth', 695.)
71. Law, 'Evil-God Challenge', 372.
72. Avicenna defended this third version of the single-divine-attribute doctrine. See Zarepour, *Necessary Existence*, 5.
73. In other areas of philosophy of religion, good-god theists take god's simplicity to constitute a significant reason to favour the good-god hypothesis. To take one example, for Avicenna and Zarepour, the unique simplicity of god rules out competing hypotheses such as polytheism. See Ibid., 51–4.
74. Miller makes a similar point in his own response to the challenge, arguing that 'for any empirical data, one can construct an enormous number of hypotheses explaining that data (some explaining it better than even the best scientific hypothesis). And yet usually the hypothesis we end up choosing is chosen on the grounds of simplicity.' ('God is Probably Good', 453.)
75. Law, 'Evil-God Challenge', 369, 372.
76. Ibid., 372.
77. Miller, 'God Is Probably Good', 458–9.
78. Lancaster-Thomas, *An Exploration*, 182.
79. Ibid.
80. Furthermore, I maintain that Lancaster-Thomas's view confuses the intrinsic value of existence with the extrinsic value of existence. I discuss this further in Section 3.5.
81. Schellenberg, *Hiddenness Argument*, 98.
82. Lancaster-Thomas, *An Exploration*, 215.
83. Ibid. (My emphasis.)
84. Note that throughout *The Prince*, Machiavelli claims that *both* goodness and evil are extrinsic great-making properties. For example, Machiavelli writes, 'When men receive favours from someone they expected to do them ill, they are under a greater obligation to their benefactor.' Niccolò Machiavelli, *The Prince*, trans. George Bull (London: Penguin Books, 1999), 43.
85. Ibid., 74. (My emphasis.)
86. Friedrich Nietzsche, 'Ecce Homo', in *The Anti-Christ, Ecce Homo, Twilight of the Idols*, trans. Judith Norman (Cambridge: Cambridge University Press, 2005), 145.
87. Since writing this section, Putin has been comparing himself to the Russian monarch, 'Peter the Great', which has inspired a flurry of headlines: 'Putin the Great'. See Anton Troianovski, 'Putin the Great? Russia's President Likens Himself to Famous Czar', *New York Times*, June 2022, www.nytimes.com/2022/06/09/world/europe/putin-peter-the-great.html.

88 Recall that 'exact parallel' or 'parody' arguments – which must adopt the principles, premises and structure of their target arguments – are not the same as 'parallel' arguments. Unhelpfully, much of the literature (both for and against) describes the evil-god challenge as a parody; although some individual arguments for evil god are parodies of their orthodox counterparts, the majority are, in fact, parallel arguments. See Sections 1.3–1.5.
89 Schellenberg, *Hiddenness Argument*, 98.
90 Lancaster-Thomas, *An Exploration*, 50. (My emphasis.)
91 A student points out to me that even if Putin were maximally powerful and intelligent (but remained malevolent), we might still consider Gandhi (solely in virtue of his moral character) to have the intrinsically greater of the two characters.
92 Bergmann and Brower, 'The God of Eth', 695. (My emphasis.)
93 The great pumpkin example (and my response) is an adapted version of an objection to Reformed epistemology that has been presented by Alvin Plantinga. See Alvin Plantinga, 'Reason and Belief in God', in *Faith and Rationality: Reason and Belief in God*, ed. Alvin Plantinga and Nicholas Wolterstorff (Notre Dame, IN: University of Notre Dame Press, 1983), 74–8.
94 Lancaster-Thomas, *An Exploration*, 215.
95 Ibid.
96 Ibid.
97 Murphree, 'Natural Theology', 81.
98 New, 'Antitheism'.
99 I believe this is why those who have responded to the challenge, such as Hendricks, have claimed that the modal ontological argument provides 'significant grounds' for rejecting the symmetry thesis. See 'Sceptical Theism', 555.
100 Bergmann and Brower, 'The God of Eth'.
101 Ward, 'A Response', 45–6.
102 Keltz, 'A Thomistic Answer', 689–98.
103 Edward Feser, *Aquinas: A Beginner's Guide* (London: Oneworld Publications, 2009).
104 Ibid., 35.
105 Saint Thomas Aquinas, *The Summa Theologica*, Fathers of the English Dominican Province Translation (London: Burns Oates and Washbourne, 1920), I.5.1.
106 Ibid.
107 Ibid., I.48.1. (My emphasis.)
108 Feser, 'Law's "Evil-God Challenge"'.
109 Aquinas, *Summa Theologica*, I.2.3. The quotation has been separated to assist the reader in identifying the argument's premises.

110 Here, I part with Aquinas's example that there must be a maximum heat. Although I think heat is a scaling property, I don't agree with Aquinas that heat has a maximum. Instead, I take heat to be a non-maximality property like mass or size.
111 I believe Feser would also accept this interpretation. See Feser, *Aquinas,* 107.
112 One may argue that the challenger does not need to reverse the orthodox privation theory, but that they can choose to reject the privation theory instead. As I explained in Section 1.4, I believe such a move is beyond the scope of the evil-god challenge. If one could successfully reject the privation theory, then there would be no need to develop a parallel account; however, the evil-god challenge proceeds by granting the good-god theist the benefit of the doubt and proceeding to show that their reasoning leads to absurd consequences (such as belief in two mutually exclusive monotheisms).
113 Collins, 'Extended and Defended', 87–9.
114 Lancaster-Thomas, *An Exploration,* 74–80.
115 In claiming that existence is intrinsically evil, Lancaster-Thomas appeals to the work of David Benatar (*An Exploration,* 84–7). However, as I argue in Section 3.5, Benatar does not claim that existence is intrinsically evil, and, therefore, the parallel is unsuccessful.
116 Arthur Schopenhauer, 'On the Vanity of Existence', in *Essays and Aphorisms,* trans. R. J. Hollingdale (London: Penguin Books, 2004a), 53–4.
117 Arthur Schopenhauer, 'On the Suffering of the World', in *Essays and Aphorisms,* trans. R. J. Hollingdale (London: Penguin Books, 2004b), 41.
118 Arthur Schopenhauer, *The World as Will and Representation,* vol. 1, trans. E. F. J. Payne (New York: Dover Publications, 1969), 196.
119 This is a parallel version of Aquinas's fourth way, as presented in *Summa Theologica,* I.2.3.
120 Hill, *Divinity,* 11.
121 See Feser, 'Broken Law'.
122 I acknowledge that many philosophers would object that apparent conceivability is not evidence of possibility – that is to say, one may argue that something may be logically coherent and yet still impossible. (In my view, logical coherence is the best evidence for possibility – how else can we prove if something is possible or not?) However, if conceivability does not entail possibility, then the evil-god hypothesis may be – as held by Feser – impossible. Nevertheless, this would not detract (but would strengthen) my wider thesis: that it is more reasonable to attribute goodness to god than it is to attribute evil to god.
123 Collins, 'Extended and Defended', 87–9.
124 Page and Baker-Hytch, 'Meeting the Evil God Challenge', 498.
125 Ibid.
126 Keltz, 'A Thomistic Answer', 696. The quotation has been amended to remove two identical grammatical errors: *if unimpeded* ~~with~~ while.

127 Ibid., 695.
128 Lancaster-Thomas, *An Exploration*, 215.
129 Miller, 'God Is Probably Good', 456.
130 Keltz, 'A Thomistic Answer', 695.
131 Lancaster-Thomas, *An Exploration*, 88.
132 Ibid.
133 Richard Swinburne, *The Existence of God*, 2nd edition (Oxford: Oxford University Press, 2014), 100–6.
134 Forrest, 'Replying to the Anti-God Challenge'.
135 Miller, 'God Is Probably Good'.
136 Luke Wilson, 'Moral Motivation and the Evil-God Challenge', *Religious Studies*, vol. 57 (4) (2021): 703–16.
137 Weaver, 'Evilism'.
138 Page and Baker-Hytch, 'Meeting the Evil God Challenge', 498.
139 Richard Swinburne, 'The Coherence of Theism', in *Philosophers on God: Talking about Existence*, ed. Jack Symes (London: Bloomsbury, 2024), 18–9.
140 Swinburne, *Existence of God* (2nd), 100.
141 Ibid., 105.
142 A similar argument is presented by Keith Ward in his 'four responses' to the evil-god challenge. See 'A Response', 46–7.
143 Weaver, 'Evilism', 9.
144 Ibid., 13.
145 Ibid.
146 A version of this argument is also presented by Miller in 'God Is Probably Good', 461.
147 This point is echoed by Page and Baker-Hytch: 'Hence, if moral motivation internalism is true, then an omniscient, wholly evil being is impossible.' ('Meeting the Evil God Challenge', 498.)
148 In 'Replying to the Anti-God Challenge', Forrest also presents a version of this argument, but relies on a stronger version of moral internalism.
149 Wilson, 'Moral Motivation', 706.
150 Collins, 'Extended and Defended', 106.
151 Hendricks, 'Sceptical Theism', 556.
152 I disagree with Hendricks to the following extent: I maintain that we should appeal to popular arguments for god before we appeal to unpopular arguments for god. That way, one can defend a significantly higher proportion of traditional theists.
153 Collins, 'Extended and Defended', 106–7.
154 Ibid., 107. (My emphasis.) In the full quotation, Weaver says the same thing about Forrest's objection.

155 Ibid., 106.
156 Miller, 'Why God Is Probably Good', 13. Typo amended: ... *we could reasonably leave it at that.*
157 Suppose that the evil-god challenger could respond to this objection. Even so, the orthodox principle – like the claim that goodness (and not evil) is a great-making property, and that evil (and not goodness) is a privation – is more intuitively appealing. For my wider argument – that there are numerous grounding asymmetries favouring good god and not evil god – to be considered successful, one may concede that their orthodox principles offer (at least in this case) *minor* asymmetries favouring good god.
158 Swinburne, *Existence of God* (2nd), 96–109.
159 Richard Swinburne, *The Coherence of Theism*, revised edition (Oxford: Oxford University Press, 1993a), 146.
160 Whether acting out of whim is rational or irrational should not concern the challenger. If it is rational to act out of whim, then this fits Swinburne and Weaver's framework: god is motivated to act rationally. If it is irrational, then the challenger may state the following: god is motivated by the value of whim (irrational decisions that result in irrational or, arguably, immoral outcomes) over moral values (rational decisions that result in rational, moral, outcomes).
161 Lancaster-Thomas, *An Exploration*, 110.
162 Ibid., 111.

Chapter Three

1 Thomas Aquinas, *Summa Contra Gentiles*, trans. Anton C. Pegis (New York: Image Books, 1955), I.11.5.
2 Alister E. McGrath, *Christian Theology: An Introduction*, 3rd edn (Oxford: Blackwell Publishing, 2001), 209.
3 To borrow from William Paley's *Natural Theology* (231), 'a power, which could create such a world as this is, must be, beyond all comparison, greater, than any which we experience in ourselves', so 'we should ascribe power to the Deity under the name of "omnipotence"'.
4 Jonathan Edwards, *The Works of Jonathan Edwards Volume 6: Scientific and Philosophical Writings* (New Haven, CT: Yale University Press, 1980), 230.
5 Ibid., 231.
6 Inevitably, any discussion of the world's values (its goods, evils, beauty and ugliness) will appeal to observations and examples from the natural order of things. Depending on the evidence one chooses to present, we can end up in very different places – as demonstrated by the longstanding debate between optimistic-theists

('the world is a wonderful place!') and pessimistic-atheists ('The world is a horrible place!'). In representing the traditional theist and the evil-god challenger, I have selected these observations in good faith, without personal commitment to any of the hypotheses discussed.

7   My discussion is limited to three popular theories; I accept that there may be other theories of moral character that sufficiently capture god's character.
8   I am heavily indebted to Lancaster-Thomas for her work on this topic, as well as our lengthy discussions and our co-presented paper on this section at the 94th Joint Session of the Aristotelian Society and Mind Association, University of Kent. For a more thorough examination of evil god's moral character, see Lancaster-Thomas, *An Exploration*, 23–35.
9   Peter Brian Barry, 'In Defense of the Mirror Thesis', *Philosophical Studies*, vol. 155 (2) (2011): 199–205.
10 John Kekes, *The Roots of Evil* (Ithaca: Cornell University Press, 2005).
11 Luke Russell, *Evil: A Philosophical Investigation* (Oxford: Oxford University Press, 2014).
12 Laurence Thomas, *Vessels of Evil: American Slavery and the Holocaust* (Philadelphia: Temple University Press, 1993).
13 The problems do not stop there. One might also think that somebody who does not perform good actions, but enjoys the happiness of others, should also be considered good (consider the non-combatant who is pleased to hear that the war has ended). An action-based approach to character cannot account for such cases. Note, however, that as god is the ultimate creator and designer of the universe – which is a performative action – we can rule god out as a simple spectator.
14 Todd Calder, 'The Apparent Banality of Evil', *Journal of Social Philosophy*, vol. 34 (3) (2003): 364–76.
15 My discussion here is limited. See Bernard Williams, 'Moral Luck', in *Moral Luck: Philosophical Papers 1973–1980* (Cambridge: Cambridge University Press, 1981), 20–39, and Thomas Nagel, 'Moral Luck', in *Mortal Questions* (Cambridge: Cambridge University Press, 1979), 24–38.
16 Peter Brian Barry, *Evil and Moral Psychology* (New York: Routledge, 2013).
17 Daniel Haybron, 'Consistency of Character and the Character of Evil', in *Earth's Abominations: Philosophical Studies of Evil*, ed. Daniel Haybron (New York: Rodopi, 2002), 63–78.
18 Luke Russell, 'Dispositional Accounts of Evil Personhood', *Philosophical Studies*, vol. 149 (2) (2010): 231–50.
19 Note that, as we have seen, some traditional theists, such as Nagasawa (*Maximal God*), are not beholden to the claim that god is omnipotent and omniscient. Therefore, on Nagasawa's account, god may not always (if ever) possess the ability to perform good (or evil) actions. For why I discuss the omni-god thesis rather than the maximal-god thesis, see Section 2.2.

20 Swinburne, *Existence of God* (2nd), 116.
21 Xenophon, *Memorabilia*, trans. Christopher Bruell (London: Cambridge University Press, 1994), 22–3. Here, Socrates's interlocutor is convinced by the argument for benevolence in design – 'by Zeus … these things very much resemble the contrivance of some wise craftsman who loves animals' (23).
22 Swinburne, *Providence*, 247.
23 Paley, *Natural Theology*, 237–76.
24 I have strengthened Paley's argument in places, and I am confident that Paley would embrace such changes. For example, as 'intrinsic goods' (beauty, consciousness, and so forth) meet his definition of 'gratuitous goods' (otherwise referred to as 'superadded goods'), I have included them within this section.
25 Paley, *Natural Theology*, 237. (My emphasis.)
26 Ibid. (My emphasis.)
27 For, according to several philosophers of mind – including Blackmore and Chalmers – ordinary conscious creatures (conscies) are no more likely to survive than their non-conscious (zombie) counterparts. See Susan Blackmore, 'The Grand Illusion' (17–8) and David Chalmers, 'The Hard Problem' (32–3) in *Philosophers on Consciousness: Talking about the Mind*, ed. Jack Symes (London: Bloomsbury, 2022).
28 Paley, *Natural Theology*, 238.
29 As stated in Section 1.4, the evil-god challenge proceeds by developing arguments that parallel arguments for traditional theism, rather than disputing their underlying principles. So, let us give Paley the benefit of the doubt: if these two principles are true, let us assume the good-god theist can ground god's goodness in nature. Before we look at some of Paley's supporting arguments, we should keep in mind that Paley gives copious examples of the beneficial design and surplus pleasures that we find in nature. Rather than providing a catalogue of examples, I have selected (in good faith) those which will allow us to understand Paley's thinking, and, therefore, illustrate what a successful parallel would look like.
30 Paley, *Natural Theology*, 238.
31 Ibid., 238–9.
32 Ibid., 241.
33 Ibid., 250.
34 Ibid., 251.
35 Ibid., 242.
36 Ibid., 241.
37 Ibid., 255.
38 Note that Paley says that we should ascribe infinite (rather than finite) benevolence to god, because 'what is benevolence at all, must in him be infinite benevolence, by reason of the infinite, that is to say, the incalculably great, number of objects, upon which it is exercised'. (Ibid.)

39 Swinburne, *Providence*, 247.
40 Ibid.
41 Ibid.
42 Cahn, 'Cacodaemony'.
43 Millican, 'Devil's Advocate', 199–204.
44 Stein, 'God, the Demon'.
45 New, 'Antitheism', 37–8.
46 Morriston, 'Evidential Argument from Goodness'.
47 Law, 'God of Eth', in which writes, 'It's obvious our creator is very clearly evil! Take a look around you! Witness the horrendous suffering he inflicts upon us. The floods. The ethquakes. Cancer. The vile, rotting stench of God's creation is overwhelming!'
48 Zande, *Infernal Names*.
49 Lancaster-Thomas, 'Mal-Design'.
50 Hume, *Dialogues*, 102–3.
51 Richard Dawkins, *River out of Eden: A Darwinian View of Life* (New York: Basic Books, 1995), 131–2.
52 Dawkins does not believe in a god, but, if we take him at his word, he claims that a morally-mixed god (and perhaps an evil god) is *slightly* more reasonable than a good god. (Note, however, that Dawkins is wrong, for the morally-mixed-god hypothesis and evil-god hypothesis face 'evil-god' challenges of their own.)
53 Richard Dawkins, *The God Delusion* (London: Bantam Press, 2006), 108.
54 Joshua Rasmussen and Felipe Leon, *Is God the Best Explanation of Things? A Dialogue* (Cham, Switzerland: Palgrave Macmillan, 2019), 210–2.
55 Thank you to Philip Goff for pointing me towards Leon's examples. See Philip Goff, *Why? The Purpose of the Universe* (London: Oxford University Press, 2023), 86.
56 Leon, *Best Explanation*, 210. (Leon borrows both examples from Dvorsky. See George Dvorsky, '9 Predators with the Most Brutal Hunting Techniques', *Gizmodo*, May 2013, https://gizmodo.com/9-predators-with-the-most-brutal-hunting-techniques–510100768.)
57 Ibid., 310.
58 See Peter Singer, *Animal Liberation* (London: Penguin Books, 2015), 25–158.
59 Arthur Schopenhauer, 'On Religion', in *Essays and Aphorisms*, trans. R. J. Hollingdale (London: Penguin Books, 2004c), 187.
60 It is contentious whether the suffering and killing of our fellow (non-human) creatures is a natural or moral evil.
61 Hume, *Dialogues*, 96.
62 Ibid., 96–7.
63 Nagasawa, 'Problem of Evil for Atheists', 159–60.
64 Ibid., 151.
65 Yujin Nagasawa, 'The Problem of Evil for Atheists', in *Philosophers on God: Talking about Existence*, ed. Jack Symes (London: Bloomsbury, 2024), 93, 100.

66 Paley, *Natural Theology*, 251.
67 Hume, *Dialogues*, 98–9.
68 Goff, *Why?*, 91.
69 To be clear, Goff's view is that there is a better action available to god: god could have created a better world. For Goff, the world contains more evil than we'd expect from a perfectly good god, but the world is still an overall good (and not an overall bad) place.
70 Schopenhauer, 'On Religion', 184.
71 Page and Baker-Hytch also discuss the value of life and consciousness in relation to the evil-god challenge. (See 'Meeting the Evil God Challenge', 503–5).
72 For the original, see John Rawls, *A Theory of Justice: Revised Edition* (Cambridge, MA: Harvard University Press, 1999), 15–8.
73 Gregory Miller, 'Why Consciousness Matters', in *Philosophers on Consciousness: Talking about the Mind*, ed. Jack Symes (London: Bloomsbury, 2022), 7.
74 Lancaster-Thomas, *An Exploration*, 139.
75 Ibid.
76 Chris Byron, 'Why God Is Most Assuredly Evil: Challenging the Evil God Challenge', *Think*, vol. 18 (51) (2019), 27–8.
77 See Lancaster-Thomas, 'Mal-Design', 107 and Lancaster-Thomas, *An Exploration*, 139.
78 David Benatar, *Better Never to Have Been: The Harm of Coming into Existence* (Oxford: Oxford University Press, 2006), VII, 202.
79 Benatar does not call this his 'master argument'. I take this label from David Lindeman, who informs me that this is widely considered to be Benatar's most powerful argument.
80 Benatar, *Better Never to Have Been*, 32.
81 I note that Lancaster-Thomas alludes to this point in *An Exploration* (183) – 'Benatar's argument from axiological asymmetry that claims that existence is extrinsically bad.'
82 I outline the structure of parallel arguments in Section 1.4.
83 However, as I claim in Section 3.8, Benatar's argument could (arguably) be used as an argument for symmetry thesis. Note that such an argument would rely on the claim that the totality of the world's goods (intrinsic and extrinsic) does not outweigh the totality of the world's evils (intrinsic and extrinsic).
84 Benatar, *Better Never to Have Been*, 73.
85 Law, 'Evil-God Challenge', 369–70.
86 Augustine, *Free Choice of the Will*, 3.5.15.56.
87 See Plantinga, *God, Freedom, and Evil*, 30 and Plantinga, *Nature of Necessity*, 166–7.
88 Law points this out. See, 'Evil-God Challenge', 369.
89 See Lancaster-Thomas, 'Objections', 2 and Nagasawa, *Maximal God*, 159.
90 Stein, 'God, the Demon', 166.

91 Ibid.
92 Law, 'Evil-God Challenge', 369. (My emphasis.)
93 Ibid.
94 G. E. Moore, *Principia Ethica* (Cambridge: Cambridge University Press, 1922), 209.
95 Law, 'Evil-God Challenge', 370.
96 Richard Swinburne, *Is There a God?* (Oxford: Oxford University Press, 1996), 106–7.
97 In fact, Swinburne claims that the victims of the Holocaust were 'of use' to a 'great good', for they 'provided the opportunity' for guards to make morally significant choices. See Richard Swinburne (1993b), 'God: For and Against', *YouTube: 'Glenn Morris'* (original footage produced by Channel 4), www.youtube.com/watch?v=aivRDaTnx8M&t, 37:15–38:46.
98 Frederick Robert Tennant, *Philosophical Theology, 2 vols* (Cambridge: Cambridge University Press, 1930), 89–93.
99 Peter Forrest, *God without the Supernatural* (Ithaca: Cornell University Press, 1996), 38–41.
100 Swinburne, *Existence of God* (2nd), 190–1.
101 Forrest, *Without the Supernatural*, 39.
102 Swinburne, *Existence of God* (2nd), 121.
103 Richard Swinburne, *The Existence of God*, 1st edition (Oxford: Clarendon Press, 1979), 150.
104 Swinburne makes use of the argument from beauty within the context of (direct) arguments for and against the existence of good god, rather than as a solution to the evil-god challenge; however, I claim that Swinburne's argument – with some minor changes – can be used to form a (seemingly plausible) solution to the challenge.
105 Swinburne, *Existence of God* (2nd), 121, 190.
106 Richard Dawkins, 'Richard Dawkins vs John Lennox: The God Delusion Debate', October 2007, *YouTube: 'Larry Alex Taunton'* (original footage produced by Fixed Point Foundation), https://www.youtube.com/watch?v=zF5bPI92-5o, 21:10–22:02.
107 Allen Carlson, 'Nature and Positive Aesthetics', *Environmental Ethics*, vol. 6 (1) (1984), 5.
108 Emily Brady, 'Ugliness and Nature', *Enrahonar*, vol. 45 (2010), 34.
109 Ibid., 32.
110 Carlson, 'Nature', 5. (My emphasis.)
111 David Attenborough in Michael Bright, *100 Years of Nature* (London: BBC Books, 2007), 184.
112 This argument is taken from Alexander Pruss's Wilde Lectures at Oxford University. See Alexander Pruss, November 2019, 'Wilde Lecture 1 (2019a)', *University of Oxford: Faculty of Theology and Religion*, www.theology.ox.ac.uk/files/wildelecture12019mp4, 01:06:15–01:11:53.

113 The example of the ugly hands is Pruss's. See 'Wilde Lecture', 01:07:25–01:07:30.
114 Claude Monet, *Woman with a Parasol* (Washington: National Gallery of Art, 1875).
115 This is Pruss's explanation. See 'Wilde Lecture', 01:07:40–01:08:20.
116 Leonardo da Vinci, *The Last Supper (restored)* (Milan: Museo Cenacolo Vinciano, 1495–98).
117 This quotation is taken from Pruss's slides. See Alexander Pruss, 'Wilde Lecture 1 (2019b) - Accompanying Slides', *AlexaderPruss.com*, www.alexanderpruss.com/papers/beauty.pdf, slides 47–9.
118 Ibid. Typo amended: ... *positive judgments* ~~can't~~ *can be confidently made based on a small part...*
119 Quentin Massys, *An Old Woman (The Ugly Duchess)* (London: The National Gallery), c. 1513.
120 Fra Angelico, *The Last Judgement* (Florence: Museum of San Marco), c. 1425–30.
121 Nagasawa, 'Problem of Evil for Atheists', 151.
122 *Breaking Bad* (television), Vince Gilligan (USA: AMC, 2008–13).
123 Vladimir Nabokov, *Lolita* (Paris: Olympia Press, 1955).
124 The reader may claim that Lolita is not, in fact, an immoral artwork; in such a case, I offer two responses. First, one may think that *Lolita* is not an 'immoral artwork', but that some other artwork is immoral. If this is the case, the reader is welcome to substitute my example for their own. Second, perhaps one rejects the existence of 'immoral artworks' altogether – maybe the reader thinks that all artworks are good. If this is the case, I ask the reader to reject my first suggestion (that there are immoral but aesthetically pleasing fictional characters).
125 William Beaudine and Harold Daniels (director), *The Lawton Story of 'The Prince of Peace'* (film), Kroger Babb and J. S. Jossey (USA: Hallmark Productions, 1949).
126 *Mr. T's Commandments*, Laurence Tureaud (artist) (USA: Columbia Records, 1984).
127 Law, 'Evil-God Challenge', 358.
128 Lancaster-Thomas, *An Exploration*, 125. (My emphasis.)
129 Bergmann and Brower, 'The God of Eth', 36–8.
130 Law, 'Law vs Peoples', 19:40–20:20.
131 Craig, 'Reasonable Faith', *Philosophers on God*, 38.
132 Ibid.
133 Ibid.
134 Bergmann and Brower, 'The God of Eth', 4.
135 Law, 'Evil-God Challenge', 370.
136 Swinburne, *Is There a God?*, 106–7.
137 Hume, *Dialogues*, 103.
138 Daniel Hill, 'What's New in .... Philosophy of Religion', *Philosophy Now*, 1998, www.philosophynow.org/issues/21/Whats_New_in_Philosophy_of_Religion.
139 Plantinga, 'Reason and Belief in God', 16–93.
140 Ibid., 17. (My emphasis.)

141 Ibid., 79.
142 Paul Helm, 'John Calvin, the *Sensus Divinitatis*, and the Noetic Effects of Sin', *International Journal for Philosophy of Religion*, vol. 43 (2) (1998), 88.
143 John Calvin, *Institutes of the Christian Religion*, trans. Ford Lewis Battles (London: SCM Press, 1960), 88.
144 Plantinga, 'Reason and Belief in God', 80.
145 It is noteworthy that a 'sense of good god' is not unique to those who identify as theists. As Deborah Kelemen – and many other studies have pointed out – children appear to be pre-disposed towards belief in god regardless of the religiosity of their cultures and home background. See Kelemen, 'Are Children "Intuitive Theists" Reasoning About Purpose and Design' in Nature, *Psychology Science*, vol. 15 (5) (2004): 295–301.
146 For summary of the project, see 'Humans "Predisposed" to Believe in Gods and the Afterlife', *ScienceDaily*, July 2011, https://www.sciencedaily.com/releases/2011/07/110714103828.htm.
147 Roger Trigg and Justin Barrett, *The Roots of Religion: Exploring the Cognitive Science of Religion*, ed. Roger Trigg and Justin Barrett (London: Routledge, 2016), 10.
148 Lancaster-Thomas, *An Exploration*, 225. Typo amended: … belief-wall ~~rests~~ can be reduced to…
149 The Superman *reductio* can be found in an exchange between Plantinga and Daniel Dennett. See Daniel Dennett and Alvin Plantinga, *Science and Religion: Are They Compatible?* (Oxford: Oxford University Press, 2011), 46–7.
150 One reference to Reformed epistemology and the Flying Spaghetti Monster can be found in Peter J. Morgan's *The Free System Corollary: Responding to Abductive Problems of Evil* (Eugene, OR: Wipf & Stock, 2019), 52.
151 Plantinga, 'Reason and Belief in God', 74.
152 Ibid., 86.
153 Law, 'Evil-God Challenge', 362.
154 Murphree, 'Natural Theology', 82. (My emphasis.)
155 The challenger may argue that *some* orthodox theists form these properly basic beliefs. For example, suffering at the hands of the Nazis during the Second World War, one might think that many Jews formed the properly basic belief that 'god is *un*justifiably punishing me'. A survey of the survivor testimonies shows that, in reality, Jews' abandonment of their faith was very rare. However, even if there are such cases, the second premise of my argument (2x) can accommodate them, for it states that there are not a '*significant* number of properly basic beliefs' which indicate that god is evil. (In other words, the following premise is sufficient for motivating my argument: positive properly basic beliefs significantly outweigh negative properly basic beliefs.)
156 Plantinga, 'Reason and Belief in God', 84.

Chapter Four

1. McGrath, *Christian Theology*, 94.
2. Law recognizes this point himself but suggests that orthodox revelation theology does not 'fit the good-god hypothesis better than the evil'. (See 'The Evil-God Challenge', 364).
3. Throughout this chapter, I use a lowercase 's' when I am referring to scriptures that are *not* specifically Christian; I use an uppercase 'S' when I am referring specifically to 'Christian Scriptures'. The term 'Old Testament' is used in place of 'Hebrew Bible' as our focus, in the case of restricted scripture, is the Christian Scriptures.
4. See Dawkins, *God Delusion*, 31.
5. Richard Dawkins, *Outgrowing God: A Beginner's Guide* (London: Black Swan, 2020), 72.
6. Ibid., 72–92.
7. Millican, 'Devil's Advocate', 206. Note that Millican uses 'Antigod' to mean 'Evil God'.
8. Ibid.
9. Isaiah, 45: 7.
10. Steve Wells, *Drunk with Blood: God's Killings in the Bible* (Moscow, ID: SAB Books, 2013), 291–7.
11. Genesis, 7: 23.
12. Steven Pinker, *The Better Angels of Our Nature: Why Violence Has Declined* (New York: Penguin Books, 2011), 697.
13. Ibid.
14. Wells, *Drunk with Blood*, 12.
15. Colin McEvedy and Richard Jones, *Atlas of World Population History* (London: Allen Lane, 1978), 344.
16. Tom Pickett, 'Population of the PreFlood World', *Lambert Dolphin's Library*, April 1998, www.ldolphin.org/pickett.html.
17. Bodie Hodge, 'Why Don't We Find Human & Dinosaur Fossils Together', in *The New Answers Volume 1: Over 25 Questions on Creation/Evolution and the Bible*, ed. Ken Ham (Green Forest, AR: Master Books, 2006), 182.
18. Raymund Schwager, *Must There Be Scapegoats? Violence and Redemption in the Bible* (New York: Crossroad, 2000), 47–60.
19. Ezekiel, 5: 13–17.
20. Schwager, *Must There Be Scapegoats?*, 47–60.
21. Matthew J. Hart and Daniel J. Hill, 'Does God Intend That Sin Occur? We Affirm', *European Journal for Philosophy of Religion*, vol. 12 (1) (2020): 143–71.
22. Exodus 4: 21. (My emphasis.)
23. Exodus 9: 16.
24. Dawkins, *God Delusion*, 31.

25 Genesis, 1.
26 For a specific example, see Matthew 14: 13–21. (It is worth noting, however, that as the world's creator, god causes *all* happiness.)
27 Romans, 8: 28.
28 Acts, 9: 1–19.
29 Mark, 10: 18.
30 Psalm, 25: 8.
31 Revelation, 19: 11–21.
32 Matthew, 25: 31–46.
33 Jeremiah, 29: 11. (My emphasis)
34 Genesis, 47: 13–27.
35 See Hart and Hill, 'We Affirm', 157–60.
36 John, 3: 16.
37 Stephen Law, 'Sceptical Theism and A Lying God: Wielenberg's Argument Defended and Developed', *Religious Studies*, vol. 51 (1) (2015): 91–109.
38 See also, Erik J. Wielenberg, 'Sceptical Theism and Divine Lies', *Religious Studies*, vol. 46 (4) (2010): 509–23.
39 Law, 'Sceptical Theism', 92.
40 Note, that this argument (as presented in Section 4.4) functions only if the target propositions depend solely on the word of god.
41 Millican, 'Devil's Advocate', 205.
42 Law, 'Evil-God Challenge', 364.
43 Lancaster-Thomas, 'Religious Experience', 149–50. (Lancaster-Thomas endorses Law's claim that evil god, but not good god, would be motivated to reveal conflicting messages.)
44 Law, 'Evil-God Challenge', 362–3.
45 Matthew, 1: 23.
46 John, 1: 1.
47 Matthew, 28: 18.
48 Qur'an, 5: 116. (My emphasis)
49 Qur'an, 4: 171. (My emphasis)
50 Matthew, 27: 32–56.
51 Matthew, 28: 1–8.
52 Qur'an, 4: 157–8. (My emphasis)
53 Damien Keown, *Buddhist Ethics: A Very Short Introduction*, 3rd edition (Oxford: Oxford University Press, 2020), 75.
54 Law, 'Evil-God Challenge', 364.
55 Qur'an, 3: 134.
56 See 'Mool Mantar', in *Guru Granth Sahib*.
57 *Bahá'u'lláh*, I.3.

58 Many of the compatibility objections against good god can also be reformulated as arguments for the existence of evil god. The latter are not my focus and, furthermore, seem to have obvious parallels for good god.
59 Law, 'Evil-God Challenge', 362. (My emphasis)
60 Craig, *Reasonable Faith*, 333–404. (A helpful list of sources on Jesus's resurrection is provided on pages 400–4.)
61 Richard Swinburne, *The Resurrection of God Incarnate* (Oxford: Oxford University Press, 2003).
62 Miller, 'God Is Probably Good', 463.
63 The argument presented is just as applicable to other restricted theologies, such as those who appeal exclusively to the Hebrew Bible or the Qur'an, as – all else being equal – a theology with fewer contradictions should be preferred over a theology with more contradictions.
64 Madden, 'Many Faces of Evil', 490–2. As Madden offers only a single anecdote/ the logical possibility of a negative experience, rather than developing a similarly reasonable parallel argument, I do not appeal to Madden's version of the argument in this section.
65 New, 'Antitheism', 40.
66 Law, 'Evil-God Challenge', 361–3.
67 Lancaster-Thomas, 'Religious Experience', 137–61.
68 The labels – 'positive experience' and 'negative experience' – are Lancaster-Thomas's terms.
69 Lancaster-Thomas, 'Religious Experience', 145.
70 Swinburne, *Existence of God* (2nd), 304.
71 Ibid., 322.
72 Genesis, 3: 8.
73 Matthew, 3: 13–7.
74 Qur'an, 17.
75 Charles Y. Glock and Rodney Stark, *Religion and Society in Tension* (Chicago: Rand McNally, 1965), 125–40.
76 William James, *The Varieties of Religious Experience: A Study in Human Nature* (Cambridge: Cambridge University Press, 2012), 71–2.
77 Ibid., 71.
78 Ibid., 68.
79 Jerome I. Gellman, *Experience of God and the Rationality of Theistic Belief* (New York: Cornell University Press, 1997), 7.
80 This presentation of the argument is an adapted version of Lancaster-Thomas's formulation (see *An Exploration*, 152–3); however, I have amended premises 3–5cc in order to reflect Swinburne's argument from religious experience.
81 Swinburne, *Existence of God* (2nd), 317.
82 Ibid., 318.
83 Ibid., 282.

84 Note that Swinburne's view – asserting the scarcity of negative experiences – appears to be accepted by Law. See 'The Evil-God Challenge', 362.
85 1 Samuel, 16: 15.
86 Luke, 13: 11.
87 Clifford N. R. Quantz, *An Investigation of Satanic Influences Upon Physically, Emotionally, and Spiritually Disturbed Christians: Selected Case Studies*, Andrews University: Dissertation (1994), 38–40.
88 Matthew, 17: 14–8.
89 Mark, 16: 9.
90 Matthew, 8: 16.
91 Matthew, 12: 22.
92 Mark, 9: 17–18.
93 Mark, 5: 1–14.
94 William M. Alexander, *Demonic Possession in the New Testament: Its Historical Medical, and Theological Aspects* (Eugene, OR: Wipf and Stock, 2001).
95 James D. G. Dunn and Graham H. Twelftree, 'Demon-Possession and Exorcism in The New Testament', *Churchman*, vol. 94 (3) (1980): 210–25.
96 Erika Bourguignon, 'Spirit Possession Belief and Social Structure', in *The Realm of the Extra – Human*, ed. Agehananda Bharati (The Hague: Mouton, 1976), 17–26.
97 Archie Wright, 'Evil Spirits in Second Temple Judaism: The Watcher Tradition as a Background to the Demonic Pericopes in the Gospels', *Henoch*, vol. 28 (1) (2006): 141–59.
98 T. K. Oesterreich, *Possession: Demoniacal and Other: Among Primitive Races, in Antiquity, the Middle Ages and Modern* (London: Kegan Paul, Trench, Trubner and Co., 1930), 3.
99 Ibid., ix.
100 Bourguignon, 'Spirit Possession', 19.
101 'Belief in Evil Spirits: YouGov Survey Results, GB', *YouGov*, September 2013, http://cdn.yougov.com/cumulus_uploads/document/12hhgu8wnd/YGArchive-devil-results-250913.pdf.
102 'Belief in the Devil: YouGov Survey Results, US', September 2013, *YouGov* http://cdn.yougov.com/cumulus_uploads/document/vhyn6fdnkp/tabs_exorcism_0912132013%20(1).pdf.
103 Erika Bourguignon, 'Possession and Trance', *Encyclopedia of Medical Anthropology*, ed. C. R. Ember and M. Ember (Boston, MA: Springer, 2004), 142.
104 Oesterreich, *Possession*, 5.
105 Merete Jakobsen, *Negative Spiritual Experiences: Encounters with Evil* (Lampeter: Religious Experience Research Centre, 1999).
106 Ibid., 29.
107 Yujin Nagasawa, *Miracles: A Very Short Introduction* (Oxford: Oxford University Press, 2017b), 42.
108 Plantinga, *God, Freedom, and Evil*, 58.

109 Plantinga's point is made in the context of explanations for natural evil; however, I see no reason why this should not extend to demonic possession.
110 Scrutton, 'Pragmatic Encroachment', 352.
111 Jakobsen, *Negative Spiritual Experiences*, 15.
112 Ibid., 3–4.
113 Lancaster-Thomas, 'Religious Experience', 146.
114 Ibid.
115 Toshiko Kaneda and Cark Haub, 'How Many People Have Ever Lived on Earth', *Population Reference Bureau*, January 2020, https://www.prb.org/howmanypeoplehaveeverlivedonearth.
116 Oesterreich, *Possession*, 376.
117 Ibid., 219.
118 Glock and Stark, *Society in Tension*, 42. (My emphasis.)
119 Cited in David Hay and Kate Hunt, 'Understanding the Spirituality of People Who Don't Go to Church: A Report on the Findings of the Adult's Spirituality Project at the University of Birmingham', Spiritual Journeys, August 2020, https://www.spiritualjourneys.org.uk/pdf/look_understanding_the_spirituality_of_people.pdf, 11.
120 Glock and Stark, *Society in Tension*, 61.
121 Cited in Jakobsen, *Negative Spiritual Experiences*, 6.
122 Alister Hardy, *The Spiritual Nature of Man: A study of contemporary religious experience* (Oxford: Oxford University Press, 1979), 78. (My emphasis.)
123 John Hick, *The New Frontier of Religion and Science: Religious Experience, Neuroscience and the Transcendent* (Basingstoke: Palgrave Macmillan, 2010), 17.
124 'Overview of the UK Population', *Office for National Statistics*, January 2021, https://www.ons.gov.uk/peoplepopulationandcommunity/populationandmigration/populationestimates/articles/overviewoftheukpopulation/january2021.
125 Note also that if the BBC's survey is reflective of the wider population (25 per cent of religious experiences are negative), then roughly 6.7 million members of the British population have had a negative religious experience – and 750 million people worldwide.
126 Swinburne, *Existence of God* (2nd), 282.
127 Lancaster-Thomas, 'Religious Experience', 146. (My emphasis.)
128 Jakobsen, *Negative Spiritual Experiences*, 15.
129 Ibid., 12.
130 Ibid., 22.
131 Ibid., 42.
132 Ibid., 10.
133 Ibid., 21.
134 Ibid., 28.
135 Ibid., 36.

136 Lancaster-Thomas, 'Religious Experience', 152.
137 Ibid., 154.
138 Ibid.
139 Lancaster-Thomas, *An Exploration*, 153.
140 Ibid., 47. (My emphasis)
141 A similar point is made by King-Farlow in his response to Madden's version of the evil-god challenge. King-Farlow writes, 'This move might be more plausible IF historical surveys of apparently "theist" and "diabolical" experiences could be made, and IF all reasonable people could thence know that the surveys produced another devilishly tired contest.' ('Cacodaemony', 60.)
142 I do not endorse the claim that parallel arguments (unlike parody arguments) must retain the logical form of target arguments. Instead, I maintain that parallel arguments which differ from target arguments in logical form increase the potential for asymmetries that may undermine the symmetry thesis.
143 Lancaster-Thomas, 'Religious Experience', 148.
144 Revelation, 13: 11.
145 In other words, I reject Lancaster-Thomas's conclusion that religious experiences 'offer stronger evidence for the existence of an evil god than they do a good god'. ('Religious Experience', 59.)
146 Law, 'Evil-God Challenge', 362–3.
147 Ibid., 362.
148 Ibid., 363.
149 Michael Rea, *The Hiddenness of God* (Oxford: Oxford University Press, 2018), 9.
150 Lougheed, 'Religious Disagreement', 184.
151 Nagasawa, *Miracles*, 18.
152 Nagasawa, *Miracles*, 19. (My emphasis.)
153 New, 'Antitheism', 39.
154 Nagasawa presents a similar objection to Hume's definition of miracles. (*Miracles*, 19)
155 Those who believe miracles can occur within the laws of nature may reject my proposed definition of negative miracles; I choose to focus on violations of natural laws as this popular definition of miracles reveals an important asymmetry.
156 Millican, 'Devil's Advocate', 205.
157 Law, 'Evil-God Challenge', 362.
158 Swinburne, *Existence of God* (2nd), 287.
159 Ibid.
160 Genesis, 7: 23 and Qur'an, 11: 37–44.
161 Exodus, 9: 8–9.
162 Exodus, 13–35.
163 Exodus, 10: 1–20.
164 Exodus, 11: 4–6.
165 Exodus, 11: 5.

166 Ezekiel, 5: 13–7.
167 Revelation, 13: 11–4.
168 Job, 1: 12.
169 Erkki Koskenniemi, 'Miracles of the Devil and His Assistants in Early Judaism and Their Influence on the Gospel of Matthew', in *Evil and the Devil*, ed. Erkki Koskenniemi and Ida Fröhlich (London: Bloomsbury, 2013), 84–97.
170 Faye C. Taylor, *Miracula, saints' cults and sociopolitical landscapes: Bobbio, Conques and post – Carolingian society*, University of Nottingham: Doctoral Thesis (2012), 119.
171 The University of Sheffield's *Miracles Database* was taken offline in 2018. The legacy CSV files were kindly sent to me by project leads Julia Hilner and Charles West, from which I was able to draw the cited data.
172 Reginald T. Davies, *Four Centuries of Witch Beliefs: With Special Reference to the Great Rebellion* (London: Routledge, 2011), 6.
173 Ibid., 4.
174 For examples of confession accounts, see Tony Bellows, *Channel Island Witchcraft: A Critical Survey*, 17th edition (London: Lulu, 2010).
175 Davies, *Four Centuries*, 4–5.
176 Law, *Believing Bullshit*, 25.
177 David Basinger, 'What Is a Miracle?', in *The Cambridge Companion to Miracles*, ed. Graham H. Twelftree (Cambridge: Cambridge University Press, 2011), 20.
178 Moreover, it follows that we should be sceptical of Swinburne's claim that a report of a negative miracle 'could not have been a real miracle'. (*Existence of God* (2nd), 287)
179 Genesis, 1.
180 Besides Jesus's early resurrection, this is the only miracle of Jesus reported in all four of the gospels. See Matthew, 14: 13–21, Mark, 6: 31–44, Luke, 9: 12–17 and John, 6: 1–14.
181 Nagasawa, *Miracles*, 37.
182 Rex Gardener, *Healing Miracles: A Doctor Investigates* (London: Darton Longman and Todd, 1986).
183 Mark, 1: 23–6.
184 Matthew, 8: 1–4.
185 Luke, 5: 17–26.
186 John, 11: 38–44.
187 Christine Overall, 'Miracles, Evidence, Evil, and God: A Twenty-Year Debate', *Dialogue: Canadian Philosophical Review*, vol. 45 (2) (2006): 355–66.
188 James Keller, 'A Moral Argument against Miracles', *Faith and Philosophy: Journal of the Society of Christian Philosophers*, vol. 12 (1) (1995): 54–78.
189 Numbers, 28: 31.
190 Matthew, 17: 24–7.
191 Maurice Wiles, *God's Action in the World: The Bampton Lecture 1986* (London: SCM Press, 1986), 66.

Bibliography

Alexander, W. M. (2001), *Demonic Possession in the New Testament: Its Historical Medical, and Theological Aspects*, Eugene, OR: Wipf and Stock.

Alvaro, C. (forthcoming), 'The Evil God Challenge: Two Significant Asymmetries', *The Heythrop Journal*.

Andrews, M. (2012), 'A Response to the Problem of an "Evil God" as raised by Stephen Law', *Sententias: Meaning, Purpose, and a Way of Thinking*, https://maxandrews.wordpress.com/2012/01/20/a-response-to-the-problem-of-an-evil-god-as-raised-by-stephen-law.

Angelico, F. (c. 1425–30), *The Last Judgement*, Museum of San Marco, Florence.

Anselm (1995), *Monologion and Proslogion: With the Replies of Gaunilo and Anselm*, ed. Williams, T., Indianapolis: Hackett Publishing.

Anselm (1998), 'Proslogion', in *The Major Works*, Oxford: Oxford University Press.

Aquinas, T. (1920), *The Summa Theologica*, Fathers of the English Dominican Province Translation, London: Burns Oates and Washbourne.

Aquinas, T. (1955), *Summa Contra Gentiles*, trans. Pegis, A. C., New York: Image Books.

Augustine (2010), *On the Free Choice of the Will, On Grace and Free Choice, and Other Writings*, ed. King, P., Cambridge: Cambridge University Press.

Babb, K. and Jossey, J. S. (1949), *The Lawton Story of 'The Prince of Peace'* (film), USA: Hallmark Productions.

Barry, P. B. (2011), 'In Defense of the Mirror Thesis', *Philosophical Studies*, vol. 155 (2): 199–205.

Barry, P. B. (2013), *Evil and Moral Psychology*, New York: Routledge.

Basinger, D. (2011), 'What Is a Miracle?' in *The Cambridge Companion to Miracles*, ed. Twelftree, G. H., Cambridge: Cambridge University Press.

Bellows, T. (2010), *Channel Island Witchcraft: A Critical Survey*, 17th edition, London: Lulu.

Benatar, D. (2006), *Better Never to Have Been: The Harm of Coming into Existence*, Oxford: Oxford University Press.

Bergmann, M. and Brower, J. (2007), 'The God of Eth and the God of Earth', *Think*, vol. 5 (14): 33–8.

Blackmore, S. (2022), 'The Grand Illusion', in *Philosophers on Consciousness: Talking about the Mind*, ed. Symes, J., London: Bloomsbury.

Bourguignon, E. (1976), 'Spirit Possession Belief and Social Structure', in *The Realm of the Extra-Human*, ed. Bharati, A., The Hague: Mouton.

Bourguignon, E. (2004), 'Possession and Trance', in *Encyclopedia of Medical Anthropology*, ed. Ember, C. R. and Ember, M., Boston, MA: Springer.

Brady, E. (2010), 'Ugliness and Nature', *Enrahonar*, vol. 45: 27–40.

Brierley, J., Law, S. and Peoples, G. (2011), 'Revisiting the Evil God Challenge - Law vs Peoples', *Unbelievable?* (podcast), www.premierchristianradio.com/Shows/Saturday/Unbelievable/Episodes/Unbelievable-10-Dec-2011-Revisiting-the-evil-God-challenge-Law-vs-Peoples.

Bright, M. (2007), *100 Years of Nature*, London: BBC Books.

Byron, C. (2019), 'Why God Is Most Assuredly Evil: Challenging the Evil God Challenge', *Think*, vol. 18 (51): 25–35.

Cahn, S. (1977), 'Cacodaemony', *Analysis*, vol. 37 (2) (1977): 69–73.

Calder, T. (2003), 'The Apparent Banality of Evil', *Journal of Social Philosophy*, vol. 34 (3): 364–76.

Calvin, J. (1960), *Institutes of the Christian Religion*, trans. Battles, F. L., London: SCM Press.

Carlson, A. (1984), 'Nature and Positive Aesthetics', *Environmental Ethics*, vol. 6 (1): 5–34.

Carrithers, M. (2001), *Buddha: A Very Short Introduction*, Oxford: Oxford University Press.

Chalmers, D. (2022), 'The Hard Problem', in *Philosophers on Consciousness: Talking about the Mind*, ed. Symes, J., London: Bloomsbury.

Chambers, T. (2000), 'On Behalf of the Devil – A Parody of Anselm Revisited', *Proceedings of the Aristotelian Society*, vol. 100 (1): 93–113.

Collins, J. (2019), 'The Evil-God Challenge: Extended and Defend', *Religious Studies*, vol. 55 (1): 85–109.

Columbia Electronic Encyclopedia (2021), 6th edition, Columbia University.

Craig, W. L. (2004), 'The Ontological Argument', in *To Everyone an Answer: A Case for the Christian Worldview*, ed. Beckwith, J. F., Craig, W. L. and Moreland, J. P., Downers Grove, IL: InterVarsity Press.

Craig, W. L. (2008), *Reasonable Faith: Christian Truth and Apologetics*, 3rd edition, Wheaton, IL: Crossway Books.

Craig, W. L. (2011), '#238 The "Evil god" Objection', *Reasonable Faith*, www.reasonablefaith.org/writings/question-answer/the-evilgod-objection/#_edn2.

Craig, W. L. (2013), *A Reasonable Response: Answers to Tough Questions on God, Christianity and the Bible*, Chicago, IL: Moody Publishers.

Craig, W. L. (2015), 'How Does One Determine What a Great Making Property Is?', *YouTube: 'Drcraigvideos'* (original footage produced by Reasonable Faith), www.youtube.com/watch?v=bcklaS61cbk

Craig, W. L. (2024), 'Reasonable Faith', in *Philosophers on God: Talking about Existence*, ed. Symes, J., London: Bloomsbury.

Da Vinci, L. (1495–8), *The Last Supper (restored)*, Museo Cenacolo Vinciano, Milan.

Daniels, C. (1997), 'God, Demon, Good, Evil', *Journal of Value Inquiry*, vol. 31 (2): 177–81.

Davies, R. T. (2011), *Four Centuries of Witch Beliefs: With Special Reference to the Great Rebellion*, London: Routledge.
Dawkins, R. (1995), *River out of Eden: A Darwinian View of Life*, New York: Basic Books.
Dawkins, R. (2006), *The God Delusion*, London: Bantam Press.
Dawkins, R. (2007), 'Richard Dawkins vs John Lennox: The God Delusion Debate', YouTube: 'Larry Alex Taunton' (original footage produced by *Fixed Point Foundation*), https://www.youtube.com/watch?v=zF5bPI92-5o.
Dawkins, R. (2020), *Outgrowing God: A Beginner's Guide*, London: Black Swan.
Dennett, D. and Plantinga, A. (2011), *Science and Religion: Are They Compatible?*, Oxford: Oxford University Press.
Descartes, R. (2017), *Meditations on First Philosophy with Selections from the Objections and Replies*, ed. Cottingham, J., 2nd edition, Cambridge: Cambridge University Press.
Dunn, J. D. G. and Twelftree, G. H. (1980), 'Demon-Possession and Exorcism in The New Testament', *Churchman*, vol. 94 (3): 210–25.
Dvorsky, G. (2013), '9 Predators with the Most Brutal Hunting Techniques', *Gizmodo*, https://gizmodo.com/9-predators-with-the-most-brutal-hunting-techniques-510100768.
Edwards, J. (1980), *The Works of Jonathan Edwards Volume 6: Scientific and Philosophical Writings*, New Haven, CT: Yale University Press.
Feser, E. (2009), *Aquinas: A Beginner's Guide*, London: Oneworld Publications.
Feser, E. (2010), 'Law's "Evil-God Challenge"', *EdwardFeser.blogspot*, www.edwardfeser.blogspot.com/2010/10/laws-evilgod-challenge.html.
Feser, E. (2011), 'Broken Law', *EdwardFeser.blogspot*, https://edwardfeser.blogspot.com/2011/11/broken-law.html.
Forrest, P. (1996), *God Without the Supernatural*, Ithaca: Cornell University Press.
Forrest, P. (1998), 'God, Anti-God and the Emotions: A Response to Murphree', *Sophia*, vol. 37 (1): 153–9.
Forrest, P. (2012), 'Replying to the Anti-God Challenge: A God without Moral Character Acts Well', *Religious Studies*, vol. 48 (1): 35–43.
Gardener, R. (1986), *Healing Miracles: A Doctor Investigates*, London: Darton Longman and Todd.
Gellman, J. I. (1997), *Experience of God and the Rationality of Theistic Belief*, New York: Cornell University Press.
Gilligan, V. (2008–13), *Breaking Bad* (television), USA: AMC.
Glock, C. Y. and Stark, R. (1965), *Religion and Society in Tension*, Chicago: Rand McNally.
Glover, D. (2022), *Answering the Evil God Challenge*, Ryerson University: MA Dissertation.
Goff, P. (2023), *Why? The Purpose of the Universe*, London, Oxford University Press.

Haight, D. and Haight, M. (1970), 'An Ontological Argument for the Devil', *The Monist*, vol. 54 (2): 218–20.

Hardy, A. (1979), *The Spiritual Nature of Man: A Study of Contemporary Religious Experience*, Oxford: Oxford University Press.

Hart, G. (2005), *The Routledge Dictionary of Egyptian Gods and Goddesses*, 2nd edition, London: Routledge.

Hart, M. and Hill, D. (2020), 'Does God Intend that Sin Occur? We Affirm', *European Journal for Philosophy of Religion*, vol. 12 (1): 143–71.

Hartshorne, C. (1961), 'The Logic of the Ontological Argument', *Journal of Philosophy*, vol. 58 (17): 471–3.

Hauskeller, M. (2020), *The Meaning of Life and Death: Ten Classic Thinkers on the Ultimate Question*, London: Bloomsbury.

Hay, D. and Hunt, K. (2020), 'Understanding the Spirituality of People Who Don't Go to Church: A Report on the Findings of the Adult's Spirituality Project at the University of Birmingham', Spiritual Journeys, https://www.spiritualjourneys.org.uk/pdf/look_understanding_the_spirituality_of_people.pdf.

Haybron, D. (2002), 'Consistency of Character and the Character of Evil', in *Earth's Abominations: Philosophical Studies of Evil*, ed. Haybron, D., New York: Rodopi.

Helm, P. (1998), 'John Calvin, the *Sensus Divinitatis*, and the Noetic Effects of Sin', *International Journal for Philosophy of Religion*, vol. 43 (2): 87–107.

Hendricks, P. (2018), 'Sceptical Theism and the Evil-God Challenge', *Religious Studies*, vol. 54 (4): 549–61.

Hendricks, P. (forthcoming), 'The Proper Basicality of Belief in God and the Evil-God Challenge', *Religious Studies*.

Hick, J. (2010), *The New Frontier of Religion and Science: Religious Experience, Neuroscience and the Transcendent*, Basingstoke: Palgrave Macmillan.

Hill, D. (1998), 'What's New in .... Philosophy of Religion', *Philosophy Now*, www.philosophynow.org/issues/21/Whats_New_in_Philosophy_of_Religion.

Hill, D. (2005), *Divinity and Maximal Greatness*, London: Routledge.

Hilner, J. and West, C. (2010), *The Miracles Database*, University of Sheffield: database offline.

Hobart, M. (1985), 'Is God Evil?', in *The Anthropology of Evil*, ed. Parkin, D., Oxford: Basil Blackwell.

Hodge, B. (2006), 'Why Don't We Find Human & Dinosaur Fossils Together', in *The New Answers Volume 1: Over 25 Questions on Creation/Evolution and the Bible*, ed. Ham, K., Green Forest, AR: Master Books.

Hume, H. (2008), *Dialogues and Natural History of Religion*, ed. Gaskin, J. C. A., Oxford: Oxford University Press.

Jakobsen, M. (1999), *Negative Spiritual Experiences: Encounters with Evil*, Lampeter: Religious Experience Research Centre.

James, W. (2012), *The Varieties of Religious Experience: A Study in Human Nature*, Cambridge: Cambridge University Press.

Kaneda, T. and Haub, C. (2020), 'How Many People Have Ever Lived on Earth', *Population Reference Bureau*, https://www.prb.org/howmanypeoplehaveeverlivedonearth.

Kekes, J. (2005), *The Roots of Evil*, Ithaca: Cornell University Press.

Kelemen, D. (2004), 'Are Children "Intuitive Theists" Reasoning About Purpose and Design in Nature', *Psychology Science*, vol. 15 (5): 295–301.

Keller, J. (1995), 'A Moral Argument against Miracles', *Faith and Philosophy: Journal of the Society of Christian Philosophers*, vol. 12 (1): 54–78.

Keltz, B. K. (2019), 'A Thomistic Answer to the Evil-God Challenge', *The Heythrop Journal*, vol. 60 (5): 689–98.

Keown, D. (2020), *Buddhist Ethics: A Very Short Introduction*, 3rd edition, Oxford: Oxford University Press.

King-Farlow, J. (1978), 'Cacodaemony and Devilish Isomorphism', *Analysis*, vol. 38 (1): 59–61.

Koskenniemi, E. (2013), 'Miracles of the Devil and His Assistants in Early Judaism and Their Influence on the Gospel of Matthew', in *Evil and the Devil*, ed. Koskenniemi, E. and Fröhlich, I., London: Bloomsbury.

Lancaster-Thomas, A. (2018a), 'The Evil-God Challenge Part I: History and Recent Developments', *Philosophy Compass*, vol. 13 (7): 1–8.

Lancaster-Thomas, A. (2018b), 'The Evil-God Challenge Part II: Objections and Responses', *Philosophy Compass*, vol. 13 (8): 1–10.

Lancaster-Thomas, A. (2018c), 'The Evil-God Hypothesis and the Argument from Maldesign', *Dialogue: The Phi Sigma Tau Honor Society*, vol. 60 (1): 101–10.

Lancaster-Thomas, A. (2019), 'The Possibility of an Evil-God: A Response to Ward', *Think*, vol. 18 (51): 37–46.

Lancaster-Thomas, A. (2020a), 'Encountering Evil: The Evil-God Challenge from Religious Experience', *European Journal for Philosophy of Religion*, vol. 12 (3): 137–61.

Lancaster-Thomas, A. (2020b), 'Truth, Consequences, and the Evil-God Challenge: A Response to Anastasia Scrutton', *Religious Studies*, vol. 56 (3): 447–54.

Lancaster-Thomas, A. (2020c), *An Exploration of the Evil-God Challenge*, University of Birmingham: PhD Thesis.

Lataster, R. (2018), 'The Problem of Alternative Monotheisms: Another Serious Challenge to Theism', *European Journal for Philosophy of Religion*, vol. 10 (1): 31–51.

Lataser, R. and Philipse, H. (2017), 'The Problem of Polytheisms: A Serious Challenge to Theism', *International Journal for Philosophy of Religion*, vol. 81 (3): 233–46.

Law, S. (2005), 'The God of Eth', *Think*, vol. 3 (9): 13–26.

Law, S. (2010), 'The Evil-God Challenge', *Religious Studies*, vol. 46 (3): 353–73.

Law, S. (2011a), *Believing Bullshit: How Not to Get Sucked into an Intellectual Black Hole*, New York: Prometheus Books.

Law, S. (2011b), 'Fumbling Feser', *StephenLaw.blogspot*, www.stephenlaw.blogspot.com/2011/11/fumbling-feser.html.

Law, S. (2015), 'Sceptical Theism and a Lying God: Wielenberg's Argument Defended and Developed', *Religious Studies*, vol. 51 (1): 91–109.
Law, S. (2019), 'Introduction to the Evil God Challenge', *Think*, vol. 18 (51): 5–9.
Law, S. (2024), 'The Evil-God Challenge', in *Philosophers on God: Talking about Existence*, ed. Symes, J., London: Bloomsbury.
Lee, R. (2013), *The Dobe Ju/'hoansi (Case Studies in Cultural Anthropology)*, 4th edition, Belmont, CA: Wadsworth Publishing.
Leibniz, G. (1969), *Philosophical Papers and Letters*, ed. Loemker, L. E., 2nd edition, Dordrecht, Holland: Kluwer Academic Publishers.
Leibniz, G. (2007), *Theodicy: Essays on the Goodness of God, the Freedom of Man and the Origin of Evil*, ed. Farrer, A., trans. Huggard, E. M., Charleston, SC: BiblioBazaar.
Leslie, A. M. (1987), 'Pretense and Representation: The Origins of "Theory of Mind"', *Psychological Review*, vol. 94 (4): 412–26.
Lougheed, K. (2020), 'Religious Disagreement, Religious Experience, and the Evil God Hypothesis', *European Journal for Philosophy of Religion*, vol. 12 (1): 184–8.
Machiavelli, N. (1999), *The Prince*, trans. Bull, G., London: Penguin Books.
Madden, E. (1964), 'The Many Faces of Evil', *Philosophy and Phenomenological Research*, vol. 24 (4): 481–92.
Madden, E. and Hare, P. (1968), *Evil and the Concept of God*, Springfield, IL: Charles C. Thomas.
Malcolm, N. (1960), 'Anselm's Ontological Argument', *Philosophical Review*, vol. 69 (1): 41–62.
Massys, Q. (c. 1513), *An Old Woman (The Ugly Duchess)*, The National Gallery, London.
McEvedy, C. and Jones, R. (1978), *Atlas of World Population History*, London: Allen Lane.
McGrath, A. E. (2001), *Christian Theology: An Introduction*, 3rd edition, Oxford: Blackwell Publishing.
Meister, C. (2018), *Evil: A Guide for the Perplexed*, 2nd edition, London: Bloomsbury.
Mendelssohn, M. (1997), 'On Evidence in Metaphysical Sciences', in *Philosophical Writings*, ed. Dahlstrom, D. O., Cambridge: Cambridge University Press.
Miller, C. (2021), 'Why God Is Probably Good: A Response to the Evil-God Challenge', *Religious Studies*, vol. 57 (3): 448–65.
Miller, G. (2022), 'Why Consciousness Matters', in *Philosophers on Consciousness: Talking about the Mind*, ed. Symes, J., London: Bloomsbury.
Millican, P. (1989), 'The Devil's Advocate', *Cogito*, vol. 3 (3): 193–207.
Millican, P. (2004), 'The One Fatal Flaw in Anselm's Argument', *Mind*, vol. 113 (451): 437–76.
Monet, C. (1875), *Woman with a Parasol*, National Gallery of Art, Washington.
Moore, G. E. (1922), *Principia Ethica*, Cambridge: Cambridge University Press.
Morgan, P. J. (2019), *The Free System Corollary: Responding to Abductive Problems of Evil*, Eugene, OR: Wipf & Stock.

Morris, T. (1991), *Our Idea of God: An Introduction to Philosophical Theology*, Downers Grove, IL: InterVarsity Press.

Morriston, W. (2004), 'The Evidential Argument from Goodness', *The Southern Journal of Philosophy*, vol. 42 (1): 87–101.

Mugg, J. (2016), 'The Quietest Challenge to the Axiology of God: A Cognitive Approach to Counterpossibles', *Faith and Philosophy: Journal of the Society of Christian Philosophers*, vol. 33 (4): 441–60.

Murphree, W. (1997), 'Natural Theology: Theism or Antitheism?', *Sophia*, vol. 36 (10): 75–83.

Nabokov, V. (1955), *Lolita*, Paris: Olympia Press.

Nagasawa, Y. (2010), 'The Ontological Argument and the Devil', *The Philosophical Quarterly*, vol. 60 (238): 72–91.

Nagasawa, Y. (2017a), *Maximal God: A New Defence of Perfect Being Theism*, Oxford: Oxford University Press.

Nagasawa, Y. (2017b), *Miracles: A Very Short Introduction*, Oxford: Oxford University Press.

Nagasawa, Y. (2018), 'The Problem of Evil for Atheists', in *The Problem of Evil: Eight Views in Dialogue*, ed. Trakakis, N. N., Oxford: Oxford University Press.

Nagasawa, Y. (2024), 'The Problem of Evil for Atheists', in *Philosophers on God: Talking about Existence*, ed. Symes, J., London: Bloomsbury.

Nagel, T. (1979), 'Moral Luck', in *Mortal Questions*, Cambridge: Cambridge University Press, 24–38.

New, C. (1993), 'Antitheism: A Reflection', *Ratio*, vol. 6 (1): 36–43.

Nietzsche, F. (2005), *The Anti-Christ, Ecce Homo, Twilight of the Idols*, trans. Norman, J., Cambridge: Cambridge University Press.

Oesterreich, T. K. (1930), *Possession: Demoniacal and Other: Among Primitive Races, in Antiquity, the Middle Ages and Modern*, London: Kegan Paul, Trench, Trubner and Co.

Office for National Statistics (2021), 'Overview of the UK Population', https://www.ons.gov.uk/peoplepopulationandcommunity/populationandmigration/populationestimates/articles/overviewoftheukpopulation/january2021.

Overall, C. (2006), 'Miracles, Evidence, Evil, and God: A Twenty-Year Debate', *Dialogue: Canadian Philosophical Review*, vol. 45 (2): 355–66.

Page, B. and Baker-Hytch, M. (2020), 'Meeting the Evil God Challenge', *Pacific Philosophical Quarterly*, vol. 101 (3): 297–317.

Paley, W. (2008), *Natural Theology: Or Evidence of the Existence and Attributes of the Deity, Collected from the Appearances of Nature*, ed. Eddy, M. D. and Knight, D., Oxford: Oxford University Press.

Pickett, T. (1998), 'Population of the PreFlood World', *Lambert Dolphin's Library*, www.ldolphin.org/pickett.html.

Pike, N. (1970), *God and Timelessness*, London: Routledge.

Pinker, S. (2011), *The Better Angels of Our Nature: Why Violence Has Declined*, New York: Penguin Books.

Plantinga, A. (1974a), *God, Freedom, and Evil*, Grand Rapids, MI: William B. Eerdmans Publishing Company.

Plantinga, A. (1974b), *The Nature of Necessity*, New York: Oxford University Press.

Plantinga, A. (1983), 'Reason and Belief in God', in *Faith and Rationality: Reason and Belief in God*, ed. Plantinga, A. and Wolterstorff, N., Notre Dame, IN: University of Notre Dame Press.

Pruss, A. (2019a), 'Wilde Lecture 1 (2019)', *University of Oxford: Faculty of Theology and Religion*, www.theology.ox.ac.uk/files/wildelecture12019mp4.

Pruss, A. (2019b), 'Wilde Lecture 1 (2019) – Accompanying Slides', *AlexaderPruss.com*, www.alexanderpruss.com/papers/beauty.pdf.

Quantz, C. N. R. (1994), *An Investigation of Satanic Influences Upon Physically, Emotionally, and Spiritually Disturbed Christians: Selected Case Studies*, Andrews University: Dissertation.

Rasmussen, J. and Leon, F. (2019), *Is God the Best Explanation of Things? A Dialogue*, Cham, Switzerland: Palgrave Macmillan.

Rawls, J. (1999), *A Theory of Justice: Revised Edition*, Cambridge, MA: Harvard University Press.

Rea, M. (2018), *The Hiddenness of God*, Oxford: Oxford University Press.

Religious Studies (2019), 'The Evil-God Challenge: Information', http://www.cambridge.org/core/journals/religious-studies/article/evilgod-challenge/E925DF20AF17F3C87B9449B25F649F27#fndtn-information.

Richman, R. J. (1958), 'The Ontological Proof of the Devil', *Philosophical Studies*, vol. 9 (4): 63–4.

Ritchie, A. (2012), *From Morality to Metaphysics: The Theistic Implications of Our Ethical Commitments*, Oxford: Oxford University Press.

Russell, L. (2014), *Evil: A Philosophical Investigation*, Oxford: Oxford University Press.

Russell, L. (2010), 'Dispositional Accounts of Evil Personhood', *Philosophical Studies*, vol. 149 (2): 231–50.

Schellenberg, J. L. (2015), *The Hiddenness Argument: Philosophy's New Challenge to Belief in God*, Oxford: Oxford University Press.

Schopenhauer, A. (1969), *The World as Will and Representation*, vol. 1, trans. Payne, E. F. J., New York: Dover Publications.

Schopenhauer, A. (2004a), 'On the Vanity of Existence', in *Essays and Aphorisms*, trans. Hollingdale, R. J., London: Penguin Books.

Schopenhauer, A. (2004b), 'On the Suffering of the World', in *Essays and Aphorisms*, trans. Hollingdale, R. J., London: Penguin Books.

Schopenhauer, A. (2004c), 'On Religion', in *Essays and Aphorisms*, trans. Hollingdale, R. J., London: Penguin Books.

Schwager, R. (2000), *Must There Be Scapegoats? Violence and Redemption in the Bible*, New York: Crossroad.

ScienceDaily (2011), 'Humans 'predisposed' to Believe in Gods and the Afterlife', https://www.sciencedaily.com/releases/2011/07/110714103828.htm.

Scrutton, A. (2016), 'Why Not Believe in an Evil God? Pragmatic Encroachment and Some Implications for Philosophy of Religion', *Religious Studies*, vol. 52 (3): 345–60.

Singer, P. (2015), *Animal Liberation*, London: Penguin Books.

Sobel, J. H. (1987), 'Gödel's Ontological Proof', in *On Being and Saying: Essays for Richard Cartwright*, ed. Thomson, J. J., London: MIT Press.

Stein, E. (1990), 'God, the Demon, and the Status of Theodicies', *American Philosophical Quarterly*, vol. 27 (2): 163–7.

Swinburne, R. (1979), *The Existence of God*, 1st edition, Oxford: Clarendon Press.

Swinburne, R. (1993a), *The Coherence of Theism*, revised edition, Oxford: Oxford University Press.

Swinburne, R. (1993b), 'God: For and against', *YouTube: 'Glenn Morris'* (original footage produced by Channel 4), www.youtube.com/watch?v=aivRDaTnx8M&t.

Swinburne, R. (1996), *Is There a God?*, Oxford: Oxford University Press.

Swinburne, R. (1998), *Providence and the Problem of Evil*, Oxford: Oxford University Press.

Swinburne, R. (2003), *The Resurrection of God Incarnate*, Oxford: Oxford University Press.

Swinburne, R. (2014), *The Existence of God*, 2nd edition, Oxford: Oxford University Press.

Swinburne, R. (2024), 'The Coherence of Theism', in *Philosophers on God: Talking about Existence*, ed. Symes, J., London: Bloomsbury.

Taylor, F. C. (2012), *Miracula, Saints' Cults and Sociopolitical Landscapes: Bobbio, Conques and Post-Carolingian Society*, University of Nottingham: Doctoral Thesis.

Tennant, F. R. (1930), *Philosophical Theology – 2 vols*, Cambridge: Cambridge University Press.

Thomas, L. (1993), *Vessels of Evil: American Slavery and the Holocaust*, Philadelphia: Temple University Press.

Trigg, R. and Barrett, J. (2016), *The Roots of Religion: Exploring the Cognitive Science of Religion*, ed. Trigg, R. and Barrett, J., London: Routledge.

Troianovski, A. (2022), 'Putin the Great? Russia's President Likens Himself to Famous Czar', *New York Times*, www.nytimes.com/2022/06/09/world/europe/putin-peter-the-great.html.

Tureaud, L. (1984), *Mr. T's Commandments*, USA: Columbia Records.

Vernon, T. (1994), *The Complete Secularist*, Fayetteville, AR: M & M Press.

Ward, K. (2015), 'The Evil God Challenge – A Response', *Think*, vol. 14 (40): 43–9.

Weaver, C. (2015), 'Evilism, Moral Rationalism, and Reasons Internalism', *International Journal for Philosophy of Religion*, vol. 77 (1): 3–24.

Wells, S. (2013), *Drunk with Blood: God's Killings in the Bible*, Moscow, ID: SAB Books.

Wielenberg, E. J. (2010), 'Sceptical Theism and Divine Lies', *Religious Studies*, vol. 46 (4) (2010): 509–23.

Wiles, M. (1986), *God's Action in the World: The Bampton Lecture 1986*, London: SCM Press.

Williams, B. (1981), 'Moral Luck', in *Moral Luck: Philosophical Papers 1973–1980*, Cambridge: Cambridge University Press, 1981, 20–39.

Wilson, L. (2021), 'Moral Motivation and the Evil-God Challenge', *Religious Studies*, vol. 57 (4): 703–16.

Wright, A. (2006), 'Evil Spirits in Second Temple Judaism: The Watcher Tradition as a Background to the Demonic Pericopes in the Gospels', *Henoch*, vol. 28 (1): 141–59.

Xenophon (1994), *Memorabilia*, trans. Bruell, C., London: Cambridge University.

YouGov (2013a), 'Belief in Evil Spirits: YouGov Survey Results, GB', http://cdn.yougov.com/cumulus_uploads/document/12hhgu8wnd/YG-Archive-devil-results-250913.pdf.

YouGov (2013b), 'Belief in the Devil: YouGov Survey Results, US', http://cdn.yougov.com/cumulus_uploads/document/vhyn6fdnkp/tabs_exorcism_0912132013%20(1).pdf.

Zande, J. (2015), *The Owner of All Infernal Names: An Introductory Treatise on the Existence, Nature & Government of our Omnimalevolent Creator*, Great Britain: CreateSpace Independent Publishing.

Zarepour, M. S. (2022), *Necessary Existence and Monotheism*, Cambridge: Cambridge University Press.

Index

Abrahamic scriptures 130, 148, 151
absurdity challenge/challenger 7–10, 13–16
aesthetic argument/argument from beauty 73, 93–106
aesthetic value 73, 95–6
   artistic values and 101–2, 104
   asymmetry argument 101
   moral/immoral and aesthetic properties 104–5
   natural instances of 96–7
Alister Hardy Religious Experience Research Centre (AHRC) 134–7
Andrews, M. 6, 10, 25
Angelico, F., *The Last Judgement* 103–4
Anselm of Canterbury 37–8
   armchair 41–4
   impossibility objection 50
   ontological argument 22–3, 43, 47
   Proslogion/Proslogion II 22–3, 43
Antichrist 141–2, 149
antitheism 119, 161 n.4
apathetic-god challenge 163 n.43
Apophis 14
Aquinas, T. 37–8, 54–7, 68, 71, 174 n.110
   god's goodness 68–9
   The Summa Theologica 173 n.108
asymmetry objections 24–5, 29, 31, 34, 39, 64, 69
atheism 83, 111
Attenborough, D. 97
Augustine of Hippo 19, 42, 89
Avicenna 172 nn.72–3

Bahá'u'lláh 127
Baker-Hytch, M. 58–60, 168 n.165, 175 n.147
balance of evidence 71, 104, 141–2, 144
Barrett, J. 111
Barry, P. B. 74–5
Basinger, D. 150

Being Itself 2, 54–7, 59, 61, 69, 157
Benatar, D. 72, 88, 93, 107, 174 n.115, 180 n.79, 180 n.83
   anti-natalism 87–8
   Better Never to Have Been 87
benevolence 27, 31, 38, 40, 47–9, 52–3, 63, 74–5, 79, 107, 118, 123, 127, 130, 151–3, 178 n.38
Bergmann, M. 52, 108, 172 n.70
betrayal and illness (evils) 60
Bible 119–21, 123
Blackmore, S. 178 n.27
Bonaparte, N. 49
Bourguignon, E. 133
Brady, E., negative aesthetic experiences 96
Brower, J. 52, 108, 172 n.70
Bruell, C. 178 n.21
Byron, C. 87
   parallel argument 88

Cahn, S. 8, 18
Calder, T. 74
Calvin, J. 110, 112, 149
Carlson, A. 95
Chalmers, D. 178 n.27
character-destroying defence 12
Christianity 134, 145
Christian Scriptures 3, 18, 118–19, 125, 128, 133, 141, 155, 184 n.3
Christian theology 128, 141
'Cognition, Religion and Theology' Project 111
Collins, J. 21, 56, 58, 64–6, 68
combined challenge 16–17, 157, 163 n.48
cosmic sin 80–6
Craig, W. L. 20, 23, 108
creation theology xiii, 1–3, 32, 69, 71, 80, 81, 108, 157–8, 169 n.174
   grounding god's moral character 115
   unorthodox 115

Daniels, C. 10, 25
Davies, R. 149
da Vinci, L., *The Last Supper* 100
Dawkins, R. 72, 81, 95, 121, 179 n.52
  The God Delusion 81
  Outgrowing God 119
Deity 76, 79, 176 n.3
demonism (evil-god theism) 26, 161 n.4
Descartes, R. 5, 19
  Meditations 5 43
diabolism 161 n.4
dualistic-divine-attribute doctrine 45
dualistic polytheism 10, 164 n.59

Edwards, J. 72
evil god 7, 10, 19, 24, 42, 48, 60–1, 66, 84, 106, 143, 160 n.2, 168 n.165
  central attributes 49
  posteriori absurdity/non-absurdity 11, 13, 27–8, 164 n.69
  priori absurdity/non-absurdity 10–11, 25–6, 28, 164 n.69
  and religious experience 129
evil-god challenge xii–xiv, 1–2, 5, 108, 163 nn.43–4. *See also* evil-god hypothesis; good-god hypothesis
  absurdity challenge 7–9, 15–16
  arguments 22–4, 173 n.87, 178 n.29
  combined challenge 16–17, 163 n.48
  exclusivity challenge 7, 9–10, 15–16, 165 n.95
  evil-god dilemma 15–16
  narrow and broad 19, 109
  presenting 6–17
  responses (*see* responses, evil-god challenge)
  simpliciter 10, 29, 49, 90
  strong challenge 8–9, 15, 163 n.48
  structure 20–2
  symmetry xii, 17–19
  virtues of 65
  weak challenge 7–8, 163 n.48
evil-god defender 12, 20–1, 23–4, 40, 53, 114, 122–3, 127–8
evil-god hypothesis 1–2, 4, 7–11, 16, 24, 39, 45, 58, 92, 109, 125, 127–9, 161 n.4
  good-god hypothesis and 14, 27, 29–30, 37, 40, 50, 64, 94, 106, 112, 126, 143–4, 158

impossibility objections 37
non-absurdity 12–13
theistic dualism in 139
evil-god literature 29, 39, 52, 86, 127, 164 n.59, 169 n.11
evil-god theism 26, 63
  good-god theism *vs.* 30, 114
  negative effects of 30
exact parallel thesis 17–20, 34
exclusivity challenge 7, 9–10, 15–16, 165 n.95
extrinsic free-will defence 12

Feser, E. 10, 25–6, 54–5, 58, 174 n.122
  evil-god challenge 55
  evil-god hypothesis 58
  Thomistic conception of god 55–6
Finch, A. xiii
Forrest, P. 10, 29, 93, 95
free will 19, 91
  intrinsic value of 73, 88–92
  limits of 93

Gandhi, Mahatma 52, 173 n.90
Gardener, R., *Healing Miracles* 152
Gellman, J. 131
global theology 128–9
Glock, C. 135
  American Piety 130–1
  Religion and Society in Tension 136
Glover, D., *Answering the Evil God Challenge* 163 n.48
god's goodness (good god) xii–xiii, 2, 5, 10, 12, 21, 23–4, 29, 42, 54, 67–9, 71, 91, 122, 160 n.2
  asymmetry 18–19
  attribution of 76, 80, 86, 88–9, 92, 94, 106, 110, 117, 130, 141, 143, 158
  'Being Itself' 2, 54–7, 61, 69
  benevolence 38, 40, 48
  compatibility 114, 127–8, 142, 144, 151–2, 186 n.58
  and evil god 7, 25, 34, 60–1, 64, 72–3, 164 n.59
  extrinsic and intrinsic goods 3, 71, 86, 91–2, 107, 115, 158
  grounding 112, 114–15, 128, 142, 144, 178 n.29
  omni 38–9

Reformed epistemology 3, 72–3, 110–15
Swinburne's argument 62–3
Goff, P., *Why? The Purpose of the Universe* 85
good-god defender 12–13, 16, 31, 40, 54, 60, 67–8, 79, 89, 91–2, 104, 108–9, 114, 123–4, 127, 136, 139, 142–5, 151–3
good-god hypothesis 1–2, 4, 7–11, 13, 19, 24–5, 53, 55, 90, 109, 157, 172 n.73
  and evil-god hypothesis 14, 27, 29–30, 37, 40, 50, 64, 94, 106, 112, 126, 143–4, 158
  monotheistic 15
good-god theism 7, 12, 16, 20–3, 46, 50, 53, 83, 136
  vs. evil-god theism 30, 114
  positive effects of 30
goodness as correct function 54
gratuitous evils 79, 83–4
great-making property 2, 23, 41, 44–5, 50–1, 68, 113, 157, 172 n.83
  benevolence 27, 31, 38, 40, 47–9, 52–3, 63, 74–5, 79, 107, 118, 123, 127, 130, 151–3, 178 n.38
  evil-world response 52
  extrinsic 48, 51, 172 n.83
  great-making objections 37–8
  intrinsic 42, 48–9, 54
  malevolence 33, 39, 44, 48–9, 52, 79, 107, 115, 127, 130, 141–2, 148–51, 155
grounding and compatibility 1–2, 6, 12, 31–4, 43, 46, 52, 60–1, 69, 73, 80, 107–12, 114–15, 118, 128, 142, 144–5, 152, 155–9
Guru Granth Sahib 127

Haight, D. 6, 8, 19
Haight, M. 6, 8, 19
Hardy, A., *The Spiritual Nature of Man* 136
Hare, P. 18
  Evil and the Concept of God 5
Hart, M. 121
Hartshorne, C. 43
Haybron, D. 75
Hay, D. 136
Heald, G. 136

Hendricks, P. 13, 16, 65, 172 n.98, 175 n.152
'Sceptical Theism' 168 n.171
Hick, J. 136
Hill, D. xii, 41, 109, 121
  Divinity and Maximal Greatness 169 n.11
  maxi-optimality properties 57
Hobart, M. 15
holy wars 126
Hume, D. 5–6, 19, 72, 81–3, 109
  Dialogues 85

imaginary evidence 50–4, 113
immoral rationalism 65
impossibility objections 25, 27, 37, 50, 64
intrinsic asymmetry 73
intrinsic value of free will 73, 88–92

Jakobsen, M. 134–6, 138
James, W., *The Varieties of Religious Experience* 131
Jones, R. 120
Judaism 134

Kalām cosmological argument 20, 22
Kekes, J. 74
Kelemen, D. 183 n.145
Keller, J. 153
Keltz, B. K. 59, 61
Keown, D. 126
King-Farlow, J. 29, 189 n.141
Koskenniemi, E. 149

Lancaster-Thomas, A. xiii, 6–11, 20, 22, 24–5, 28–9, 31, 38, 40, 48, 51–3, 56, 60–1, 67–8, 72, 86, 88, 107, 112–13, 125, 127, 129–30, 132, 134–5, 137–40, 143–4, 153, 166 n.120, 172 n.79, 177 n.8, 180 n.81, 186 n.80
  'The Evil-god Hypothesis and the Argument from Mal-design' 86–7
  An Exploration 180 n.81
  impossibility objections 25
  principle of the inferiority of existence 47, 87
  strong evil-god challenges 8–9, 163 n.48
  weak evil-god challenges 7–8, 163 n.48

Law, S. xii–xiii, 1, 5, 7–8, 11–14, 16–19, 26–8, 33, 43, 45–6, 52, 73, 88–93, 106–9, 113, 123–7, 129, 134, 143–4, 148, 150, 153, 160 n.2, 184 n.2
   character-destroying defence 12
   evil god's absurdity 12
   'God of Eth' 179 n.47
   symmetry thesis 1, 18–19
Lee, R. 31
Leibniz, G. 21
Leon, F. 81–2
Lindeman, D. 180 n.79
Lougheed, K. 10, 145, 164 n.59
loyalty and health (goods) 60

Machiavelli, N. 48
   Machiavellian intuition 48
   The Prince 48, 172 n.83
Madden, E. 6, 8, 18, 129, 189 n.141
   Evil and the Concept of God 5
Magdalene, M. 133
Malcolm, N. 43
malevolence 33, 39, 44, 48–9, 52, 71, 79, 107, 115, 127, 130, 155
   maximal 142
   miraculous 148–51
Massys, Q., *An Old Woman (The Ugly Duchess)* 102–3
maximal-god thesis 37–41, 68, 169 n.5, 177 n.19
maximally good god 5, 54–6, 73–6, 141, 157
maximal moral character 73–6, 115
   action-based account 73, 75
   disposition-based account 73–5
   motivation-based account 73–5
Maxwell, M. 136
McEvedy, C. 120
McGrath, A. 71
Metaphysics ii 55, 57
Miller, C. 46, 60, 66, 128, 172 n.74
Miller, G. 86
Millican, P. 8–9, 22, 43, 119, 125, 127, 147, 153, 171 n.69
miracles 112, 118, 129, 145–9
   benevolence 151–3
   immoral 153–5
   malevolence 148–51
   negative 3, 118, 146–53, 155, 158
   positive 118, 146–7, 150–6, 158

mis-match thesis 45–7
mixed-god challenge 163 n.43
Monet, C., *Woman with a Parasol* 98–9
monotheistic deity 15
Moore, G. E., *Principia Ethica* 92
moral goodness 54
moral motivation 2, 37–8, 65, 67–9, 72, 169 n.174
moral rationalism 63–5, 68
Morris, T. 33, 42
Morriston, W. 8, 26–8
motivation 2, 12, 64–6, 69, 73–5, 86, 89, 115, 121, 123–4, 168 n.171
Mugg, J. 28
Murphree, W. 6, 53, 113, 163 n.44, 166 n.115, 166 n.119

Nabokov, V., *Lolita* 182 n.122
Nagasawa, Y. 20, 38–9, 41–2, 72, 83–4, 134, 146–7, 169 n.11, 171 n.69, 177 n.19
natural order 82
   humans in 82
   of things 77–9, 82, 85–6, 105, 147, 176 n.6
natural world 3, 12, 19, 71–2, 76, 78–9, 83, 95–6, 106–7, 114, 158
   beauty 95–7, 106
   ugliness 96, 98–101
New, C. 8, 53, 129, 146–7
New Testament 125–6, 133
Nietzsche, F. 48
non-Humean-Kantian approach 63
non-Humean moral motivation 62, 68

Oesterreich, T. K. 133, 135
Old Testament 118, 120, 184 n.3
omni-god thesis 37–41, 68, 170 n.12, 177 n.19
ontological argument 18, 22–3, 38, 42–3, 47, 50, 56, 173 n.98
orthodox privation theory 58–9, 174 n.111
orthodox theism 12, 20, 30–1, 34, 38, 46, 53–4, 58, 67, 83, 117, 122, 128, 153, 166 n.116
   maximal-god thesis 37–41, 68
   omni-god thesis 37–41, 68
   proponents of 54
Overall, C. 153

Page, B. 58–60, 168 n.165
Paley, W. 6, 11, 19, 27, 72, 81, 83–4, 108, 178 n.24, 178 n.29, 178 n.38
   good-god defender 79
   humans and non-human animals 76–7
   Natural Theology 76, 176 n.3
   pains and evils 79
   world's creatures 76–8
perfect-being theology xiii, 1–2, 23, 32, 34–5, 38, 42–5, 47–9, 55–6, 71, 87, 108–9, 117, 145, 157–8, 169 n.174
   goal of 52
   grounding god's moral character 69, 71
   ontological argument 56
   orthodox and unorthodox 47, 49, 53, 68, 71
   and rationality 67
   reengineering 50
   traditional 52
Philosophers on God: Talking about Existence xiv
philosophical theology xiii–xiv, 1, 31–3, 157, 159
Philosophy and Phenomenological Research 5
Pickett, T. 120
Pike, N. 41–2, 80, 88–9
Pinker, S. 120
Plantinga, A. 43, 89, 110, 112, 114, 134, 172 n.92, 188 n.109
polytheism 10, 111, 164 n.59
Pope Innocent VIII, *Summis desiderantes affectibus* 149
privation of intuition 58–61
privation theory of evil 38, 54, 56–61, 69
privation theory of good 38, 55–60, 69
Pruss, A. 98–9, 101–2
public philosophy xiii–xiv
Putin, V. 49, 51–2, 172 n.86, 172 n.90

Qur'an 125–8

Rawls, J. 86
Rea, M., *The Hiddenness of God* 145
reasons internalism 63–4, 68
Reformed epistemology 72–3, 92, 107, 109, 110–14, 158, 169 n.174, 172 n.92
   plausibility of 112
   reductio objections 112

religious experience 3, 32, 158, 186 n.80, 189 n.145
   demonic possessions 129, 132–7
   evil deities 132, 137, 142, 144
   evil god 137–42
   negative and positive 129–31, 135, 137, 158, 188 n.125
   numinous 129, 132, 139
   orthodox argument 131
   parallel argument 132
   quasi-sensory 129, 132, 137–8
   universal distribution 143–5
religious extremism 126
Religious Studies xii, 1
responses, evil-god challenge 24–31
   asymmetry objections 24, 34
   fideistic objections 25, 29
   impossibility objections 25–7, 35
   well-being objections 25, 29–30
revelation theology xiii–xiv, 1, 3, 32, 34, 71, 92, 108–9, 115, 117, 157–8, 169 n.174
   divine intervention 117
   grounding god's moral character 115, 155–6, 158
   miracles 118–19, 145–8
      anti-miracle 146
      benevolence 151–3
      immoral 153–5
      malevolence 148–51
      positive and negative 118, 146, 148, 150–1, 153, 155–6, 158
      Scriptural 151
   orthodox 147, 184 n.2
   religious experience 118, 129–32
   restricted revelation 124, 128
   Scriptures 118–19, 121–2
      explicit and teleological 122, 124, 127, 155, 158
   universal revelation 124, 127
   unorthodox 117
   war, huh (good god) 124–9
Ritchie, A. 6
Russell, L. 74–5

Sandler, A. xiv
Santa Claus 91
sceptical theism 68, 118, 123–4, 168 n.171

Schellenberg, J. L. 42, 48, 51
Schopenhauer, A. 14, 56–7, 59, 82, 85
   'On the Vanity of Existence' 56
Schulz, C. 112
Schwager, R. 120–1
Scrutton, A. 30–1, 134
sense of good god 183 n.145
sensus divinitatis 110–14
single-divine-attribute doctrine 44–5, 47, 172 n.72
Socrates 76, 178 n.21
Soul of Britain survey (BBC) 136
Stark, R. 135
   American Piety 130–1
   Religion and Society in Tension 136
Stein, E. 18, 90
   'all or nothing' phenomenon 90–1
surface-level goods and evils 84
Swinburne, R. 11, 27, 37, 62–4, 66–7, 72, 75–6, 79, 83–4, 93, 95, 109, 129, 131–2, 134, 137, 140, 148, 150, 176 n.160, 181 n.97, 181 n.104, 186 n.80, 190 n.178
   credulity and testimony 130
   The Existence of God 94
   Is There a God? 93
   Providence and the Problem of Evil 79
   suicide and the intrinsic value of life 85, 87
symmetry thesis 1–2, 7, 16–21, 25, 29, 34, 71, 109, 111, 145, 169 n.174, 180 n.83
Synoptic Gospels 133
systemic evil 83

Taylor, F. 149
teleological evils 82
Tennant, F. R. 93, 95
theism xiii–xiv, 34, 37, 52, 65, 90, 94, 111–13, 160 n.1. *See also* evil-god theism; good-god theism; orthodox theism
Thomas, L. 74
threshold argument 40
totality of goods and evils 3, 34, 71–3, 88, 90, 93, 106–10, 114–15, 158, 180 n.83
transcending moral principles 51
Trigg, R. 111
Tschudin, V. 136

University of Sheffield, *Measuring the Miraculous?* 149, 190 n.171
unorthodox theologies 2

Ward, K. 10, 18, 25, 175 n.142
Weaver, C. 10, 25, 37, 62–8, 176 n.160
Wells, S., *Drunk with Blood* 119–21
Wielenberg, E. 123
Wiles, M. 154
worst-being theology 45, 47
worst conceivable being 38, 44–50

Xenophon, *Memorabilia* 178 n. 21

Yahweh 120
YouGov 133

Zarepour, M. S. 44–5, 172 n.73

www.ingramcontent.com/pod-product-compliance
Lightning Source LLC
Chambersburg PA
CBHW052110300426
44116CB00010B/1610